MONETARY POLICY AND FINANCIAL SECTOR REFORM IN AFRICA:

GHANA'S EXPERIENCE

MAHAMUDU BAWUMIA

**To the memory of my late father,
Alhaji Mumuni Bawumia.**

ACKNOWLEDGEMENTS

I owe a lot to my parents for bringing me into this world and encouraging me to be the best that I could be. My father was a teacher and a lawyer by training and he never missed an opportunity to emphasize the benefits of education if even in harsh disciplinary terms. We nicknamed him "Sarge" as in a military Sergeant Major. Without his discipline, this book could not have been written. My mother has always been a source of constant loving and unquestioning support. Thank you, mum.

I also owe a lot to all my teachers at different stages of my education. This book is a product of their collective work.

My thanks also go to the University of British Colombia (Fisheries Centre, the Liu Centre for Global Studies and Green College) St. Antonys College, University of Oxford, and the Centre for the Study of African Economies, University of Oxford for providing me the support to write this book. In particular, I would like to thank without implicating Professor Rashid Sumaila, Professor Paul Collier, Professor Daniel Pauly, Ms. Julie Wagemakers, Professor Mark Vessy, Professor Mahmoud Hasan Khan, H.E. Mr. Darren Schemmer, Canada's High Commissioner to Ghana, Mr. Zakari Mumuni, Dr. Benjamin Amoah, Dr. Kenneth Attafuah, Dr. Joseph Atta-Mensah, Mr. Adrian Alhassan, Senanu Mortty, and Mr. Richard Oppong for their kind support and for sharing their ideas.

Professionally I have benefited a lot from too many people to mention but I would like to acknowledge with thanks the support and kindness of Dr. Kwabena Duffuor, who as Governor, gave me the opportunity to work at the Bank of Ghana. I have also benefited immensely from working closely with Governor Dr. Paul A. Acquah. Dr. Acquah is a professional's professional. He had a clear vision of where he wanted to take the Bank of Ghana in the area of monetary policy and financial sector reform and pursued it with passion, humility and the utmost integrity. I learnt so much from him (but may be after reading this book, he would say I did not learn well!) and it was a privilege to be part of his team. Many thanks also go to my former colleague Deputy Governors Mr. Lionel Van Lare Dosoo as well as Mr. Emmanuel Asiedu-Mante. The Board of Directors of the Bank of Ghana was also very central in driving the vision and mission of the Bank of Ghana and I am thankful to them. My thanks also go to all past Governors and Deputy Governors and staff of the Bank of Ghana who collectively left a solid legacy.

My sincere thanks also go to His Excellency former President John Agyekum Kufour, for having the confidence to appoint me as Deputy Governor of the Bank of Ghana at an age that was considered by many in Ghana as relatively young.

I am also very grateful to Nana Addo Dankwa Akufo-Addo for the honour in selecting me as his Vice-Presidential Candidate in the 2008 Ghanaian Presidential elections. I am also thankful for his friendship and kindness. His passion for the transformation of Ghana's economy and the strengthening of its democracy runs deep and this book has benefited from his many incisive questions about the future direction of Ghana's economy.

I am also thankful for the kind support and kindness of Dr. J.L.S. Abbey, Mr. C.K. Tedam, Naa Professor J.S. Nabila, H.E. Alhaji Aliu Mahama, Mr. Kwame Pianim, Mr. E.O. Appiah, H.E. Ambassador R.I. Alhassan and Auntie Jane, and Alhaji Ahmed Ramadan.

I have many people I would like to mention who in various ways contributed to making this book possible and for fear of leaving anyone out, I will just like to say a big thank you to all of you. You know who you are.

My brothers and sisters, nieces, nephews and in-laws have been very supportive and I am thankful for their support.

To my dear wife Samira and my children, Abdul, Nadia and Mahmoud, I say a very big thank you for bearing with me through thick and thin. This could not have been possible without your patient support.

TABLE OF CONTENTS

List of Tables

List of Figures

List of Abbreviations and Acronyms

ACH	Automated Clearing House
ADB	Agricultural Development Bank
AfDB	African Development Bank
AfDF	African Development Fund
AFRC	Armed Forces Revolutionary Council
ARB	Association of Rural Banks
ATMs	Automated Teller Machines
BCC	Bank for Credit and Commerce
BED	Bank Examinations Department
BHC	Bank for Housing and Construction
BOG	Bank of Ghana
BSD	Bank Supervision Department
CAR	Capital Adequacy ratio
CCC	Codeline Cheque Clearing
CG	Consultative Group
CMC	Capital Market Committee
CSD	Central Securities Depository
CUA	Credit Union Association
CUs	Credit Unions
CPI	Consumer Price Index
CPP	Convention Peoples Party
CVCs	Citizens Vetting Committees
DAA	Dutch Auction System
DFI	Development Finance Institution
DSA	Debt Sustainability Analysis
eFASS	Electronic Financial Analysis and Surveillance System
ERP	Economic Recovery Programme
FI	Financial Institution
FSAC	Financial Sector Adjustment Credit
FIC	Financial Intelligence Centre
FINSAP	Financial Sector Adjustment Programme
FINSSP	Financial Sector Strategic Plan

GCB	Ghana Commercial Bank
GDP	Gross Domestic Product
GGILBs	Government of Ghana Index-Linked Bonds
GHIPSS	Ghana Interbank Payments and Settlement System
GNI	Gross National Income
GoG	Government of Ghana
GPRS	Ghana Poverty Reduction Strategy
GSE	Ghana Stock Exchange
ICT	Information and communication technology
IFC	International Finance Corporation
IFRS	International Financial Reporting Standards
IMF	International Monetary Fund
LIFFE	London International Financial Futures Exchange
LAR	Liquid asset ratio
LTS	Long-Term Savings
M2+	Broad money
MCA	Millennium Challenge Account
MDGs	Millennium Development Goals
MBG	Merchant Bank Ghana
MEFP	Memorandum of Economic and Financial Policies
MFIs	Micro Finance Institutions
MPC	Monetary Policy Committee
NBFI	Non-Bank Financial Institution
NDA	Net Domestic assets
NDC	National Democratic Congress
NFA	Net Foreign Assets
NGOs	Non-Governmental Organizations
NHIS	National Health Insurance Scheme
NIB	National Investment Bank
NIC	National Insurance Commission
NLC	National Liberation Council
NPA	Non Performing Asset
NPART	Non Performing Assets Recovery Trust
NPL	Non-Performing Loan

NPP	New Patriotic Party
NPV	Net Present Value
NSCB	National Savings and Credit Bank
NYEP	National Youth Employment Programme
ODA	Overseas Development Assistance
OMO	Open Market Operations
PDs	Primary Distributors/Dealers
PDCs	Peoples Defense Committees
PIN	Personal Information Number
PNDC	Provisional National Defense Council
PNP	Peoples National Party
PP	Progress Party
PRGF	Poverty Reduction and Growth Facility
PSBR	Public Sector Borrowing Requirement
REPOS	Repurchase Agreements
RCBs	Rural and Community Banks
RTGS	Real Time Gross Settlement System
SAP	Structural Adjustment Programme
SCB	Standard Chartered Bank
SEC	Securities & Exchange Commission
SIC	State Insurance Company
SMC	Supreme Military Council
SOE	State Owned Enterprise
SSA	Sub-Saharan Africa
SSB	Social Security Bank
SSNIT	Social Security and National insurance Trust
SSR	Secondary Reserve Requirement
TOT	Terms of Trade
TSA	Treasury Single Account
UGCC	United Gold Coast Convention
WACB	West African Currency Board
WDCs	Workers Defense Committees

PREFACE

Ghana obtained independence from British colonial rule in 1957, the first African country south of the Sahara to do so. The country was full of promise and the expectations of Ghanaians were high. In the words of Dr. Kwame Nkrumah, the first President, Ghana wanted to show the world that the black man can handle his own affairs. Some 53 years later, the optimism has somewhat waned and harsh reality has set in with the wide chasm between what is Ghana today and what could have been.

At the time of Ghana's independence it was the world's leading exporter of cocoa; it produced 10 percent of the world's gold; it had diamonds, bauxite, and manganese, and a flourishing trade in mahogany. Its income per capita was almost exactly equal to South Korea's at $490 (in 1980 dollars). Fifty three years later, the economic fortunes of the two countries could not be more different. The World Bank's purchasing power parity calculations show that South Korea's gross national income per capita was $28,120 while Ghana's was at $1,430 at the end of 2008. This basically tells the story that while South Korea has been growing very fast, Ghana has for long periods stagnated. GNI/Capita has been increasing on average by $20 annually in Ghana since independence while it has been increasing by an average of $545 annually in South Korea over the last 53 years. If Ghana performs along the same trajectory observed since independence then it will take at least 500 years to get to South Korea's per capita income in 2008! On the other hand if the recent growth performance of the economy continues and some 7.0 percent plus real GDP growth rate is maintained, Ghana could attain the 2008 South Korean GDP/Capita levels in less than 60 years (but South Korea will not be standing still.). However, this means that whether it takes 500 years or 60 years, most policy makers and most of the population will not live long enough to see this future Ghanaian economy even though policy actions today will determine the path and timing of its attainment. This implies that there would have to be a significant amount of altruism, selflessness and forward thinking at the heart of policy making today.

Indeed, many institutions that are in place in many of the developed countries today have a very long history. The first central register for large credit transactions (the forerunner to the modern credit reference agency) was established in England by the Statute of Burnell in 1293, over 700 years ago. This does not however mean that African countries should be looking at that that time horizon. One of the advantages of being a latecomer is the opportunity to leapfrog as we are observing the areas of mobile telephony and the internet for example.

In the financial markets, Ghana's economy has been characterized by long periods of high and volatile inflation and macroeconomic instability which has reflected in high and variable interest rates and significant exchange rate volatility and depreciation. The question for many is why the financial sector cannot deliver the low interest rate regime that has been observed in many other countries.

For example, the average interest rate in the Britain in the 200 year period between 1750 and 1950 was in the region of 4-6 percent! While Bank lending rates in Ghana in 2009 were at some 35% (annual percentage rate), those in the United Kingdom were at an average 8% (for personal unsecured loans) and some 3% for mortgages. Lending rates in Japanese Banks were less than 2% on average in 2009 and close to zero a few years earlier. In Singapore, lending rates were on average 0.9 % at the end of 2009.

The developed economies also appear to have inflation largely under control. EU annual inflation was 1.4% in December 2009. A year earlier the rate was 2.2%. In December 2009, the lowest annual rates were observed in Ireland (-2.6%), Estonia (-1.9%) and Latvia (-1.4%), and the highest in Hungary (5.4%), Romania (4.7%) and Poland (3.8%). U.S. Inflation was 2.7 % for 2009 while Japan and China registered -1.90% and 0.60% inflation rates respectively in November 2009.

People in developing countries like Ghana look at the economic performance of the developed countries and the emerging market economies like China with awe. "Why can't we have what they have?" Why can't we have low inflation and low interest rates with exchange rate stability and high economic growth?

The answers to these questions are not straightforward. However, a sound monetary/fiscal policy framework and a developed financial sector would have to be part any comprehensive answer. This book examines monetary policy and financial sector reform in Ghana since independence in 1957 in the context of developments in the international monetary system. During this period Ghana has adopted three monetary regimes; direct controls, indirect monetary instruments, and inflation targeting. Financial sector development and reform has also taken place alongside the monetary policy regimes. These include regulatory and legal reforms, capital market and money market reforms, banking reforms, currency redenomination, reforms, payment system reform, rural banking reforms, and accessing the international capital markets. Why were these monetary policy regimes adopted? What role did the political economy play in the reforms and outcomes? What was the impact of the different monetary regimes and financial sector reforms on the performance of Ghana's economy? The book provides a detailed and chronological account of these issues and draws out the lessons for African countries.

CHAPTER 1

DIRECT CONTROLS AND THE EVOLUTION OF GHANA'S FINANCIAL SECTOR (1957-1983)

Formal banking took roots in the colonial Gold Coast towards the end of the nineteenth century with the establishment of the British Bank of West Africa in 1897 (known as Standard Chartered Bank today) and Barclays (Dominion, Colonial and Overseas) in 1917. These two banks basically served the needs of the expatriate community to the exclusion of the local indigenous population. Prior to the establishment of the British Bank of West Africa, the Post Office Savings Bank was established in 1887 and was more widely used by the local population. By 1913, there were 13 branches of the Post Office Savings Bank, growing to 32 branches by 1918 (Uche, 1996).

The exploitative nature of the colonial economic structure became increasingly apparent to the indigenous population and a surge of national self-consciousness and increasing discontent among the populace led to the popularity of the idea of political independence. The United Gold Coast Convention (UGCC) was formed in 1947 to spearhead the fight for independence. It was Ghana's first political party. In 1949, after a split with the UGCC, Kwame Nkrumah formed the Convention Peoples Party (CPP). The constitution of the CPP stipulated the establishment of "a Socialist State in which all men and women shall have equal opportunity and where there shall be no capitalist exploitation". The CPP was victorious at elections held to the Legislative Assembly in 1951, ushering in a period of "self-government".

By the early 1950s, political agitation also began for the establishment of a bank to serve local Ghanaian interests. This led to the establishment of the Bank of the Gold Coast (now Ghana Commercial Bank (GCB)) in 1953 to serve the indigenous population, especially the farmers and entrepreneurs who felt ignored by the foreign banks. GCB was instructed to extend its branch network to the rural areas to provide the rural population with access to banking facilities. Indeed, by 1960 the branches of commercial banks in Ghana totaled 105. Ghana Commercial Bank had 7 branches, Bank of West Africa had 42 branches, and Barclays Bank D.C.O. had 55 branches spread all over the regions of Ghana. The Post Office Savings Bank on the other hand had 402 branches by 1960 (Bank of Ghana, 2007).

Given the CPP's development strategy, fiscal policy was expansionary. Expenditure on education, health, and physical infrastructure dramatically increased from their colonial levels. Government expenditure increased from 5.5 percent of GDP in 1950 to 9.5% by 1956 (Frimpong Ansah, 1991).

During this period, the Gold Coast was operating with the colonial international economic arrangements. The British West African Currency Board (WACB) was constituted in 1912 to control the supply of currency to the British West African Colonies; Nigeria, Ghana, Sierra Leone and Gambia. It was headquartered in London and was given the mandate to "provide for and to control the supply of currency to the British West African colonies, Protectorates and Trust Territories". Uche (1996) notes that in practice, the WACB was no more than a money changer, issuing as much local currency as the banks wanted to buy for sterling and vice-versa.

The exchange rate of the West African Pound to sterling was fixed and there were no capital controls as far as the sterling area was concerned. Under this regime, changes in foreign assets were automatically reflected in changes in the domestic money stock and Ghana's inflation was directly linked to inflation in the sterling area. This framework kept inflation barely noticeable. At the time of independence in 1957, Ghana's inflation was less than 1 percent and a year later was zero (Table 1.1).

It should be noted that when a country decides to be part of a fixed exchange rate regime, it implies that it cannot have an independent monetary policy. This is because monetary policy is basically subjugated to maintaining the fixed exchange rate. This was the case when countries of the world operated on the gold standard and later on the Bretton Woods System. Ghana operated under this type of fixed exchange rate system at independence. Price stability and parity conversions however had their cost because the ability of the WACB to create credit was severely hampered.

Establishment of the Bank of Ghana

The Bank of Ghana (BOG), the central bank, was established in 1957 when the Bank of Ghana Ordinance (1957, no.34) was passed by the British Parliament. Under the Ordinance, the Bank of Ghana was established as an independent central bank with orthodox central bank functions of regulating the money supply, containing inflation, and stabilizing the monetary system. The Ordinance was designed to protect the central bank from political interference and prevent the use of the Banks' and the country's' resources indiscriminately.

President Kwame Nkrumah however had a different view and vision of the role of the banking system. At the opening ceremony for the Bank, he stated inter alia that *"it is essential to our own independence that we have a government-owned bank and that the central bank follows a policy designed to secure our economic independence and to further the general development of our country"* (Bank of Ghana, 2007).

Nkrumah therefore wanted a banking system that would complement the government led development strategy. By 1960, the Convention Peoples Party was becoming increasingly frustrated by the apparent autonomy of the Bank of Ghana. The Bank of Ghana Ordinance 1957 (no.34) basically left little room for the government to use the central bank to advance the development objectives of the country as the politicians saw it. The Ordinance was cast as neo-colonialist and obstructive to the country's development. It was argued that one of the major functions of a central bank in a developing country such as Ghana was to provide development finance to accelerate economic growth.

In fact, this frustration with the 1957 Ordinance became more strident by 1960 as Government finances were coming under severe pressure and the foreign exchange reserves were declining. The Government deficits were rising and unlike the earlier years when foreign exchange reserves were relatively plentiful, the option of resorting to a drawdown in foreign reserves to finance the deficit was largely foreclosed by 1960. Government also exhausted its bank balances and started borrowing from the banking system. The Government of Ghana began to issue Treasury Bills in 1960. Exchange controls and import licensing were introduced in 1961 under the Exchange Control Act. As Leith and Soderling (2003) point out, with the introduction of exchange controls, Ghana had effectively taken itself out of the sterling area. This meant that increases in the money supply would not result in a capital movement but would result in inflation since with no foreign reserves to buy imports; the excess demand would be reflected in the prices of domestic goods.

The stage was set for a change in the Bank of Ghana Ordinance to bring it into line with CPP government policy. A committee was set up to draft a new central bank bill which was enacted as the Bank of Ghana Act, 1963 (Act 182). This Act required the central bank to operate in consultation with government. It also empowered the Bank of Ghana to direct lending to priority sectors of the economy and set ceilings on advances or investments by commercial banks. This policy was driven by the belief that the market imperfections and nature of the colonial financial system could not support the desired pattern and level of investment without government intervention.

As part of the agenda of using the banking system to drive the development agenda, Government through the Bank of Ghana facilitated the establishment of a number of development banks, established for specific purposes. In fact, all the banks that were established between the 1950s and the late 1980s were wholly or majority owned by the government. These included the National Investment Bank (NIB) in 1963 to assist industry, and the Agricultural Credit and Cooperative Bank (Agricultural Development Bank) in 1965 to assist agriculture.

Monetary Policy in the Nkrumah Era- Direct Controls

As a result of the Great Depression, (which begun with a catastrophic collapse of stock-market prices on the New York Stock Exchange in October 1929), many banks went into insolvency. The failure of so many banks, combined with a general loss of confidence in the economy, led to significantly reduced levels of spending and demand and hence of production, thus aggravating unemployment. Before the Great Depression, the dominant view in economics (the classical school) was that the interplay of market forces would naturally result in the economy attaining full employment output. The classical economists did not however have an answer to the problem of unemployment resulting from the Great Depression.

John Maynard Keynes in the *Great Depression* (1936) argued that the thinking of the classical school was fundamentally flawed. Market forces, in the presence of uncertainty, would not necessarily yield full employment. With interest rates near zero, one could not expect further cuts in interest rates to stimulate private investment. What was needed, Keynes argued, was an injection of aggregate demand i.e. an increase in government spending (what is referred to today as a "stimulus package"). Keynes' view was that the interest rate, being essentially a monetary phenomenon with potentially vast real effects, could and should be manipulated in order to increase investment. In his opinion,

"...the rate of interest, unless it is curbed by every instrument at the disposal of society, would rise too high to permit an adequate inducement to investment."

The Keynesian view became the dominant paradigm after the Great Depression and Roosevelt's New Deal and the Marshall Plan for Europe were examples of this new thinking. One way to increase aggregate demand was to increase investment and this could be accomplished by governments directing banks to lend to specific sectors of the economy or setting ceilings on interest rates. This ushered in an era of direct controls as the monetary policy framework of most countries in the 1950s and 1960s.

Direct Controls

Direct Controls refer to the one-to-one correspondence between the instrument (such as a credit ceiling) and the policy objective (such as a specific amount of domestic credit outstanding). Direct instruments operate by setting or limiting either prices (interest rates) or quantities (amounts of credit outstanding) through regulations, The most common direct instruments are interest rate controls, credit ceilings, and directed lending (lending at the behest of the authorities, rather than for commercial reasons), and capital controls. In addition, there were restrictions on market entry into the financial sector, and government ownership or domination of banks.

Direct methods of monetary control were appealing for several reasons. By having a direct control over the financial system, the government could have access to funds more cheaply. More specifically, by restricting the behaviour of existing and potential participants of the financial markets, the government could create monopoly or captive rents for the existing banks and also tax some of these rents so as to finance its overall budget.

Direct controls also forced banks to allocate subsidized credit to industries that were perceived to be strategically important for industrial policy. It was also more cost effective than going through the public sector's budgetary process. Government directives and guidance sometimes included detailed orders and instructions on managerial issues of financial institutions to ensure that their behaviour and business was in line with industrial policy or other government policies. The policy of nationalization or control of banks was another way of ensuring that credit was directed appropriately.

At the same time, governments also imposed a ceiling on the interest rate banks could offer to depositors. Interest ceilings function in the same way as price controls, and thereby provide banks with economic rents.

Direct controls were generally perceived by governments to be reliable, at least initially, in controlling credit aggregates or both the distribution and the cost of credit. They were relatively easy to implement and explain, and their direct fiscal costs were relatively low. Direct controls were therefore attractive to governments that wanted to channel credit to meet specific objectives.

Bank of Ghana's Monetary Policy of Direct Controls

After independence in 1957, economic policies in Ghana generally followed the dominant paradigm in development economics of the time. The case for adopting an import-substituting interventionist strategy of development was persuasive and many developing countries embraced it. Ghana's first President, Kwame Nkrumah, captured this consensus when he commented that "Government interference in all matters affecting the economic growth in less developed countries is today a universally accepted principle"[1]. Economic policies of this era emphasized controls over interest rates, exchange rates, commodity prices, state ownership of enterprises and import substitution as the vehicles for economic development with social equity.

To give concrete expression to its independence, Ghana issued its own currency, the Ghana Pound on July 14th 1958 with the same value as the West African Pound. As noted earlier, however, the Bank of Ghana did not have an independent monetary policy at this time as a result of the fixed exchange rate regime that it was strictly enforcing as part of the Sterling Area arrangements. Changes in Ghana's foreign assets were automatically reflected in changes in the domestic money stock and Ghana's inflation was directly linked to inflation in the sterling area.

---

[1] Nkrumah, Kwame (1963, pp.109-110). Africa Must Unite. International Publishers. New York

The Bank of Ghana Act of 1963 was a break from the rules based monetary policy of the colonial era to the use of discretion. Nonetheless the discretion given the Bank of Ghana was within limits. The framers of the 1963 Act recognized the dangers of unbridled discretion. The Act recognized the importance of limiting the growth of the money supply because of its inflationary consequences. It gave the Bank of Ghana powers to impose reserve requirements on total deposits as an instrument of monetary control. Furthermore, there was an implicit monetary growth target of a maximum of 15 percent set for the Bank of Ghana. Under the Act, if monetary growth in any year exceeded 15 percent, the Board of the Bank was required to write a letter to the Minister of Finance explaining the reasons for the increase and recommending measures to deal with the inflationary consequences of such an increase in the money supply.

With its new powers under the Bank of Ghana Act 1963, formal monetary policy started with the introduction of credit control regulations in April 1964. This ushered in the era monetary policy through direct controls that was to last through the early 1980s. Under this monetary policy regime, credit was controlled and directed to government's priority areas. There was the desire to direct credit away from trade (mainly imports of consumer goods) finance towards the "productive" sectors.

Specifically, the credit control regulations of 1964 stipulated inter alia that Banks were required to:

- Hold 100 per cent foreign currency cover with the Bank of Ghana for sight balances due to banks abroad.

- Hold 48 percent of their deposit liabilities in the form of liquid reserves between March and August and 54 percent between September and February (cocoa season)[2].

---

[2] Liquid reserves were defined to include cash reserve assets, Treasury bills, approved industrial and agricultural loans and balances in special deposit accounts.

- Maintain a cash ratio of 8 per cent
- Obtain approval from the Bank of Ghana Credit Control Committee for individual loans exceeding ¢10,000 for purposes other than agriculture and industry.

Importers of consumer goods were required to deposit with banks a minimum down payment of 15 percent with the Bank of Ghana. This policy was meant to discourage the import of "non-essential" consumer goods.

The credit control regulations proved to be ineffective because they were flouted by the Government itself, which put pressure on the banks (which were government-owned) to grant loans to state enterprises which were running at losses.

During this period, the interest rate tool was dormant, remaining fixed at 4.5 percent between 1961 and 1965 even though inflation rose from 6.2 per cent to 22.7 percent over the same period (Table 1.1).

Real interest rates therefore turned negative between 1961 and 1966 (Table 1.1) with the incentives for borrowers and disincentives for savers. The demand for credit was consequently high.

Nkrumah's ambitious development program had taken its toll on the economy. The external reserve position deteriorated significantly between 1957 (when net reserves stood at $269 million) and 1966 when they were negative (-$39 million- Figure 1.1). This reflected a deteriorating fiscal and balance of payments position.

Table 1.1 Selected Macroeconomic Indicators. 1957-1983

	Inflation	Money Growth %	Real GDP Growth	Gross Reserv	Net Reserve	Nom. Int.	Real int. Ra	Exchange Ra	Exch. Rate Depre	Gov. Bal
1957	1	-10.6		273	269			0.73	0.00	2.70
1958	0	-7.3		281	277			0.72	-1.39	1.90
1959	2.9	13.6		304	295			0.72	0.00	1.10
1960	0.9	11.4		294	259	4	3	0.71	-1.41	-1.70
1961	6.2	15.4	3.3	163	159	4.5	-1.6	0.71	0.00	-4.80
1962	5.9	13.3	4	197	180	4.5	-4.4	0.74	4.05	-8.70
1963	5.6	0	4.3	219	187	4.5	-0.1	0.77	3.90	-8.00
1964	15.8	41.2	2.1	136	89	4.5	-6.9	0.87	11.49	-5.60
1965	22.7	0	1.3	118	-10	4.5	-17.4	1.04	16.35	-6.40
1966	14.8	4.2	-5.1	113	-39	7	-5.5	1.14	8.77	-5.00
1967	-9.7	-4	2.6	95	-51	6	15.7	1.01	-12.87	-5.90
1968	10.7	8.3	0.3	106	-62	5.5	-2.2	1.07	5.61	-6.10
1969	6.5	11.5	5.5	80	-101	5.5	-1.7	1.09	1.83	-3.30
1970	3	6.9	9.2	74	-23	5.5	2.4	1.05	-3.81	-2.20
1971	8.8	3.2	5.3	53	-6	8	-1.4	1.1	4.55	-3.50
1972	10.8	43.8	-3	115	98	8	-1.9	1.18	6.78	-5.70
1973	17.1	28.3	2.8	194	184	6	-9.9	1.26	6.35	-5.30
1974	18.8	18.6	7.7	108	2	6	-10.3	1.3	3.08	-4.20
1975	29.8	44.3	-4.3	167	110	8	-16.8	1.49	12.75	-7.60
1976	55.4	41.6	-3.5	109	17	8	-30.8	2.1	29.05	-11.30
1977	116.5	67.1	1.8	169	-3	8	-50.1	3.72	43.55	-9.50
1978	73.1	72.8	9.3	190	9	13.5	-34.4	6.08	38.82	-9.00
1979	54.5	13.3	-1.6	302	118	13.5	-26.5	8.3	26.75	-6.40
1980	50.2	30.1	0.5	232	85	13.5	-24.4	10.8	23.15	-4.20
1981	116.5	54.5	-2.9	198	-72	19.5	-44.8	21.52	49.81	-6.50
1982	22.3	19	-6.7	215	-6	10.5	-9.6	24.1	10.71	-5.60
1983	122.8	49.3	-4.5	220	-193	14.5	-48.6	50.84	52.60	-2.70

Source: Bank of Ghana

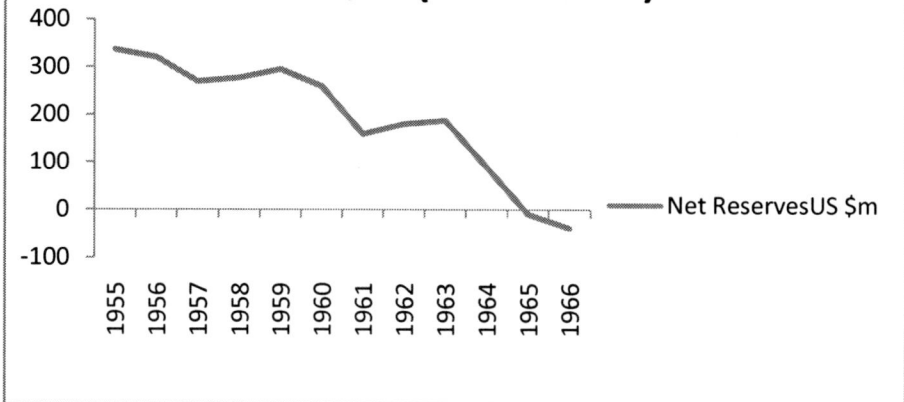

Figure 1.1. Net International Reserves US $m (1955-1966)

The fiscal position also deteriorated as Government spending increased from 9.5 percent in 1957 of GDP to 25.8 percent of GDP by 1965. The government budget balance deteriorated from a surplus of 14.5 percent of GDP in 1954 to a deficit of 6.4 percent of GDP by 1965 (Table 1.1, Figure 1.2).

Inflation also rose from zero in 1958 to 22.7 percent by 1965 (Table 1.1). With rising inflation and a fixed exchange rate, this resulted in a significant real appreciation of the currency. The real exchange rate was 50.0 percent less than at independence and exports declined from 30.0 percent of GDP in 1957 to 18.0 percent of GDP by 1965 (Leith and Soderling, 2003).

In January 1966, against the background of increasing inflation and declining foreign exchange reserves, the Bank of Ghana decided to bring the interest rate tool into play. There was an increase in the Bank discount rate from 4.5 percent to 7.0 percent and commercial banks were asked to reflect this in their lending rates.

Figure 1.2. Budget Balance /GDP % (1950-1966)

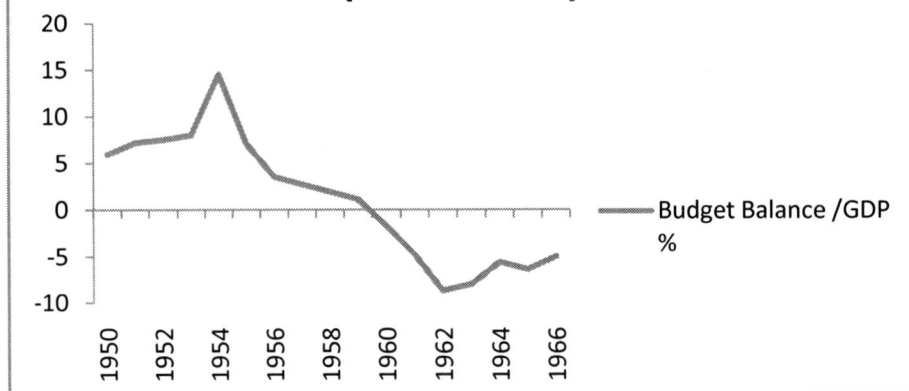

This was an acknowledgement that the policy of trying to maintain artificially low interest rates to supposedly help the productive sectors of the economy had failed. Notwithstanding the low nominal interest rates, output was on the decline, foreign reserves were depleted and there was a shortage of consumer goods. The Bank of Ghana could not meet the targets of monetary policy because the Government's own fiscal policy was inconsistent with the monetary policy objectives of the Bank as laid down in the Bank of Ghana Act, 1963. This is a major lesson which unfortunately successive governments have failed to learn; fiscal policy and monetary policy have to be coordinated for policy success.

The deteriorating economic and political situation was used by a group of military and police officers as an excuse to stage a coup d'état and overthrow the CPP on February 24, 1966. The new military government was named the National Liberation Council (N.L.C).

On coming into office, the NLC immediately embarked on an IMF supported stabilization aimed at improving the adverse balance of payments, cutting the budget deficit, reducing the government sector, and stimulating private enterprise. There was a reduction in absolute investment, tighter control over import licenses and a devaluation of the cedi. The objective of the stabilization was largely achieved. The balance of trade moved into surplus and the current account and the government budget deficits were reduced. Inflation fell from an average of 18.0 percent during 1964-66 to a single digit average of 9.0 percent for the years 1967-69 (Killick, 1978).

The NLC replaced Ghana's currency which at the time bore the effigy of deposed President Nkrumah. The New Cedi (N¢) was introduced on February 23, 1967, a year after the overthrow. The old and new cedis were allowed to circulate simultaneously for three months, with the old currency demonetized on May 23, 1967.

However, the stabilization during the NLC era was attained at the cost of economic growth. GDP per capita fell by -0.4 percent in 1967 and rose only by 0.7 percent in 1968. Worker discontent with the economic achievements of the regime was reflected by 27 strikes in 1967, 36 in 1968, and 51 in 1969. The strikes significantly undermined support for the regime, and the NLC announced a transition to civilian rule with general elections to be held in 1969.

The 1969 elections were won by the Progress Party (PP) led by Dr. K.A. Busia. The PP continued the NLC policy of providing incentives for the development of a market economy and privatization.

Monetary policy in the NLC-Busia era however was operated, as under the Nkrumah era, under a regime of direct controls. The key difference however was that there was better coordination between fiscal and monetary policy. The Bank of Ghana, with the support of government fiscal policy, kept monetary growth between 1966 and 1971 at an average of 5.0 percent (Table 1.1), well within the 15.0 percent maximum set under the Bank of Ghana Act 1963. As inflation declined, the Bank of Ghana also reduced interest rates from 7.0 percent in 1966 to 5.5 per cent by 1970.

To further tighten monetary policy, the Bank of Ghana in December 1969 increased the cash ratio for commercial banks from 15.0 percent to 30.0 percent (bringing the total liquidity reserves ratio to 50.0 percent) and a limit of 21.0 percent was set as the ceiling for credit expansion.

In July 1971, the Bank of Ghana discount rate was also increased to 8.0 percent. The minimum savings deposit rate was raised from 2.5 percent to 7.5 percent and banks were required to pay interest on demand deposits (current accounts) with balances above ¢50.00 at a minimum rate of one per cent per annum. These measures were expected to reduce the demand for credit while increasing savings in the banking system (Bank of Ghana, 2007).

By 1971 however, the economy found itself in the same position as it was in 1965 with increasing fiscal and current account deficits. The economic situation was aggravated by a dramatic drop in cocoa prices in 1971 resulting in a balance of trade deficit. The Busia government responded with a devaluation of the cedi by 42.0 percent in December 1971. Also a new nationwide tax on development was levied on annual profits above ¢1,000. Bank interest rates were raised, and gasoline prices were increased. Government employees and servicemen lost their discounts for rent and upkeep of cars. Severe cuts in military expenditure were also implemented.

The devaluation and economic difficulties provided the pretext for a coup d'état on 13th January 1972 by the National Redemption Council in 1972 under Colonel I.K. Acheampong, and later reconstituted as the Supreme Military Council (SMC I.). A palace coup in 1978 replaced Colonel Acheampong with General F.W. Akuffo in 1978 (SMC II).

In the midst of these political developments, the state continued to be interventionist in the financial sector. A merchant bank, Merchant Bank Ghana, was set up in 1972 as a partnership between ANZ Grindlays, the government and public sector financial institutions. A Bank for Housing and Construction was set up in 1974 to provide loans for housing, industrial construction and companies producing building materials. The National

Savings and Credit Bank (NSCB) and the Cooperative Bank (CO-OP) were set up in 1975 to provide consumer loans and credit for SMEs and co-operatives. The Social Security Bank (SSB) was set up in 1977 to provide credit and long term loans to businesses and individuals. In 1975 the government issued an indigenization decree which allowed it to acquire a 40.0 percent equity stake in the two foreign-owned banks (Barclays and SCB) which were established in the colonial era.

The Rural Banking System

As the Ghanaian Banking system evolved after independence, it was increasingly clear by the 1970s that the financial system was developing to the exclusion of the rural population. The Bank of Ghana, under the then Governor Dr. Amon Nikoi, actively promoted and set up the rural banking system. The objectives were to institutionalize financial intermediation in the rural areas, mobilize rural savings for on-lending to agriculture and cottage industry, and inculcate the banking habit among rural households. In 1976, the first two rural banks were established at Agona Nyakrom and Biriwa, both in the Central Region. By 1980 there were 20 rural banks.

Rural banks are unit banks incorporated as limited liability companies. They are owned by the communities in which they are located and they operate generally within a 20 mile radius of their headquarters. To avoid the dominance of large shareholders in the community, no single individual or company was allowed to own more than 10 percent and 20 percent of the share capital respectively.

Rural Banks were subject to the same regulatory oversight as the deposit money banks and operated under the Banking Act 1970. Rural banks had to maintain a primary reserve in the form of cash and balances with other banks of not less than 10 percent of deposit liabilities and secondary reserves in the form of treasury bills and other money market instruments of not less than 52 percent of their deposit liabilities, transfer a minimum of 50 percent of their annual net profit after tax to their reserve fund, and seek ratification of the

Bank of Ghana before the disbursement of loans above specified amounts to a single party and all loans to directors or companies in which they have an interest.

Under the policy of directed lending, rural banks were required to comply with sectoral guidelines in respect of their loan portfolio. In the mid-1980s these requirements were 45 percent for agriculture and 30 percent for cottage industry.

For Ghana's economy, the period between 1970 and 1983 was characterized by a dramatic economic decline (Figure 1.3).

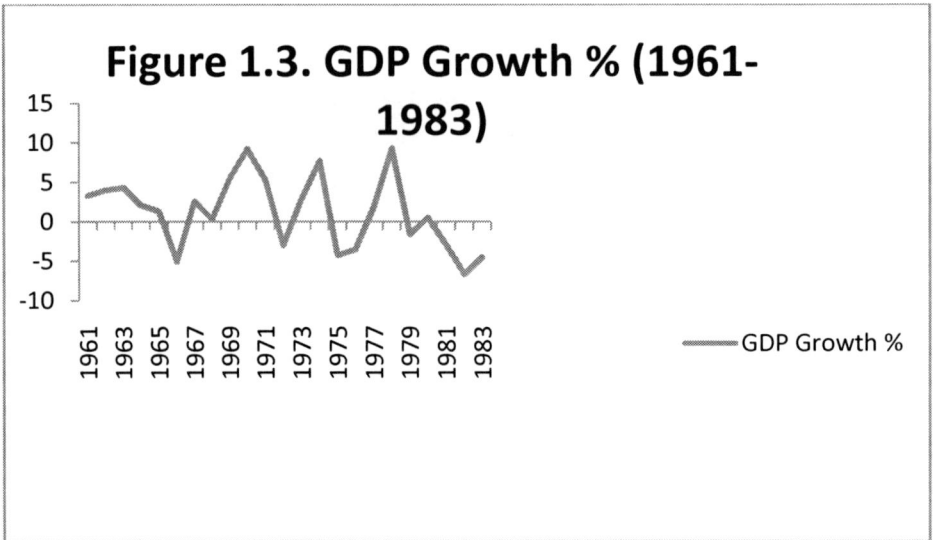

Figure 1.3. GDP Growth % (1961-1983)

This entailed a decline in GDP per capita by more than 3 percent a year, in industrial output by 4.2 percent a year and in agricultural output by 0.2 percent a year. The main foundation of the economy, cocoa, was on the decline. Central government revenues which amounted to 21 percent of GDP in 1970 fell to only 5 percent of a smaller GDP in 1983 (Tabatabai, 1986). The revenue collapse increased the reliance on the banking system to finance expenditures. Between 1974 and 1983 the monetary base expanded from 697 million to 11,440 million cedis[3].

Figure 1.4. Inflation and Monetary Growth (1967-1983)

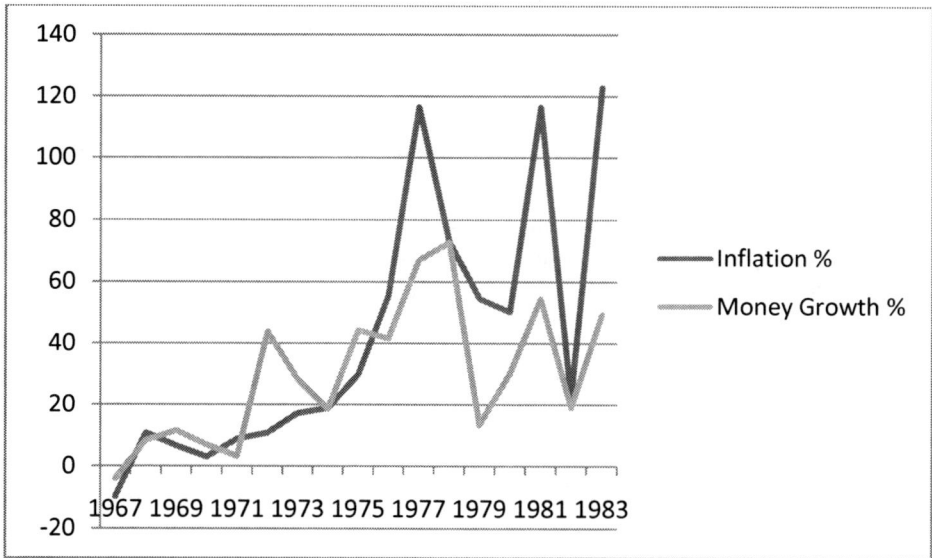

The loss of monetary control accelerated inflation, which increased from 6.5 percent in 1969 to 116.5 percent by 1977 and 122 percent by 1983, in the midst of a regime of controlled prices (Figure 1.4). The period of economic decline was also characterized by negative real interest rates (Table 1.1), and domestic savings and investment decreased from 12 and 14 percent of GDP respectively to less than 4 percent (IMF, 1987)[4]. The Bank of Ghana determined the structure and level of bank interest rates (deposit and lending) and set preferential rates for priority sectors like agriculture.

---

[3] ibid
[4] International Monetary Fund, *Ghana, Recent Economic Developments,* May 1987

In the face of excessive monetary financing of the fiscal deficit, the Bank of Ghana's monetary policy tools proved to be ineffective. Various measures, including increases in interest rates, the cash ratio, the liquid reserve ratio, credit ceilings etc. were implemented but they all proved futile. In the twelve-month period to June 1978 for example, the level of currency issued by the Bank of Ghana increased by 110 percent, doubling the currency in circulation (Bank of Ghana, 2007).

As the currency crisis worsened with the Bank of Ghana appearing powerless, Government announced a currency reform to replace the existing currency notes and to cut-off counterfeit notes inside and outside the country. A nationwide exercise was undertaken over a fifteen day period. Old notes up to ¢5,000 were discounted at 30.0 percent, while those in excess of ¢5000 were discounted at 50.0 per cent. Many who could not change their notes within the given deadline suffered heavy losses. This exercise was a traumatic experience for many. The enduring lesson was clear. Government could not be trusted to redeem its obligation for its currency. For many people, it was better to keep a significant portion of their savings in foreign currency rather than risk arbitrary direct confiscation or indirect confiscation through an inflation tax. The currency reform, notwithstanding all its stated objectives, failed because it was only dealing with the symptom of an underlying problem and not the problem itself. So while monetary growth declined from 72.4 percent in 1978 to 13.3 percent in 1979, it quickly rose to 54.7 percent by 1981 (Table 1.1).

In the meantime, successive governments continued the policy of overvaluing the cedi. The current account deficit of US$ 2.7 million in 1975 increased to US$ 294 million by 1983. The current account deficits not only depleted gross official foreign reserves but also involved an accumulation of external debts. Arrears amounted to the equivalent of 90% of annual export earnings in 1982 (IMF, 1987). Successive governments responded with import controls which fell disproportionately on consumer goods.

SMC II was overthrown by another coup d'état in 1979 by the Armed Forces Revolutionary Council (AFRC) under the leadership of Flt. Lt. Jerry John Rawlings. After four months in office, the AFRC handed over power to a democratically elected government of the Peoples National Party (PNP) under the leadership of Dr. Hilla Limann. The PNP government was however overthrown in another coup d'état, by Flt. Lt. Jerry John Rawlings in December 1981, this time under the banner of the Provisional National Defense Council (PNDC).

Between January 1982 and November 1983 the PNDC was characterized by socialist revolutionary policies and measures tinged with populism. The business community, large scale farmers and professionals were the regime's declared enemies. Economic policy was interventionist and anti foreign capital. Price controls, import duties and tariffs were imposed on a wide range of goods. The PNDC was hostile toward the prescriptions of the International Monetary Fund and World Bank. Rent controls were instituted and Workers Defense Committees (WDCs) and Peoples Defense Committees (PDCs) were established as revolutionary organs to mobilize the population.

In a rather interesting attempt to stem the rate of monetary expansion, the PNDC implemented the following policies in 1982:

- All ¢50 notes were demonetized without compensation.
- The Bank rate was reduced from 18.0 percent to 13.5 percent
- The minimum deposit rate was reduced from 18.5 percent to 14 percent
- The ceiling on bank lending rates was reduced from 26.0 percent to 18 percent

Furthermore, Citizens Vetting Committees (CVCs) were empowered to investigate people "whose lifestyle and expenditure substantially exceeded their known incomes". Specifically, anyone with more than ¢50,000 ($1,250 at the prevailing black market exchange rate of some ¢50/$) had to appear before the CVC to explain how they acquired it. Banks were required to provide details of all such bank accounts in excess of ¢50,000. Meanwhile, all such accounts were frozen and those associated with corruption, or any other crime as determined by the CVC, were confiscated to the state. The wealthy became the targets of a vindictive Public Tribunal system. Again, government had dealt a devastating blow to the very foundations of the banking system. The one ingredient that is fundamental to the growth of the banking system (confidence) was eroded.

Notwithstanding all these "anti-corruption" measures, the economy turned for the worse and it soon became obvious that the populist socialist policies were not sufficient to stabilize a monetary system or grow an economy. Inflation reached 122.8% at the end of 1982 and monetary growth reached 49.2 percent in 1983 (Table 1).

During the period, banks were regulated under the Banking Act 1970. This Act stipulated minimum capital requirements for foreign and locally-owned banks of ¢2 million and ¢500,000 (later raised to ¢750,000) respectively. These capital requirements were worth very little by the early 1980s because of the inflationary spiral during this period. By the end of 1983, the minimum paid-up capital for a local bank was the equivalent of $16,000 (Brownbridge and Gockel, 1998).

The period between 1965 and the early 1980s had economic and political instability as its hallmark. Frequent military coup d'état, and significant price distortions emanating from price controls, interest rate controls, negative real interest rates, directed credit, high reserve requirements, fixed nominal exchange rate, appreciating real exchange rate, high inflation, high fiscal deficits, and a resort to monetary financing of the deficit which led to high monetary growth rates. The Banking system was also used primarily as a tool for financing government expenditure to the disadvantage of the private sector, which many governments regarded with suspicion. For the most part, the financial sector was in the throes of financial repression, with controls on interest rates.

There was a mistaken belief by many policy makers of the day that ceilings on interest rates, as inflation spiraled, would lower the cost of borrowing to agriculture and industry, business, consumers and government. Unfortunately all that this succeeded in doing was to keep potential savers away from the banking system and fuel liquidity outside the banking system. This was inflationary because the excess liquidity was manifested in the demand for goods and services which themselves were in short supply.

Figure 1.5. Bank Deposits and bank Claims on the Private Sector (1970-1983)

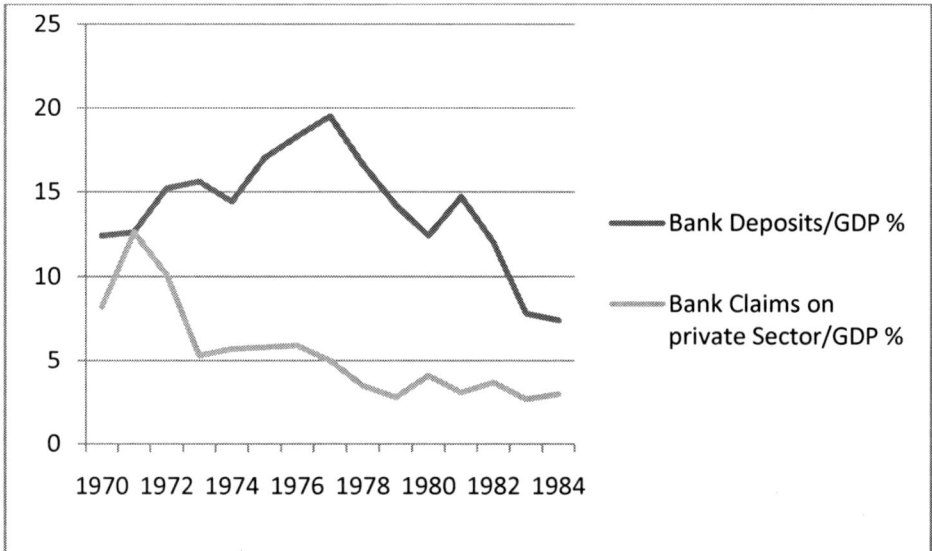

People also shied away from the banking system, as discussed earlier, because of the lack of confidence in the banking system. The passage of AFRC decree 17 which allowed the government to access individual bank accounts without the knowledge of the account holder resulted in many depositors withdrawing their savings from banks and many more not depositing their savings in the banking system.

As Figure 1.5 shows, the economy recorded a dramatic decline in Bank deposits/ as a percentage of GDP from 19.5% of GDP in 1977 to 7.8 percent of GDP by 1983. Similarly, bank lending to the private sector declined from 12.6% of GDP in 1971 to just 2.7% of GDP by 1983.

By late 1983, a combination of frequent coup attempts against the regime, a severe Sahelian drought, sporadic bush fires, the flight of capital from the country, and continuing miserable performance of the economy had threatened the very existence of the PNDC regime (Ray 1986)[5].

---

[5] Ray, Donald I. *Ghana: Politics Economics and Society*. London: Frances Pinter (Publishers Ltd), 1986

CHAPTER 2

INDIRECT MONETARY POLICY INSTRUMENTS REGIME

The end of the Bretton Woods system by 1971 unleashed two decades of financial globalization, encouraged by the deregulation and the liberalization of financial and other markets. The dominant view and ideology was that of the efficiency of free markets and the inefficiency of the state. The World Bank and the IMF both headquartered in Washington DC, became the poster boys for this free market ideology. So dominant was this view that John Williamson noted that there appeared to be a consensus about policy making in a number of key areas. This was later to be described as the "Washington Consensus".

Williamson (2004) summarises the "Washington Consensus" in the following 10 points:

1. Fiscal Discipline

Budget deficits, properly measured to include those of provincial governments, state enterprises, and the central bank, should be small enough to be financed without recourse to the inflation tax.

2. Public Expenditure Priorities

Policy reform consists in redirecting expenditure from politically sensitive areas, to neglected areas with high economic returns and the potential to improve income distribution, such as primary health and education, and infrastructure.

3. Tax Reform

Tax reform involves broadening the tax base and cutting marginal tax rates. The aim is to sharpen incentives and improve horizontal equity.

4. Financial Liberalisation

The ultimate objective of financial liberalisation is market-determined interest rates but a sensible interim objective is the abolition of preferential interest rates for privileged borrowers and achievement of a moderately positive real interest rate.

5. Exchange Rates

Countries need a unified (at least for trade transactions) exchange rate set at a level sufficiently competitive to induce a rapid growth in non-traditional exports, and managed so as to assure exporters that this competitiveness will be maintained in the future.

6. Trade Liberalisation

Quantitative trade restrictions should be rapidly replaced by tariffs, and these should be progressively reduced until a uniform low tariff in the range of 10 percent (or at most around 20 percent) is achieved.

7. Foreign Direct Investment

Barriers impeding the entry of foreign firms should be abolished; foreign and domestic firms should be allowed to compete on equal terms.

8. Privatisation

State enterprises should be privatised.

9. Deregulation

Governments should abolish regulations that impede the entry of new firms or restrict competition, and ensure that all regulations are justified by such criteria as safety, environmental protection, or prudential supervision of financial institutions.

10. Property Rights

The legal system should provide secure property rights without excessive costs, and make these available to the informal sector.

On 28 August 1983, Flt. Lt. Rawlings delivered an address on national radio and television to the people of Ghana. As Attafuah (1993) notes, the speech was essentially a close-up analysis and critique of the populist and economically unproductive elements in the "31st December Revolution" as it had evolved to date:

> *We can no longer postpone the time for halting the populist nonsense and for consolidating the gains of the past 20 months and making a noticeable leap forward... Production and efficiency must be our watchwords. Populist nonsense must give way to popular or unpopular sense ... to scientific sense, whether it is popular or not. Many of us have spent too much time worrying about who owns what. But there can be no ownership without production first. The only resources which do not have to be produced are those given to us by nature, and these must be used for the benefit of all the people of today and tomorrow. Everything else has to be produced, and until we all fully recognize and act upon this fact, we shall be deceiving ourselves with empty theories. (West Africa, September 12, 1983.).*

Rawlings' rejection of "popular nonsense" reflected a recognition of the simple truth, that revolutionary rhetoric and "mobilization" are by themselves inadequate vehicles for growing and sustaining an economy.

The PNDC's 1983 Budget, announced by Dr. Kwesi Botchwey, the Finance Secretary, signaled the governments' adoption of the "Washington Consensus". This Budget contained a significant devaluation of the cedi (an act which was anathema to Rawlings in 1979), and an increase in the prices of basic foodstuffs. This marked the beginning of Ghana's market-oriented Structural Adjustment Programme (SAP). With it, the PNDC moved Ghana away from Kwame Nkrumah's socialist economic philosophy towards the capitalist free market philosophy that the government railed so much against at its inception. The major policies underpinning the SAP were as follows:

Exchange Rate Policy

At the onset of the SAP, there was a wide divergence between the parallel market and the official exchange rate of the cedi, reaching some 2,100 percent in 1982 (IMF, 1991). The official exchange rate was adjusted in stages from ¢2.75/US$ in 1983 to ¢90.0/US$ by January 1986. A two window exchange rate system was introduced on September 19, 1986. The first window exchange rate, (fixed at ¢90.0/US$) covered official transactions like debt service payments and the importation of drugs and petroleum products. The second window covered all other transactions; Quantitative restrictions were also eliminated with most goods no longer requiring a Special Import License. In February 1987, the official exchange rates were unified at ¢150/US$. To bridge the gap between parallel and official exchange rates, foreign exchange bureaus were established in February 1988, leading to the virtual absorption of the parallel foreign exchange market.

Fiscal Policy

Fiscal policy under the SAP aimed at correcting the fiscal imbalances through reforming the tax system, and rehabilitating the nation's physical and social infrastructure. By 1983, the government's total revenue had declined to 5.6% of GDP and the tax revenue to 4.6% of GDP (IMF, 2000). Tax polices under SAP were gradually restructured, with an emphasis on broadening the tax base and lowering tax rates. These measures resulted in an increase in tax revenue to 16.9% of GDP by 1993. On the expenditure side, some emphasis was given to cost recovery measures in areas such as health and education. Fees for hospital beds and consultations were sharply raised in 1985 in advance of the World Bank's Health and Education Rehabilitation project. The credit for this project contained the formal requirement that 15.0 percent of the recurrent revenues should be met from cost recovery measures.

Privatisation

Given Nkrumah's state-centered approach to economic development, many public enterprises (about 350) were established to undertake production across all sectors of the economy, including mining, agriculture, manufacturing, trade, construction, energy, telecommunication, housing, finance and banking. By the early 1980s the public sector completely dominated production, accounting for 75 percent of formal employment (IMF, 2000).

The public enterprise reform process in Ghana aimed to reduce the managerial and financial burden these enterprises placed on public resources while promoting efficiency of the economy. To speed up the privatization process, the government set up the Divestiture Implementation Committee in June 1988. However, divestiture required approval of final sale by the President's Office.

Over the period 1989-1999, an additional 192 enterprises were divested: 46 through the sale of shares, 88 through outright sale, 15 through joint ventures and 38 through liquidation (Table 2.1).

Table 2.1. Ghana: Divestiture of State-Owned Enterprises, 1989-1999

	1989-1992	1993-1999	1989-1999
Number of SOEs Divested	59	133	192
Joint Ventures	3	12	15
Lease	2	3	5
Liquidation	26	12	38
Outright Sales	11	77	88
Sale of Shares	17	29	46
Divestiture Proceeds			
Cedis	11,554	183,396	194,950
US dollars	14.8	610.6	625.4
UK pounds	3.4	0.0	3.4
German Marks	8.1	0.0	8.1
French francs	0.0	21.0	21.0
Total (in million of US$*	61.4	726.17	747.7

Source: Divestiture Implementation Committtee, IMF. * using exchange rates for the period.

The divestiture included the sale of Government's interests in Ashanti Goldfields Company, (US$462.4 million), state-owned banks (US$65.2 million) and a 30% strategic stake in Ghana Telecom (US$38 million), Ghana National Trading Corporation (GNTC), State Fishing Corporation, Achimota Breweries Company, Star Hotel, Continental Hotel, Juapong Textiles, Lever Brothers, GIHOC, GHACEM, Aluworks, Neoplan Ghana Ltd,

TABLE 2.2. SELECTED LIST OF DIVESTED STATE ENTERPRISES – 1989-1999

Leyland DAF Ghana Ltd	Ghana Aluminium	GNTC	Ghana Rubber Estates Ltd	L'air Liquide
Kwahu Dairy Farms	Neoplan Ghana Ltd	New Edubiase Oil Palm	Kingfisheries Tema	Willowbrook Ghana Ltd
NIC Textiles	GIHOC Electronics	New Match Factory	Aluworks Ghana Ltd	African Timber & Plywood
GIHOC Ice and Cold	GIHOC Metals factory	GIHOC Paints	Ghana Union Assurance	Nkawkaw Rattan Factory
NIC Metal Fabrication	Nestle Ghana Ltd	Ghana Cotton Company Ltd	Coca Cola (GNTC) Bottling	GIHOC Cannery Wechi
State Fishing Corporation	Guiness Ghana Ltd	Ghana Pioneer Aluminium	Komenda Sugar Factory	Gilksten West Africa Ltd
NIC Soap and Detergent	Pioneer Tobacco Ltd	Ghana Textile Printing	BARDEC Livestock Project	Produce Buying Company
Ghamot Enterprises	Irani Brothers & Others	Tema Food Complex	State Construction Company	Ashanti Goldfieds Company
Ghamot Motor Engineering	Meat Marketing Board	Atlantic Hotel	Barclays Bank Ghana Ltd	Ghana Telecom
Ghamot Textiles	Tarkwa Goldfields	Star Hotel	Ghana Bauxite Company	Ghana Commercial Bank
West Coast Shrimping	GHACEM	Ambassador Hotel	Ghana Printing Company	Merchant Bank
GIHOC Farms	Prestea Goldfields	African Timber and Plywood	Black Star Line	Social Security bank
Continental Hotel	West African Mills Company	Dunkwa Goldfields	State Transport Company	Twifo Oil Plam
Saltpond Ceramics limited	Kumasi Glue Factory	Kumasi a Furniture & Joinery	Ghana Oil Palm Devt. Co	Medie Horticulture Nursery
Reiss & Co. (Ghana) Ltd	Naja David Veneer & Lumber	Juapong Textiles	City Express Services	Gradecorp Quarry-Weija
GIHOC Glass Factory	GIHOC Paper and Printing	Ghana National Manganese	Overseas Knitwear & Fabrics	Winneba Animal Production Far
GEA General Chemicals	GIHOC Mosquito Coil	GIHOC Brick and Tile	DL Steel Ltd	Fafia Auto Parts
GIHOC Machine Shop	Ghana Seed Company Ltd	GIHOC Marble Works	Metalico Ltd	Ayinasi & Mpem Rubber Plant
Achimota Brewery Company	La Beach Complex	Tamale Catering Rest House	Victory Industries	Cape Cost Catering Rest House
GIHOC Boatyards Sekondi	GIHOC Phamaceutical	RT Briscoe	Broadway Enterprises Ltd	Emil Ghana Limited
Eveready Plastics	GIHOC Vegetable Oil	Tema Shipyard and Drydock	GHASEL Asutuare Factory	Two Worlds Manufacturing
National Tobacco Company	Rice mills Tamale	Ghana Film Industry	Tricotex Ltd	Wire and Metal Production Ltd
NIC Kool Bottling	NIC Vehicle Assembly Plant	Meridian Hotel	Umarco	GAVA Farms
Bibiani Industrial Complex	GIHOC Nsawam Cannery	Tomos Ghana Ltd	NIC Chemical and Paints	Golcha Films Ltd
GIHOC Steelworks	Juaben Oil Palm Plantation	City Hotel, Kumasi	Central Parts Depot	Lever Brothers Ghana Ltd

Source: IMF, Divestiture Implementation Committee

Pioneer Tobacco, Ghana Aluminium, Tema Food Complex etc. (see Table 2.2—for list of some of the enterprises divested). The PNDC also committed itself to the sale of the Tema Oil Refinery by the end of 1999. The divestiture was ultimately meant to reduce the burden of the state enterprises on the budget and the attendant monetary implications as well as allow the enterprises to operate more efficiently under private sector incentives. It also yielded revenue to the budget.

The total divestiture proceeds for all the 192 state enterprises divested between 1989 and 1999 was the equivalent of some US$747.7 million, including $462.4 million from AGC (Table 2.1).

The Move from Direct Controls to Indirect Instruments (Monetary Targeting).

The Keynesian policy prescription following the Great Depression and the resulting unemployment was to increase aggregate demand (mainly through an increase in government spending). There was recognition however, that as the economy moved towards full employment increases in aggregate demand would result in inflation. There was an apparent trade-off between unemployment and inflation as captured by what is referred to as the Phillips Curve relationship. This appeared to hold in the 1950s and 60s. By the 1970s however, this received wisdom was increasingly questioned when the oil price shocks of 1973/74 and 1979 resulted in increasing unemployment and rising inflation, a phenomenon described as *stagflation* (i.e. stagnation together with inflation). There was, after all, no trade-off between unemployment and inflation and Keynesian policy prescriptions were inadequate to deal with the problem of stagflation. On the one hand, higher unemployment seemed to call for Keynesian demand stimulus, but on the other hand rising inflation seemed to call for a withdrawal of such stimulus.

Milton Friedman, the Nobel Prize winning economist was the intellectual father of a monetarist view that countered Keynesian economics. Friedman argued that the Keynesian solution to unemployment was only a short-run solution and in the long run there was no trade-off between inflation and unemployment. For Friedman, the Keynesian approach resulted in too much money injected in the economy chasing too few goods. Friedman argued that "inflation was always and everywhere a monetary phenomenon" (Friedman and Schwartz, 1963). Monetarism and neoclassical economics paralleled one another in their belief that the market functioned well provided that money supply remains stable. In their pursuit for quick votes or lack of understanding that economies may slowdown, government officials break a cardinal rule by changing the supply of money circulating in the economy.

The control of inflation therefore began taking centre stage on the agenda of central banks around the world. Internationally, direct controls became discredited as a monetary policy regime. The classic theory of financial repression developed by Mckinnon (1973) and Shaw (1973) argued that under financial repression (interest rate ceilings below the equilibrium interest rate) the financial system was unable to mobilize the requisite amount of savings for investment while at the same time increasing the demand for loanable funds (savings). Financial institutions, in the presence of a market shortage of loanable funds (savings), resort to non-market means of rationing credit. The economy as a whole is not able to mobilize sufficient savings for investment and economic growth is lower as a result. It was therefore argued that financial liberalization, with a market determination of interest rates and prices, would result in an allocation of resources to their most efficient uses. Competition in the banking sector should increase, there should be more product innovation and financial intermediation will be enhanced as credit is channeled to its most efficient use.

Control of the money supply (Monetary Targeting) was to be undertaken through *indirect monetary instruments* like open market operations, reserve requirements, and central bank lending facilities. The move to the use of indirect monetary instruments was the counterpart in the monetary area of the widespread movement toward enhancing the role of the free market and price signals in the economy. It was part of a broader set of reforms, which included not only liberalization of the financial sector but also macroeconomic stabilization and liberalization of the economy in general. In addition, the adoption of indirect instruments took place in an increasingly open economic environment characterized by widespread adoption of current account convertibility and progress in moving to full external account convertibility, especially following the collapse of the Bretton Woods System.

Bank of Ghana's Monetary Targeting through Indirect Monetary Policy Instruments

The Bank of Ghana's strategy for inflation management under the indirect monetary instruments regime was based on the monetarist view that inflation is mainly a monetary phenomenon. This means that to control inflation you have to control the growth of the money supply in the economy. Since the central bank cannot control the money supply directly, it uses a number of instruments to do so indirectly. The indirect monetary instruments that have been used include reserve requirements, open market operations (OMO), repurchase agreements (Repo), and rediscount facilities. These instruments are used to impact base money (the operating target) which in turn impacts broad money (the intermediate target) and finally prices (the final target) as represented in the diagram below.

Figure 2.1: Monetary Targeting Strategy

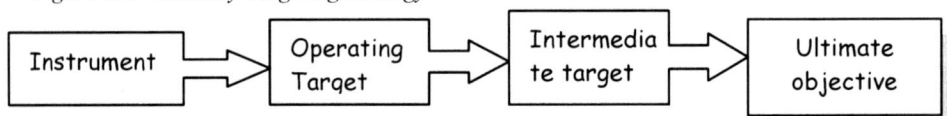

Reserve Requirements

Reserve requirements oblige banks to hold a specified part of their portfolio as reserves at the central bank. Ghana has a long history of using reserve requirements for both prudential and monetary management purposes. During the period of direct controls, they were used as a supplement to credit controls. The central bank continued to use reserve requirements after the introduction of indirect monetary control. However, the ratio (base and method of calculation) has evolved over the years. Prior to March 1990, the ratios discriminated between types of deposit. The ratios applied on demand deposits were higher than those for savings and time deposits (quasi money). The idea was to encourage commercial banks to mobilize long-term funds, which could be channeled into term lending. After 1990, the two ratios were merged into a single ratio on total deposits (demand, time and savings deposits). Finally in 1997, the coverage was extended to foreign currency deposits. This was in response to the central bank's decision to target the broader definition of money supply, M2+, which also includes foreign currency deposits. Thus, the central bank was able to have a better control over the money supply, while at the same time leveling the playing field for the mobilization of both domestic and foreign currency deposits.

The level of the ratio itself fluctuated over the years, reflecting liquidity conditions in the banking system, reaching its highest level of 27 per cent in 1990. After 1990, the ratio was progressively lowered until it reached its lowest point of 5 per cent in 1993. The reserve ratio was again raised to 10 per cent in 1996 and lowered to 8 per cent in 1997 when foreign currency deposits were included in the total deposit base for the calculation of reserves. In July 2000 in response to rising inflation and the sharp depreciation of the cedi, the ratio was raised to 9 per cent (Yahya, 2001).

Reserves against Foreign Currency Deposits

There are two main issues that frequently come up with foreign currency deposits: whether the reserves against these deposits should be held in foreign or domestic currency; and whether foreign currency deposits should be included in the monetary target. Generally, when reserves against foreign currency deposits are held in domestic currency, banks may be exposed to foreign currency risks. On the other hand, denominating some reserves in foreign currency can complicate monetary policy implementation by removing some of the central bank's control over base money. The second issue of whether foreign currency deposits should be included in the monetary target is an empirical issue, depending on the substitutability of foreign and domestic currencies.

Reserve requirements against foreign currency deposits were introduced in Ghana in 1997 with the main aim of leveling the playing field for the mobilization of domestic and foreign currency deposits. Requirements against foreign currency deposits were applied at the same ratio as cedi deposits and are not remunerated. However, the Bank of Ghana required banks to keep reserves for foreign currency deposits in cedis for a number of reasons. First, keeping reserves in foreign currency is operationally difficult because the central bank will have to monitor the banks' several (nostro) accounts in different currencies. Also, there was the need at the time to further tighten liquidity in order to sustain the downward trend in inflation. This measure apparently provided an avenue for the central bank to tighten liquidity conditions without appearing to increase overall reserve requirements.[6]

Open Market-Type Operations

Open market operations (OMO) are the purchase and sale of financial instruments by the central bank in either the primary market or the secondary market. The instruments commonly used for OMO include government treasury bills, central bank bills or prime commercial paper. In conducting monetary policy, Bank of Ghana intervenes mainly through the primary auction of government securities (treasury bills). This has been the underlying instrument for open market intervention and for meeting the public sector borrowing requirement (PSBR) since 1996. The auction system has gone through several transformations. Originally, weekly auctions of treasury bills were held on Fridays, with the amount offered based on the position with regard to targeted reserve money, maturing bills, as well as the PSBR.

---

[6] In order to satisfy the requirement, banks would either have to call in loans or sell foreign exchange, in either case impacting negatively on money supply.

Investors could also purchase on tap directly from BOG between tenders (auctions) at the weighted average price declared at the preceding auction. The tap was supposed to be open only when targets were not met, but were, in practice, always open in view of the large liquidity overhang. This situation discouraged the development of the secondary market, and therefore in 1997, and BOG abolished the tap for the non-bank sector. The weekly auctions were initially open to both banks and the non-bank public, although the non-bank public had to submit their bids through their bankers. Since March 1996, tenders have become restricted to only primary dealers, comprising commercial banks, discount houses and four brokerage firms. The primary dealers underwrite the whole issue at the tender and act as market makers in government and central bank securities.

Like any other market-determined price, the Treasury bill rates are arrived at through the interplay of market forces of demand and supply in a weekly auction system. The demand side comes from the Government through its Public Sector Borrowing Requirement (PSBR) and from the Central Bank (for its monetary policy operations), popularly referred to as the open market operations (OMO). Thus the sum of the PSBR and OMO at any given week will determine how much the BOG needs to borrow from the investing public to satisfy both the needs of Government and the BOG. The supply side of the equation, on the other hand, comes from the investing public (i.e. those who are ready to give up their cash (money) holdings for treasury bills), which includes the financial institutions, other corporate bodies and individuals.

In March 1996, Bank of Ghana introduced the wholesale auction system. Tenders became restricted to only primary dealers comprising commercial banks, discount houses and four brokerage firms. The public participates in the auction process through Primary Dealers/Distributors (PDs). Targets for the auction (a direct function of the PSBR and OMO) are published in some of the print media every Monday. Thus, the PDs are aware, well ahead of time, of the revealed demand/preference of the Government and Bank of Ghana. On that basis, the PDs submit their bids on Thursday. The bids (amount and accompanying interests, i.e. the rates at which they will be ready to lend those funds to Government and BOG) are based on their own perception about the underlying inflationary trends in the economy. Subsequently, the auction is conducted on Friday to either accept or reject some bids based on the Dutch Auction System (DAS). DAS is an auction system in which the investor obtains the price quoted when successful. These are then ranked in ascending order of the rates quoted with the cut off at the rate at which the market is cleared. A weighted average of the discount rates of accepted bids are then calculated for the different maturity profiles and this ultimately results in the published rates the following Monday.

The workings of the auction process clearly demonstrate that a higher demand for cash (credit) by the Government and BOG will result in a higher interest rate. The high interest rate thus provides an incentive offered to investors to part with their funds. Conversely, interest rates on treasury bills will move downward with decreasing demand (i.e. reduced borrowing by the Government and the central bank). In the same vein, the rate (price) could also fall following an increased (excess) supply of funds by the public (for example due to higher past interest rates).

Money Market Instruments

The underlying financial instrument for open market interventions usually is government or central bank securities. With the introduction of indirect monetary management during 1988/89, the main instrument for open market operations was government securities. However, following the unwillingness on the part of government to issue treasury bills in amounts sufficient to mop up existing excess liquidity, Bank of Ghana introduced its own debt instruments. Not long after its introduction, BOG securities became the main instrument of monetary policy. Thus, the proportion of Government of Ghana instruments declined from 67% of total open market instruments in 1990 to 20% 1994, while Bank of Ghana securities rose from 34% to 80% over the same period.

Beginning in 1996, there was a shift in composition from Bank of Ghana securities to Government of Ghana securities i.e. Treasury bills. This followed a deliberate central bank policy of replacing BOG bills with treasury bills apparently because of the Government's increasing concerns over interest payments on these instruments. Thus, from 1996 treasury bills became the main instrument of intervention while at the same time serving the purpose of Government's debt management.

The phasing out of the BOG bills brought into focus the issue of over-financing of the deficit, with the difference between the deficit and the actual issue representing the central bank's monetary intervention. BOG addressed this issue by opening a separate account into which proceeds from intervention are put and sterilized. The BOG's decision to switch to treasury bills was taken on the basis of Government's increasing concerns about the interest payments on the BOG bills. There was therefore the danger that in future Government may decide to stop paying the interest cost on BOG bills, an action that may affect the profitability of the central bank and potentially compromise the conduct of monetary policy.

Money Market Rates

While a lot was achieved in laying down the infrastructure for market intervention, there was not much success in achieving money supply and inflation targets. Again, the main problem was the continued presence of Government on the market, as well as the inability of the central bank to vary rates to achieve the desired targets. The central bank was limited in its ability to use the Bank Rate effectively due to cost considerations. Since the cost of intervention was financed by Government, it (Government) could resist interest rate increases to levels that were necessary to clear the market.

Repurchase Agreements (REPOS)

In 1998, Bank of Ghana introduced repurchase agreements (repos) instrument, which has since become the principal instrument for the provision of central bank funds. As part of these transactions, BOG purchases government securities from the commercial banks on condition that the sellers simultaneously repurchase the securities forward.

Bank of Ghana sets the repurchase rate itself, while the banks merely state in their request the amount for which they wish to sell securities to BOG. The tenor of the repos usually ranges from overnight to 14 days and BOG provides funds to the market so as to meet its liquidity requirements.

Since its inception, repos have proved to be a very flexible cash management tool used by the central bank to manage the reserves and excess cash positions of the commercial banks. Repos, unlike outright purchases of securities, are reversible over short periods specified in advance. Furthermore, the terms of a repo transaction (the maturity, rate structure and total amount) are varied in accordance with current liquidity situation and policy stance of the Bank of Ghana.

CHAPTER 3

FINANCIAL SECTOR REFORM: 1984-2000

As part of a comprehensive macroeconomic adjustment program with the support of the International Monetary Fund and World Bank, financial market liberalization in Ghana began in the late 1980s, under the Financial Sector Adjustment Programme (FINSAP), with the restructuring of distressed banks and cleaning up non-performing assets to restore banks to profitability and viability. The programme set prices right, initiated structural reforms, including fiscal and monetary operations, and privatizations (including banks).

The adoption of the FINSAP was part of a strategy to move the Ghanaian financial sector from an era of financial repression towards one of financial liberalization. This included the removal of interest rate ceilings, abolishing of directed credit and credit controls, restructuring of seven financially distressed banks, improving the regulatory and supervisory framework, privatization of banks, development of money and capital markets, and the move towards indirect and market determined instruments of monetary policy.

Liberalization of interest Rates

Interest rate liberalization under the FINSAP was implemented gradually. First, the maximum and minimum deposit interest rates were abolished in September 1987, (the minimum saving deposit rate was temporarily maintained at 12% however). All sectoral credit allocations were also phased out. Interest rate controls were gradually relaxed and full liberalization was achieved in February 1988. In November 1990, the Bank of Ghana liberalized all bank charges and fees. A foreign exchange auction was introduced in 1986 and the establishment of forex bureaus was permitted in 1988.

Restructuring Financially Distressed Banks

The restructuring of the distressed banks involved the reconstitution and strengthening of their board of directors, closure of unprofitable branches, reduction of operating costs through retrenchment of staff, cleaning of balance sheets by offloading non-performing loans granted to state-owned enterprises, non-performing loans granted to the private sector, and loans guaranteed by the government of Ghana, upgrading of managerial capacity, intensified staff training of affected banks, and providing enough capital and adequate liquidity to enable the distressed banks to operate in a self-sustaining manner after restructuring..

Strengthening of the Regulatory and Supervisory Framework of the Central Bank

The existing regulatory framework was governed by the Banking Act of 1970. This Act however did not provide clear guidelines on minimum capital requirements, risk exposure, prudential limits for banks, and provisioning for loan losses, inter alia. A new Banking Law, the Banking Act 1989, was passed to remedy these deficiencies. The new Banking Act laid out the basic regulatory framework for the banking system: minimum capital requirements, capital adequacy ratios (banks required to maintain a minimum capital base of 6% of risk-weighted assets), prudential lending ratios, exposure limits, and uniform accounting and auditing standards. Supervisory activities of the Bank of Ghana were also strengthened and the banks were required to submit accounts for off-site monitoring. Annual on-site inspections, as well as off-site surveillance were to be conducted to verify banks' compliance with regulations.

Specifically the Banking Act 1989 provided inter alia that:

- The minimum paid-up capital for commercial banks with at least 60% Ghanaian ownership was set at ¢200 million

- Foreign banks with Ghanaian ownership of less than 60% had to maintain a minimum paid-up capital of ¢500 million
- The minimum paid-up capital for development banks was set at one billion cedis.
- All banks were required to maintain a minimum capital adequacy ratio of 6.0 percent.
- Banks were not allowed to lend more than 25.0 percent of their net worth by way of secured loans and 10.0 percent of their net worth as unsecured loans.
- Banks were not allowed to undertake non-bank activities. They could only do so through subsidiaries.

A revised Bank of Ghana Law (PNDCL 291) was also enacted in 1992 to give more supervisory powers to the central bank. These two laws together provided the legal and regulatory framework for the banking business in Ghana.

Recovery of Non-Performing Assets

A major part of the process of restructuring the banks involved removing nonperforming loans (NPLs) from their balance sheets. This was accomplished either through swapping such loans for government-guaranteed interest-bearing bonds issued by the Bank of Ghana or offsetting such NPLs against liabilities to the government. A total of ¢62 billion NPLs ($170 million or 4.4 per cent of GDP) were removed from the banks' portfolios under the exercise. These NPLs were transferred to a newly created Non-Performing Assets Recovery Trust (NPART), whose mandate was to realize these assets to the extent possible. In return, the government issued the distressed banks with interest bearing FINSAP bonds redeemable in annual installments.

Table 3.1 indicates that the NPAs of the foreign owned banks or banks with foreign equity participation (Barclays, SCB, and MBG) were the lowest while the NPAs of the state-owned banks (GCB, SSB, BHC, and NIB) were the highest (accounting for 91.6 per cent of the NPAs transferred to NPART).

This was because the foreign owned banks applied stricter commercial criteria in their lending decisions. The local banks were characterized by poor credit decisions especially due to government encouragement to lend to the agricultural sector. The foreign banks were also able to avoid political pressures.

The experience in Ghana is that the politicians are generally not able to approach the foreign banks with propositions they know will be rejected (because they are not commercially viable) but have no qualms presenting the same propositions to government-owned banks as the managing directors can easily be "persuaded" to oblige. The foreign banks were also helped by a directive that all state enterprises move their accounts to Ghana Commercial Bank, the perennial government milking cow of the Ghanaian banking industry. This experience with the performance of the state-owned banks provided the rationale for the reduction of state direct involvement in the banking system under FINSAP.

Table 3.1. Non-Performing Assets Transferred to NPART by Banks (¢ millions)

Bank	Total Amount of NPAs	% of Total
GCB	14,321	28.4
SSB	12,585	25.0
NSCB	725	1.4
ADB	1,293	2.6
NIB	6,623	13.1
BHC	12,853	25.5
Barclays	689	1.4
SCB	462	0.9
MBG	881	1.7
TOTAL	50,433	100

Source: Ziorklui et al (2001)

Institutional Restructuring and Divestiture of Government Shares in Commercial Banks

As was noted earlier, one of the major problems plaguing the financial sector was the domination of the sector by government banks and the attendant political influence and lack of competition. Government therefore undertook as part of FINSAP, to divest its shares in commercial banks in 1992. On the block for divestiture were Social Security Bank (SSB), GCB, ADB, NIB, BHC, CO-OP. 40 percent of SSB were sold to a strategic investor and 21 percent of shares were divested through a public offer. In February 1996 42 percent of shares in GCB were floated on the stock exchange. The divestiture of ADB and NIB stalled while BHC and COOP banks were liquidated following a check fraud scandal (The A-Life scandal). Government also divested 40 percent of its shares in Barclays bank in June 1998.

In 1995, the Social Security Bank merged with the National Savings and Credit Bank (NSCB). The money market was formalized with the creation in 1991 of a second discount house, the Security Discount Company (SDC) to compete with the Consolidated Discount House (CDH), which was created in 1987. Both were wholly owned by the banks in Ghana and charged with carrying out interbank market operations. These institutions played their traditional role of facilitating the intermediation process and reducing imbalances in the money market.

NON-BANK FINANCIAL INSTITUTIONS

The liberalization of the financial sector resulted in a rapid growth of non-bank financial institutions. To streamline the regulatory framework, a Financial Institutions (Non-Banking) Law (PNDCL 328) was also enacted in 1993 to govern the operations of non-banks (savings and loans companies, finance companies, discount houses, acceptance houses, building societies, mortgage finance companies, credit unions, venture capital funds, and leasing and hire-purchase companies under the oversight of the Bank of Ghana. NBFIs had not previously been covered by legislation.

The NBFI Law of 1993 provided for the following amongst others:

- The minimum capital requirement for an NBFI was set at ¢100 million.
- The minimum capital adequacy ratio was set at 10.0 percent of risk assets.
- Non-Banks were not allowed to lend more than 15.0 percent of their net worth by way of secured loans and 10.0 percent of their net worth as unsecured loans.

The Banking Act of 1989 and the NBFI Law of 1993 resulted in the emergence of new financial institutions which have added diversity and depth to the financial system, including acceptance houses, discount houses, finance houses, mortgage finance, savings and loans companies, venture capital companies (see Table 3.2).

Table 3.2. Licensed NBFIs at the end of 2000

Type of Institution	Number
Building Societies	2
Discount Houses	3
Finance Houses	10
Leasing Companies	6
Mortgage Finance	1
Savings and Loans	8
Venture Capital Funds	2
Credit Unions	225
Total	**257**

Source: Bank of Ghana

Rural Bank Reforms

The Bank of Ghana also continued to support the development of the rural banking system. The number of rural banks increased from 20 in 1980 to 111 by 1999 (Table 3.3).

TABLE 3.3.   **REGIONAL DISTRIBUTION OF RURAL BANKS 1987-2008**

REGION	1987	1995	1999	2008
ASHANTI	20	22	21	22
CENTRAL	22	22	20	21
EASTERN	19	22	19	21
BRONG AHAFO	15	18	17	20
WESTERN	10	14	12	14
VOLTA	12	14	8	11
GREATER ACCRA	5	6	6	6
UPPER EAST	2	2	3	4
UPPER WEST	2	2	3	4
NORTHERN	0	3	3	6
TOTAL	**107**	**125**	**111**	**129**

Source: Bank of Ghana

The main catalysts for the increase in the number of Rural Banks were the 1983 Economic Recovery Programme (ERP), the pressures exerted on the Bank of Ghana in the early 1980's by the Cocoa Board to facilitate cocoa purchases in the rural areas, and the demands of prominent local citizens to have rural banks in their communities.

Rural banks are unit banks incorporated as limited liability companies. They are owned by the communities in which they are located and they operate generally within a 20 mile radius of their headquarters. To avoid the dominance of large shareholders in the community, no single individual or company was allowed to own more than 10 percent and 20 percent of the share capital respectively. Rural banks have on average about 1,000 shareholders.

Even though the number of rural banks is large, their regional coverage is unequal, with a high concentration in the Ashanti, Central, Brong Ahafo, Eastern regions while the northern regions (Northern, Upper East and Upper West) are not well served (Table 3.3).

Rural Banks are subject to the same regulatory oversight as the deposit money banks and operated initially under the Banking Act 1970. The minimum capital requirement for rural banks was ¢50 million and rural banks had to maintain a primary reserve in the form of cash and balances with other banks of not less than 10 percent of deposit liabilities and secondary reserves in the form of treasury bills and other money market instruments of not less than 52 percent of their deposit liabilities, transfer a minimum of 50 percent of their annual net profit after tax to their reserve fund, and seek ratification of the Bank of Ghana before the disbursement of loans of ¢20 million or more to a single party and all loans to directors or companies in which they have an interest.

Consistent with the financial sector reform programme (FINSAP) the sectoral lending requirements which required rural banks to allocate 45 percent of their loan portfolio for agriculture and 30 percent for cottage industry were discontinued at the beginning of the 1990s.

Notwithstanding the increase in the number of rural banks, the high reserve requirements, along with high Treasury Bill interest rates, limited the ability as well as willingness of rural banks to extend credit. With Treasury Bill rates high and close to the lending rates for agriculture, manufacturing and trading, rural banks maintained a high share of their deposits as primary and secondary reserves, ranging between 65 and 80 percent of deposits between 1994 and 1998 (Table 3.4)

Outstanding credit (including on lent funds under externally assisted projects) increased from ¢6.8 billion in 1993 to 54.0 billion by 1998 while deposits over the same period increased from ¢13.2 billion to ¢114.0 billion. While the increase in deposits was significant (nearly nine times) rural bank deposits only accounted for 3.0 percent of total formal banking system deposits by the end of 1998.

Table 3.4 : Selected Financial Indicators of Rural Banks, 1993-1998 (¢ billion)

	1993	1994	1995	1996	1997	1998
Total Assets	-	-	45.3	72.5	101.8	164.3
Deposits	13.2	16.0	33.5	50.1	76.0	114.0
Outstanding Credit	6.8	7.8	14.4	24.3	36.4	54.0
Primary/Secondary Reserves	9.4	10.5	23.4	37.7	49.5	91.3
-in % of Total Deposits	71	66	70	75	65	80
Shareholders' Funds	-	1.3	3.2	4.7	7.4	11.4

Source: Bank of Ghana

The distribution of loans and advances by the rural banks was heavily skewed towards salaried workers; accounting for at least 50 percent of the total outstanding loans while the share of credit to agriculture, at between 16-20 percent was relatively small. For rural banks, lending to salaried (mainly urban) workers is relatively low risk while the experience with lending to agriculture has been very risky.

Ghana Stock Exchange

Under the direction of the government, the first feasibility study on establishing a stock exchange in Ghana was conducted in 1968 (the Pearl Report). The Report recommended the establishment of a stock exchange. In 1971, the Stock Exchange Act was passed and the Accra Stock Exchange Company was incorporated. However, because of frequent changes in government and political instability, the stock exchange envisaged in the Pearl Report was not established until 1989 when the Ghana Stock Exchange was incorporated under the Companies Code (Mensah, 1997). The incorporation of the Ghana Stock Exchange (GSE) by the PNDC government in July 1989 (and officially launched in January 1990) was a landmark event in the financial sector development of Ghana. The presence of a stock exchange was seen as increasing the possibilities for raising financial savings and contributing to capital formation. The GSE was also seen as a way to accelerate the government's privatization programme, allowing participation by local investors. The GSE has no shareholders but is incorporated as a public company limited by guarantee (i.e. it is a not-for profit organization).

There are three categories of members, namely Licensed Dealing Members (LDM), Associate Members and Government Securities Dealers (Primary Dealers- PDs). An LDM is a corporate body licensed by the Exchange to deal in all securities. An Associate member is an individual or corporate body which has satisfied the Exchange's membership requirements but is not licensed to deal in securities. In 1993 the GSE was the sixth-best performer among emerging stock markets, with a capital appreciation of 116 percent. In 1994 the GSE was the best performer among emerging stock markets, with a capital appreciation of 124 percent. After a slump in performance in 1995 following high inflation and interest rates, the GSE recovered in 1998 with the GSE index increasing by 70 percent to become the best performing market in Africa (IMF, 2000). After the floatation of AGC in 1994, it became the most important stock on the GSE, accounting for more than 70 percent of the market. The GSE was also fairly illiquid, with a turnover rate of just 4 percent in 1998.

Securities Industry Law

A Securities Industry Law (SIL) was passed in 1993 (P.N.D.C.L 333.) to provide for the establishment of a Securities Regulatory Commission (SRC) to serve as a watch dog over the industry. Its main functions include maintaining surveillance over the securities market to ensure orderly, fair and equitable dealings in securities; and to license and authorize stock exchanges, unit trust and mutual funds and securities dealers and investment advisers. The SRC was charged under the SIL with the responsibility of protecting the securities market against any abuses arising from the practice of insider trading. Takeovers, mergers, acquisitions and all forms of business combinations are subject to the review, approval and regulation of the SRC (Mensah, 1997).

The SRC was vested with significant powers to enable it acquire and gather information. The SIL gave it power to order production of books by stock exchanges and certain persons and imposes criminal sanctions on anyone who fails to obey such orders of the SRC.

The FINSAP reforms were very important financial sector reforms that transformed Ghana's financial sector. FINSAP provided a good foundation for subsequent financial sector reforms.

CHAPTER 4

MACROECONOMIC PERFORMANCE UNDER THE MONETARY TARGETING REGIME (1984-2000)

The performance of the economy in the 1984-2000 era can broadly be divided into two periods; 1984-1991 which was characterized by relative macroeconomic stability and the 1992-2000 period which was marked by relative macroeconomic instability.

A major plank of the home grown Economic Recovery Program (ERP) and World Bank's SAP was the rehabilitation and provision of physical infrastructure to help improve productivity. This programme was guided through the Public Investment Programme launched in 1984 with a focus on roads, highways, water, sanitation and electrification projects.

At the inception of the SAP/ERP, most of Ghana's roads and highways were in a state of disrepair (Huq, 1990)[7]. More than half the serviceable vehicles were off the road for lack of tires, batteries, or fast moving spare parts. The railways were in their worst condition since the system was established. Cocoa and other export products produced in the hinterland could not find their way to the ports for lack of adequate transportation facilities (Government of Ghana, 1991)[8]. It was therefore a priority of the SAP/ERP to rehabilitate the nations' infrastructure.

---

[7] Huq, M.M. . *The economy of Ghana: the first 25 years since independence.* Basingstoke: Macmillan, 1990

[8] Ghana Government, 1991. *The Economy and People of Ghana.* Government Printer. Accra.

To improve the accessibility of rural areas, particularly cocoa, timber and food producing areas, a programme of construction of bailey and steel assembly bridges throughout the country was instituted. The   roads   and highway rehabilitation programme was successful in opening up many rural areas. Priority was given to roads linking export producing regions however.

Agricultural pricing policies, together with good rainfall resulted in increases in the output of cocoa as well as cereals and starchy staples from the pre-1983 levels (Alan Roe et al, 1992)[9]

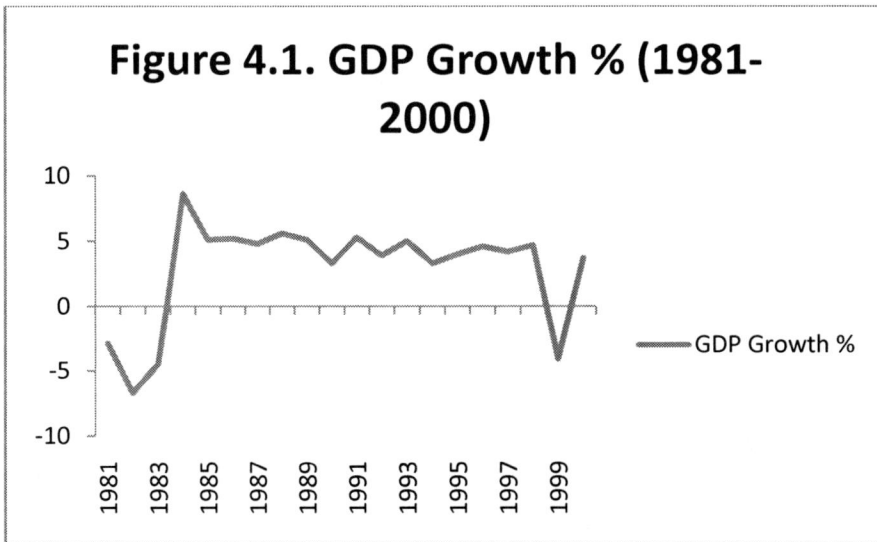

Figure 4.1. GDP Growth % (1981-2000)

The economy responded positively to the policies implemented under the SAP/ERP, and output increased. GDP growth, which was negative and declining in the three years before the SAP, recorded a remarkable recovery to register an average of some 5.0 percent per annum between 1984 and 1991. The turnaround in economic performance was masterminded by technocrats

---

[9] Alan Roe, Hartmut Schneider, and Graham Pyatt, 1992. *Adjustment and Equity in Ghana.* Development Studies Center, OECD Paris.

like Dr. Kwesi Botchwey and Dr. J.L.S. Abbey who working within a military (socialist) government, reoriented Ghana onto a path of market reform under the IMF/World Bank SAP and the homegrown ERP (the very path that the Nkrumahist Peoples National Party under the leadership of Dr. Hilla Liman was prevented from pursuing by the 1981 PNDC coup d'état) . This one can imagine was no small feat.

Growth however declined after 1991 to 3.7 percent by 2000 (Figure 4.1). The decline in growth in 2000 notwithstanding, the growth performance of the 1983-2000 period was a significant improvement over the growth record a decade earlier.

Macroeconomic stability was also restored between 1984 and 1991 and the stability was not attained at the expense of growth. Inflation declined from some 122 percent in 1983 to 10.0 percent by 1991 reflecting partly the expansion in output following the removal of infrastructure bottlenecks and fiscal discipline.

The performance of public finances also improved during the 1984-1991 period, with the government budget moving from a deficit 2.9 percent of GDP in 1983 to a surplus of 0.1 percent of GDP by 1986. The budget remained marginally in surplus between 1986 and 1991 when it registered a budget surplus of 1.6 percent of GDP, underpinned by an increase in total revenue and grants.

Relative stability also returned to the foreign exchange markets with exchange rate depreciation declining from 40.0 percent in 1984 to 11.7 percent by 1991.

Credit to the private sector (as a percentage of GDP) was however relatively static during this period, increasing from 3.0 percent in 1984 to 5.6 percent by 1989 and declining subsequently to 3.2 percent by 1991, reflecting in part the weaknesses and lack of confidence in the financial sector.

However, the economic policy framework which had brought about macroeconomic success in the 1983-1991 began to unravel however with the transition from the PNDC to the NDC after the 1992 elections. The economic and structural reforms slowed just as the gains of the market reforms became evident. The subsidies in the energy and utility sectors continued. Fiscal and monetary policy were not firm, and the public sector's borrowing led to a large build up of external as well as domestic debt, with an increased dependence on external donor inflows. The core problem of economic management that had plagued successive governments between 1957 and 1983 had reared its ugly head once again.

In the run-up to the 1992 elections, government expenditure increased dramatically as tax administration weakened. Revenue and grants declined from 16.7 percent of GDP in 1991 to 15.2 percent of GDP in 1992, with tax revenue falling from 12.4 percent of GDP to 10.8 percent. Notwithstanding the decline in government revenue, government expenditure increased at a rapid pace in the election year. Total government expenditure increased from 18.0 percent of GDP in 1991 to 24.6 percent of GDP in 1992. As a result of these developments, the overall government budget deficit, which had declined to 1.3 percent of GDP in 1991 increased sharply to 9.4 percent of GDP in 1992. The domestic debt stock increased from a low of 4.0 percent of GDP in 1991 to 16.0 percent of GDP by 1993 when expenditure increased further from 24.6 percent of GDP in 1992 to 29.0 percent of GDP in 1993 (Leite et al, 2000).

Government also undertook significant new medium-term non-concessionary borrowing in late 1992 in response to a shortfall in expected external foreign assistance. The shortfall in donor assistance was a result of policy slippages that the IMF/World Bank and other donors refused to support. The IMF and World Bank suspended financial support to Ghana between 1992 and 1994. The fiscal imbalances were also reflected in the external accounts whose deterioration was compounded by a sharp decline in cocoa prices (Leite et al, 2000).

Fiscal Dominance

The government resorted to monetary financing of the deficit. Money supply growth was 53.0 percent in 1992, 50.3 percent in 1994, and 45.4 percent by 1997. Inflation, which had fallen to 10.0 percent by the end of 1992, began to increase, reaching 74.3 percent by 1995 (Figure 4.2).

Figure 4.2. Inflation and Monetary Growth (1984-2000)

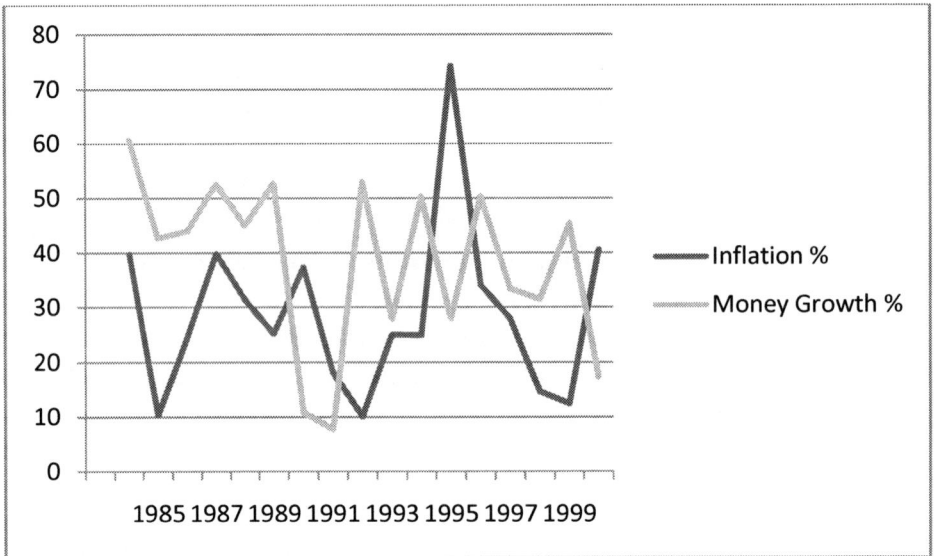

The programme with the IMF was restarted in 1995, and this together with financing pressures, resulted in the acceleration of the divestiture of a number of state companies, including Social Security Bank, Ashanti Goldfields and a 15 percent stake in Ghana Telecom.

In the run up to the 1996 elections however, large fiscal slippages occurred again (as in 1992). As in 1992, there was significant erosion in the government's revenue base. Total revenue and grants declined from 24.1 percent of GDP in 1995 to 20.2 percent of GDP in 1996 driven by non-tax revenue, which fell from 5.8 percent of GDP in 1995 to 2.5 percent of GDP by 1996 (IMF, 2000). The shortfall in petroleum tax was the result of the suspension of the automatic price adjustment formula as the elections drew closer. Again, notwithstanding the revenue shortfall, expenditure was maintained at about the same levels as a percentage of GDP (some 30 percent of GDP) as had been the case since 1993.

The fiscal stance in 1996 resulted in an overall budget deficit of 9.5 percent of GDP (the same as in 1992) and a primary deficit of 4.4 per cent of GDP. In response to the policy slippages, the IMF and World Bank suspended programme support yet again.

Between 1994 and 1998 Ghana benefited from a significant improvement in its terms of trade from an index of 99 in 1994 to 137.7 by 1998 (IMF, 2003). Notwithstanding the significant improvement in the terms of trade over this period, the fiscal policy stance meant that foreign exchange reserve cover, rather than increasing in this boom period, rather saw a decline from 4.1 months of imports in 1994 to 2.1 months of imports by 1998.

This left the economy in a very vulnerable state. The vulnerability of the Ghanaian economy in the face of persistently high fiscal deficits and declining foreign exchange reserves was to be exposed when after the economy was hit by a terms of trade shock in 1999/2000 with falling prices for Ghana's two main exports, cocoa and gold and rising prices for oil (IMF, 2003).

The excessive fiscal expansion in the run-up to the 2000 Presidential and Parliamentary elections tipped the economy into a cycle of inflation and currency depreciation, and this coincided with a sharp deterioration in the commodity terms of trade. In the short span of one year ending December 2000, the national currency, the cedi, lost 50 percent of its value vis-à-vis the US dollar. The country's gross international reserves were so depleted that it could not cover a month's imports. Foreign exchange reserve cover further declined from 2.1 months in 1998 to 0.9 months by 2000, and external payments arrears were building up.

Table 4.1. Selected Macroeconomic Indicators –
(1984-2000)

	Inflation %	Money Growth %	Real GDP Growth	Credit to Private Sector/GDP	External Debt/GDP	Nom Int. Rate Sav	Real Int. Rate Sav	Exchange Rate	Exch. Rate Depreciation	Gov. Balance
1984	39.7	60.6	8.6	3	21.7	14.5	-25.2	50.0	40.00	-1.8
1985	10.3	42.7	5.1	4.5	23.2	15.5	5.2	60.0	16.65	-2.2
1986	24.6	44	5.2	5.2	30.9	18.5	-6.1	90.0	33.35	0.1
1987	39.8	52.6	4.8	4.3	54.2	21.5	-18.3	176.1	48.87	0.5
1988	31.4	45	5.6	3.6	49.3	19.25	-12.2	229.9	23.42	0.4
1989	25.2	52.7	5.1	5.6	51.8	17	-8.2	308.0	24.14	0.7
1990	37.3	10.8	3.3	3.9	55.9	16	-21.3	344.8	12.12	0.2
1991	18.1	7.7	5.3	3.2	61.3	15	-3.1	390.6	11.72	1.6
1992	10.05	53	3.9	4.6	77.6	13.5	3.4	520.8	25.00	-5.2
1993	25	27.9	5	4.6	100.8	18.75	-6.3	819.7	36.46	-2.6
1994	24.9	50.3	3.3	5.3	103.8	18.1	-6.8	1052.6	22.13	-9.3
1995	74.3	27.9	4	6.5	99.2	26.25	-48.1	1449.3	27.37	-6.7
1996	34	50.3	4.6	8.33	85.4	28.25	-5.8	1754.4	17.39	-10.4
1997	27.9	33.4	4.2	7.38	87	28.5	-0.6	2272.7	22.81	-10.3
1998	14.6	31.4	4.7	10.62	79.1	16.5	-22.5	2325.6	22.7	-8.1
1999	12.4	45.4	-4.1	14.3	125.8	13	-6.8	3448.3	32.56	-8.2
2000	40.5	17.3	3.7	14.2	158.4	18	-4.0	7047.7	51.07	-7.9

Source: Bank of Ghana

Headline inflation was running at 41 percent; the fiscal deficit had increased from some 6.0 percent of GDP in 1999 to 9.0 percent of GDP (Table 4.1).

The debt burden of the economy increased dramatically during the structural adjustment period, with external debt/GDP ratio rising from 27 percent of GDP in 1984 to 103 percent of GDP by 1994 and rose further to 158 percent of GDP by 2000 (Figure 4.3). The country was having difficulty servicing its debts.

Figure 4.3. External Debt/GDP % (1984-2000)

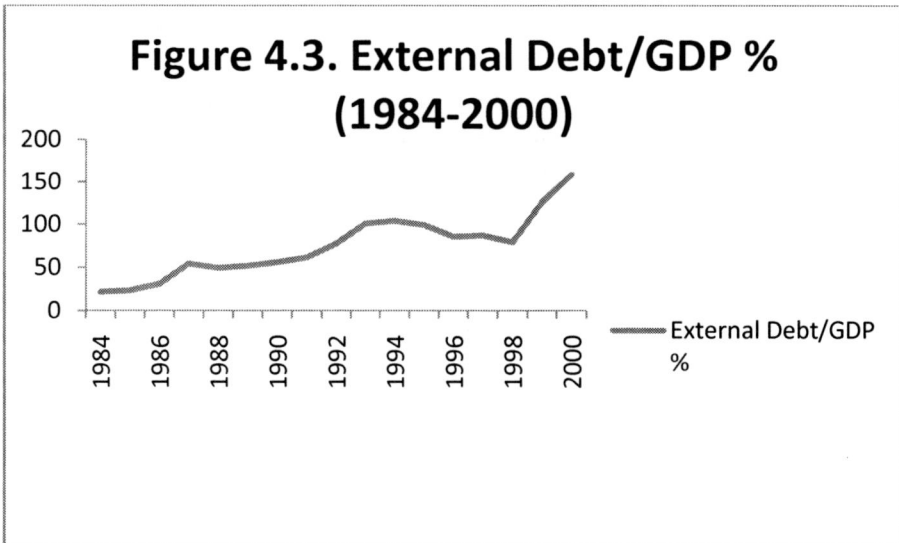

By the end of 2000 Ghana's total public external debt stock stood at $6.1 billion in nominal terms. The external public debt stood at 158.0 percent of GDP, and the domestic public debt at 29.0 percent of GDP. In Net Present Value (NPV) terms, this debt amounted to 558 percent of government revenues, and 152 per cent of exports (IMF, 2001).

For the year 1999 and 2000, statutory debt servicing for external and domestic debts accounted for 32 percent and 39 percent respectively of total government expenditure. External debt servicing alone accounted for 24 percent of total government expenditure in 2000. A major consequence of this debt overhang was not only the sacrificed economic growth, but also a reduction in social and poverty related spending. For example, the external debt service expenditure of 2,454.6 billion cedis was far bigger than the budgeted social services sector allocation of 1,370.1 billion cedis for the year 2000. Total gross reserves amounted to $264 million at the end of 2000 and the debt service due for 2001 was $560 million.

A Debt Sustainability Analysis (DSA) was conducted by the IMF in 2000 and it clearly indicated that Ghana's external debt was unsustainable. The ratio of present value of Ghana's external debt stock to its domestic budget revenue was 571 percent. This was far in excess of the 250 percent threshold considered as a sustainable debt level. The situation was not sustainable and something had to give.

It was against this background that the December 2000 Presidential and Parliamentary elections took place and were won by the New Patriotic Party (NPP) under the leadership of President John Agyekum Kufuor. The new NPP government therefore opted to take advantage of the debt relief available under the IMF/World Bank's Highly Indebted Poor Country (HIPC) Initiative in March 2001. This decision generated a lot of public debate and was taken against considerable opposition. The term "HIPC" was considered pejorative (synonymous with being declared bankrupt) but the government argued that it was a necessary course of action given the state of the economy.

The Highly Indebted Poor Country Initiative (HIPC)

The Highly Indebted Poor Country (HIPC) Initiative was launched by the International Monetary Fund (IMF) and the World Bank in 1996 with the goal to provide a permanent exit from repeated debt reschedulings of HIPCs.

The HIPC Initiative involves two stages. The first stage is a three-year period during which a HIPC works in coordination with the support of the World Bank and the IMF to establish a record of good economic policies and sustained poverty reduction. At the end of this three-year period the World Bank and the IMF determine whether a country's debt level is sustainable. For those countries whose debt burden remains unsustainable after full use of traditional debt relief mechanisms, a package of debt relief is identified. This is known as the Decision Point. While full HIPC debt relief will be provided at the Completion Point, some creditors might provide interim debt relief (the period between the Decision Point and the floating Completion Point). Under the enhanced framework, the completion point is "floating" as it is tied to the implementation of key structural reforms and poverty reduction policies.

The principal objective of the HIPC Initiative is to bring a poor country's debt burden to a sustainable level. The HIPC framework is limited to external debt that is public and publicly guaranteed; hence it excludes all domestic debt and all private debt that is not publicly guaranteed. The criterion for being "poor" is to be an "IDA-only" country, which is defined as a country that relies on highly concessional financing from the World Bank's concessional lending-arm, the International Development Association ((IDA).

The enhanced HIPC Initiative considers a country's debt to be sustainable if the net present value (NPV) of the debt-to-export ratio is below 150 percent, based on the debt sustainability analysis at the enhanced HIPC decision point. In cases where a country has both (a) an export-to-GDP ratio of at least 30 percent and (b) a government revenue-to- GDP ratio of at least 15 percent, the enhanced HIPC framework considers also a fiscal window, whereby it is assumed that a country's debt is sustainable if the NPV debt-to government revenue ratio is maximal 250 percent.

HIPC STAGES:

Stage 1: 3-Year satisfactory performance track record by HIPC country. Reduction of non-ODA debt of 67 percent in NPV terms (Naples Terms).

Stage 2: *Decision Point*. The debt relief is fixed at this point. The international financial community (Paris Club Creditors) will make a commitment to provide 90% flow reduction of debt in NPV terms after a 3 year satisfactory performance track-record and at least a full one year implementation of its Poverty Reduction Programme (Cologne Terms).
Stage 3: *Completion Point*. Paris Club will provide a reduction of the eligible stock of debt of 90% or more in present value terms.

In addition to adopting the HIPC Initiative, the NPP Government also continued with the IMF's Poverty Reduction and Growth Facility (PRGF) programme which was negotiated under the previous NDC government.

The Government however, adopted a policy stance that had an emphasis on the private sector as the engine of growth. It declared a commitment to macroeconomic discipline, to development based on the participatory process, and dialogue with development partners and civil society.

- The platform of the new regime was based on a philosophy of economic liberalism, good governance, rule of law, and respect for property rights.

- Press freedom was encouraged, the criminal libel law was abolished and there was increased policy scrutiny by civil society and market participants.

- The state was expected to play a sharply focused role, concentrating on creating the enabling environment for private sector activity to flourish, and developing the social and other supportive infrastructure to promote income generation and poverty reduction.

Ghana Poverty Reduction Strategy (GPRS)

The economic policy framework of the NPP was captured in the Ghana Poverty Reduction Strategy ("GPRS I") which was published in 2003. The GPRS set the overall framework for medium-term poverty reduction and growth in the country. In 2005, Ghana published the Growth and Poverty Reduction Strategy II, highlighting the policy objectives and the detailed activities for the period 2006-2009. Following the attainment of relative macroeconomic stability and modest economic growth under the GPRS I, the key objective of Ghana's socioeconomic development agenda under the GPRS II was to attain middle income status (with a per capita income of at least US$1000) within a decentralized democratic environment by the year

2015, to be complemented by the adoption of an overall social protection policy aimed at ensuring sustained poverty reduction.

The GPRS II represented a shift of strategic focus from the GPRS I, which was directed primarily towards the attainment of the anti-poverty objectives of the UN's Millennium Development Goals ("MDGs"). The central goal of the GPRS II is to accelerate the growth of the economy so that Ghana can achieve middle-income status within a measurable planning period. In short, the shift from the GPRS I to the GPRS II represents a shift in objectives, from stability to accelerated growth with stability. The policy emphasis was on Macroeconomic Stability, Private Sector Growth Human Resource Development, Infrastructure, Good Governance and Social Responsibility.

Given that GPRS I was focused on macroeconomic stability and poverty reduction, the immediate focus of the government was to restore macroeconomic stability. This meant a major shift in macroeconomic policies from one of considerable fiscal relaxation and monetary accommodation to one of fiscal and monetary stringency. The task of restoring macroeconomic stability was anchored on a fiscal and monetary policy framework.

On the fiscal side, the central government budget was cast in a medium term framework right from the start, and public finances were set on the course of fiscal consolidation to cut the budget deficit and stabilize the domestic public debt. This called for robust revenue mobilization (to increase the flexibility of the revenue base and reduce fiscal vulnerability) and prudent spending. On the monetary side, the central bank adopted an inflation-targeting framework for the conduct of monetary policy.

CHAPTER 5

INFLATION TARGETING

Inflation targeting is simply a formalized comprehensive framework defining precisely the coordinated effort needed to contain inflation in pursuit of the broader economic objectives of sustainable high economic growth and employment creation. This is predicated on the well-known view in economics of the long-run neutrality of money and that there is no long-run trade-off between unemployment and inflation. However, there is nevertheless a trade-off between inflation variability and output variability in the short run.

Mishkin (2001) defines inflation targeting as a monetary policy strategy that encompasses five main elements:

1. A public announcement of medium-term numerical targets for inflation,
2. An institutional commitment to price stability as the primary goal of monetary policy, to which other goals are subordinated.
3. An information inclusive strategy in which many variables, and not just monetary aggregates or the exchange rate, are used for deciding the setting of policy instruments.
4. Increased transparency of the monetary policy strategy through communication with the public and markets about the plans, objectives, and decisions of the monetary authorities, and
5. Increased accountability of the central bank for attaining its inflation objectives.

Mechanics of implementation of Inflation Targeting

In general, under inflation targeting, a central bank reacts to deviations of targeted inflation from a forecasted inflation by adjusting its policy instrument, mostly a short term interest rate. The magnitude of adjustment in policy rate in turn depends on a view on the level of the deviation and more importantly, a view of the transmission mechanism of monetary policy. This makes inflation targeting a forward-looking strategy of monetary policy (Diagram below).

Figure 5. 1:

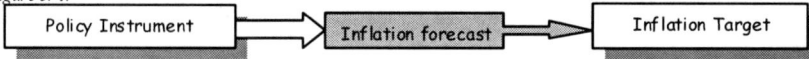

Prerequisites for Inflation Targeting

In order for inflation to be able to serve its purpose as a nominal anchor, and to be successful, some prerequisites need to be met. These can be categorized broadly as: the basic (relating to the relationship between government and the central bank) and other prerequisites. The basic prerequisites are a strong degree of central bank independence, the absence of fiscal dominance and a clearly defined objective of achieving price stability together with the absence of other nominal objectives. The others include well-developed financial and money markets, reasonably low inflation, public support for price stability, and the capacity of the central bank to model and forecast inflation.

Independence of the central bank here is seen essentially in relation to instrument independence (i.e. the ability of the central bank to choose the instruments) independently of political pressures. Additionally, the absence of fiscal dominance will imply minimal burden of financing government deficits on the central bank or generally that the fiscal policy does not dictate monetary policy. In this respect, most central bank legal frameworks in inflation-targeting countries tend to limit or even prohibit financing of government borrowing from the central bank. Ways in which countries have tended to approach this issue has generally been to maintain strong fiscal discipline and or developing deep financial markets with the capacity to absorb the public sector's borrowing requirement. Similarly, fiscal reforms to maintain a broad revenue base and thus reduce the need for seignorage revenue become crucial.

It is equally important to ensure that the objective of monetary policy remains price stability. A number of issues arise including a clear definition of price stability with respect to the price index chosen (CPI or some core CPI); whether a point or range target and the time horizon. As there are trade-offs in the choice of one or another of these options, it becomes important to strike a good balance in order to ensure credibility and transparency to anchor expectations.

Other prerequisites include the ability of the central bank to model and forecast inflation and the presence of well developed financial markets. Since inflation targeting countries react to deviations of forecasted inflation from the target, accurately forecasting the inflation becomes crucial in the process. Monetary policy impulses are also carried through the financial market and therefore the process will work better with a relatively well developed financial system.

Inflation Targeting in Ghana

Given the background of macroeconomic instability that the NPP inherited, the immediate focus of the new NPP government was to stabilize the economy. A fiscal and monetary policy framework was put together in 2001 to engineer a switch from a high inflation, interest rate and exchange rate depreciation regime to a low inflation and interest rate regime with exchange rate stability. The assessment was that monetary targeting had not yielded the desired results judging from the frequent divergence of actual monetary growth from target (Figure 5.2) and thus the non-achievement of the ultimate goal of policy. The Bank of Ghana, in line with its mandate under the new

Bank of Ghana Act to maintain a primary focus on price stability, opted for an inflation targeting monetary policy framework.

Figure 5.2. Money Growth: Actuals versus Targets

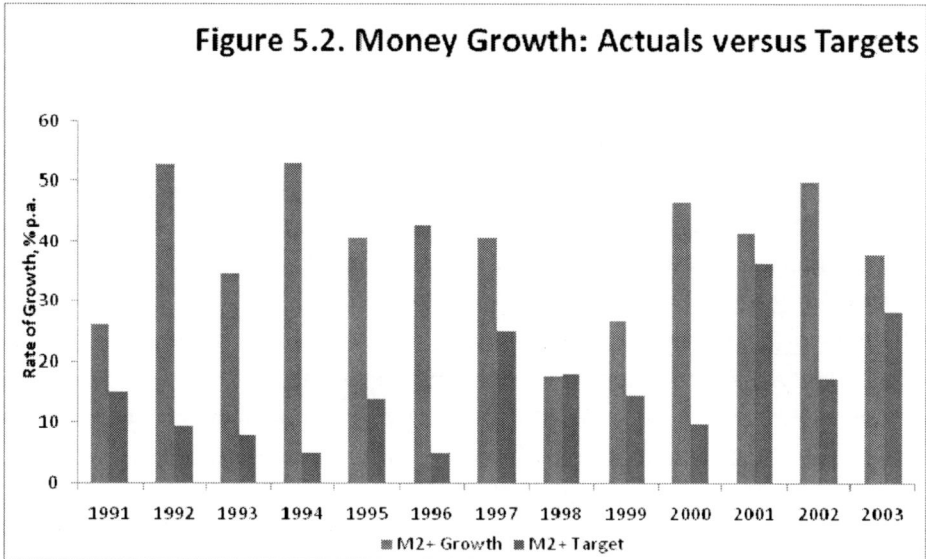

However, Ghana's Poverty Reduction Growth Facility (PRGF) programme with the IMF was cast in the framework of monetary targeting. Ghana was only the second Sub-Saharan African country to adopt the inflation targeting regime following South Africa, and was the first low income country in the world to do so. The IMF was not quite ready for Ghana's move. There was no agreed framework at the Fund to handle inflation targeting low income countries. This meant that while the Bank of Ghana pursued inflation targeting, the IMF set its targets in terms of monetary targeting. In practice, this meant that the Bank of Ghana continued to use both sets of instruments.

The effectiveness of monetary policy based on monetary targeting crucially depends on finding a stable money demand function. A stable money demand function ensures a predictable impact of money supply on other economic variables such as inflation, national income, private investments, etc. Therefore, the stability issue in the money demand function becomes an interesting research area for researchers to test the effectiveness of a given monetary programme.

In most economies, however, it has been observed over the past couple of decades that the relationship between monetary aggregates and inflation weakened and resulted in instability in the money demand function. This weak relationship between monetary aggregates and inflation made it impossible to target monetary aggregates with the view to controlling inflation. The probability of missing the final target (inflation) by achieving a specific intermediate target (monetary aggregate) significantly increased and thus resulted in central banks abandoning this framework.
.

Given its pivotal role in the policy setting, the demand for money is one of the most widely researched topics in monetary economics. Stability of the money demand function is sine qua non if the transmission mechanism for monetary policy is to be effective under a monetary targeting regime. In this regard, in most developed and developing countries, policy makers have frequently questioned whether or not the demand for money is stable with considerable effort being spent on establishing the stability of the money demand function. In general, the consensus view of the studies in developed countries during the 1990s was that of instability in demand for money following the financial liberalization and innovations. This has therefore led to a downgrading of the role of the monetary aggregates as policy targets in the conduct of monetary policy. The notable exception however, is that of the European Central Bank (ECB), with its two pillar approach.

Ghana's economy since the inception of the structural adjustment programme in 1983 has undergone a period of consistent substantial deregulation, culminating in the adoption of the use of indirect instruments in the conduct of monetary policy in 1992 and increased monetization of the economy (Figure 5.3). One of the sectors that saw major transformation was the financial sector with the launch of the Financial Sector Adjustment Programme (FINSAP) in 1988.

Figure 5.3: Ghana Broad Money as per cent of GDP

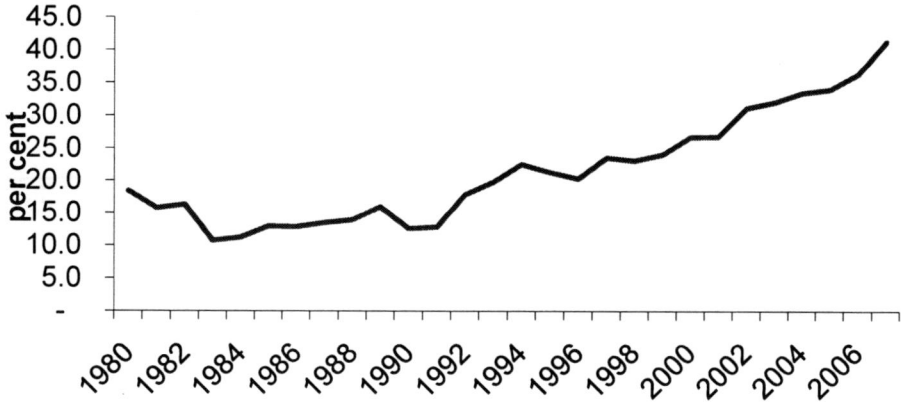

An examination of the demand for money function for Ghana points to significant parametric shifts in the demand for money in Ghana since the late 1990s (Bawumia, Amoah and Mumuni, 2008). This finding is not surprising as it has followed a period of consistent structural reforms and deregulation of the financial sector. The finding has an important consequence on the viability of framing monetary policy around monetary aggregates as it showed that money growth rates can be poor predictors of future inflation and real output (Figure 5.4).

Figure 5.4 Evolution of the Relationship between Money Supply and Inflation

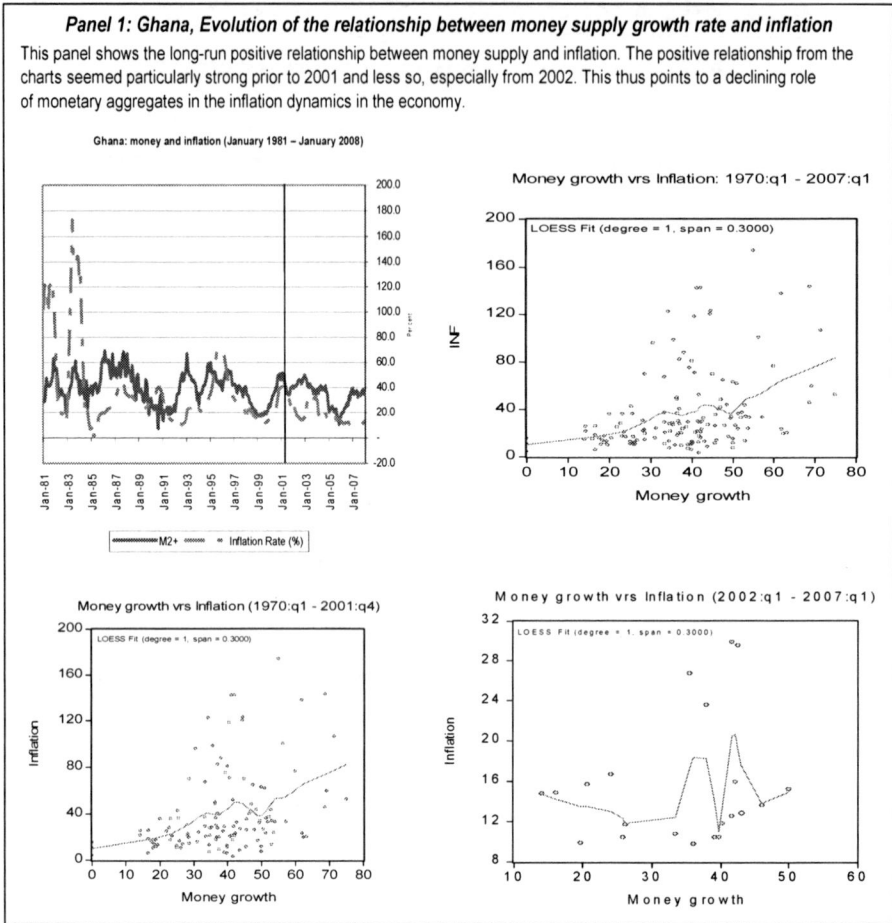

Panel 1: Ghana, Evolution of the relationship between money supply growth rate and inflation

This panel shows the long-run positive relationship between money supply and inflation. The positive relationship from the charts seemed particularly strong prior to 2001 and less so, especially from 2002. This thus points to a declining role of monetary aggregates in the inflation dynamics in the economy.

Ghana: money and inflation (January 1981 – January 2008)

Money growth vrs Inflation: 1970:q1 - 2007:q1

Money growth vrs Inflation (1970:q1 - 2001:q4)

Money growth vrs Inflation (2002:q1 - 2007:q1)

GHANA AND THE PREREQUISITES FOR INFLATION TARGETING

Independence of the central bank:

To strengthen the central bank in the conduct of monetary policy, parliament passed into law a Bank of Ghana Act in 2002. This Act gives operational independence to the Bank of Ghana. This historic Act specifies among other provisions that:

- *"The primary objective of the Bank is to maintain stability in the general level of prices"*. In addition, the law states *"Without prejudice to the above, the Bank shall support the general economic policy of the Government and promote economic growth and effective and efficient operation of banking and credit systems in the country, "independent of instructions from Government or any other authority"*. This refocused the central bank on the major task of inflation control and away from the developmental activities which characterized the Banks' operations in the past.

- A Monetary Policy Committee will be responsible for formulating monetary policy, which should bring transparency to the central bank's operations and its communications with the public

- One of the key challenges to monetary policy as identified by many studies has been the accommodation of fiscal deficits by central banks. To deal with the issue of fiscal dominance which had plagued monetary policy, the Bank of Ghana Act placed explicit limits on central bank financing of Government deficits. Government borrowing from the central bank in any year shall be limited to 10 percent of its revenue, which ties the hands of government and the central bank in a way that is

Table 5.1. Financial Indicators for Inflation Targeters

	Date of Adoption of IT	Seignorage to GDP 1980-95	Fiscal Balance to GDP %	Quasi-Money to GDP %	Private Credit to GDP %	Reserve Money to GDP %	Stock Market Cap to GDP 1997
Industrial Countries							
Australia	April 1993	0.42	-5.6	43.3	69.5	5.3	153
Canada	February 1991	0.19	-7.2	35.8	51.6	4.2	88
Finland	February 1993		-7.1	32.3	83.6	7.9	59
New Zealand	July 1989	0.12	-3.7	32.1	68.9	2.3	99
Spain	Nov. 1994	1.61	-6	44.4	77.7		50
Sweden	January 1993	0.65	-11.8	49.1	43.7	11.4	115
United Kingdom	October 1992	0.20	-6.5	86.4	114.2	3.9	147
Average		**0.58**	**-6.9**	**46.2**	**72.7**	**5.8**	**101.6**
Emerging Market Countries							
Brazil	June 1999	5.13	-5.7	24.8	28.4	6.6	29.7
Chile	Sept. 1999	1.66	-1.5	40.5	66.2	37.7	92.3
Czech Republic	Dec. 1997	2.13	-1.2	45	65.7	20.5	28.6
Hungary	June 2001	1.24	-3	28.2	33.8	10.5	35.8
Israel	June 1997	1.57	-4.3	78.7	73.9	56.7	41.2
Poland	Sept. 1998	1.22	-0.9	28.5	23.6	8.6	9.8
Average		**2.16**	**-2.8**	**41.0**	**48.6**	**23.4**	**39.6**
Sub-Saharan Africa							
South Africa	Feb. 2000	0.68	-1.9	26.6	73.0	4.9	192.2
Ghana	Nov. 2002	3.5	-4.9	14.6	12.9	11.8	12.7

Source: Horska (2004), Masson, Bank of Ghana

- Much stricter than the 20 percent ceiling which prevails in the CFA zone countries, for example.

These provisions grant the Bank of Ghana sufficient independence to deploy its instruments of monetary policy in the best ways possible to achieve its primary goal of price stability.

Relatively developed financial sector

The financial system tends to play a crucial role in the transmission of monetary policy impulses in the economy.

In this regard, the inflation targeting framework works better with well developed financial systems.. Table 5.1 compares some key financial indicators of the Ghanaian economy with those of some developed and emerging market countries including South Africa. The Ghanaian financial system remains relatively well-developed and compares favorably with indicators in other emerging market inflation targeting countries.

Practical aspects of implementation of inflation targeting in Ghana

Inflation targeting countries tend to differ in the practical aspects of implementation of the strategy. This particularly relates to issues bordering on definition and setting of the target variable, monetary policy decision making process, degree of transparency and level of accountability. In general, strategies are designed in ways that help anchor inflation expectations.

The determination and announcement of the target

Inflation targeting countries differ widely with respect to the determination and announcement of the inflation target. While in some countries, the target is determined and announced by government; in others government does so in consultation with the central bank. In a few cases, the target is determined by the central bank (Table 5.2).

Table 5.2 Inflation Targeting Countries (2007)

	Since	Target Set By	Instrument Independent	2007 Target %	Target variable
Australia	1993	Govt & Central Bank	Yes	2-3	CPI
Brazil	1999	Government	Yes	4.5 (+/- 2.0)	CPI
Canada	1991	Govt & Central Bank	Yes	2 (+/- 1.0)	CPI
Chile	1990	Central Bank	Yes	2-4	CPI
Colombia	1999	Central Bank	Yes	3.5-5.5	CPI
Czech Republic	1997	Govt & Central Bank	Yes	2-4.5	CPI
Ghana	2002	Govt & Central Bank	Yes	7-9	CPI
Hungary	2001	Govt & Central Bank	Yes	4 (+/- 1.0)	CPI
Iceland	2001	Government	Yes	2 .5 (+/- 1.0)	CPI
Israel	1991	Government	Yes	1-3	CPI
Mexico	1995	Central Bank	Yes	3 (+/- 1.0)	CPI
New Zealand	1990	Govt & Central Bank	Yes	1-3	CPI
Norway	2001	Central bank	Yes	2.5	CPI
Peru	2002	Central bank	Yes	2.5 (+/- 1.0)	CPI
Philippines	2002	Govt & Central Bank	Yes	4-5	CPI
Poland	1998	Central Bank	Yes	2 .5(+/- 1.0)	CPI
Republic of Korea	1998	Govt & Central Bank	Yes	3 (+/- 1.0)	CPI excl. food and energy
South Africa	2000	Govt & Central Bank	Yes	3-6	CPIX
Sweden	1993	Central Bank	Yes	2 (+/- 1.0)	CPI
Thailand	2000	Central Bank	Yes	0-3.5	CPI excl. food and energy
United Kingdom	1992	Government	Yes	2	CPI (HICP)

Sources: Horska (2004), Truman (2003) and Heikensten (1999)

In Ghana, the target is determined jointly by government and the central bank during the preparation of the annual budget. This remains similar to the practice by countries such as South Africa, New Zealand, Hungary, Canada and the Republic of Korea where the target is determined jointly by government and the central bank. Joint target determination has the advantage of strengthening the target's credibility by indirectly committing the government to conduct fiscal policy in a way that would support the achievement of the inflation objective. Unstable fiscal policy hinders not only the effective management of monetary policy but also hurts the credibility of inflation targets as witnessed in past regimes.

A downside risk to credibility is that government may tend to have short term incentives to alter the target and therefore impair long term credibility. In general however, irrespective of how the target is set, the central bank is ultimately held responsible for achieving it.

In terms of the target variable, the Consumer Price Index (CPI) has been used in all inflation targeting countries. However, there are differences in the range of items included in the measurement of the CPI. A number of countries have opted for a "core" consumer price index, which excludes prices affected by exogenous shocks over which the central bank has no direct control, the first-round effects of indirect tax changes and the first-round effects of interest rate changes. The major consideration in this case is preferably to include the range of products that fully reflect the domestic cost of living and are generally accepted by the public.

While the Bank of Ghana targets the CPI inflation officially, it also critically monitors developments in a number of core inflation series before taking its interest rate decisions[10].

The decision-making process

The decision on the appropriate monetary policy stance is taken by the Monetary Policy Committee (MPC). This committee was constituted shortly before Ghana adopted the inflation targeting framework for monetary policy. The Committee consists of 7 members: The Governor, two deputy governors, the heads of monetary policy analysis (Research) and banking operations of the Bank and two independent members. The Committee normally meets every other month (or six times per year) and had its first meeting in November 2002.

---

[10] In particular the CPI excluding energy and utility prices.

The MPC meetings are normally held over three days, during which period a wide range of indicators are presented and carefully analyzed. For the first two days, staff members of the bank make presentations on a wide range of economic indicators and present conditional forecast of inflation to the committee. The information is carefully examined by committee members who then follow up with a deliberation and appropriate positioning of the bank's prime rate. The decision is taken by consensus unlike in some other inflation targeting central banks where it is by majority vote (Table 5.3).

In general, information usually presented to the committee includes among others detailed assessment of developments under the following broad headings:

a. Global economic outlook and Ghana's external sector developments.
b. Fiscal developments.
c. Monetary and financial developments.
d. Financial stability reports (Banking sector, Non-banks and credit conditions surveys).
e. Real sector developments (including the composite indicator of economic index, business and consumer confidence surveys).
f. Inflation outlook and developments including inflation forecast.

In forecasting inflation, a number of models are used including an autoregressive (AR) forecasting model, error correction forecasting model, and a calibrated macroeconomic model. Results from these models are then used to construct a fan chart with varying degrees of probabilities. The final decision is nevertheless not based mechanically on the forecasts, but usually one of judgment after a careful analysis of all relevant economic data and risks.

Table 5.3 Monetary Policy Meetings and Minutes

	No. of Members	Decision Taken By	Press Notice	Minutes Published
Australia	9	Consensus	Yes	No
Brazil	9	Vote	Yes	Yes
Canada	6	Consensus	Yes	No
Chile	5	Vote	Yes	Yes
Colombia	7	Vote	Yes	No
Czech Republic	7	Vote	Press Conference	Yes
Ghana	7	Consensus	Press Conference	No
Hungary	6	Vote	Yes	No
Iceland	3	Vote	Yes	No
Israel	5	Governor	Yes	No
Mexico	5	Vote	Yes	No
Norway	7	Consensus	Yes	No
New Zealand	Variable	Governor	Speech by Governor	No
Peru	7	Vote	Yes	No
Philippines	7	Vote	Yes	No
Poland	10	Vote	Press Conference	Yes
Republic of Korea	7	Vote	Press Conference	Yes
South Africa	8	Vote	Press Conference	No
Sweden	6	Vote	Yes	Yes
Thailand	7	Consensus	Press Conference	No
United Kingdom	9	Vote	Yes	Yes

Sources: Horska (2004), Truman (2003) and Heikensten (1999)

The transparency and accountability of monetary policy

One of the key aspects of inflation targeting is its ability to anchor expectations. This is usually expected to be achieved through the central bank's commitment and consistent policy arrangements, bolstered by its policies regarding transparency and accountability.

Increased communication with the public about the monetary policy decision making process keeps the public well informed and therefore anchors their expectation. Various approaches are adopted by various central banks including the advance publication of monetary policy meeting dates, publication of minutes of the MPC, press conferences or press releases and publication of monetary policy reports (Table 5.4).

Table 5.4 Inflation Report/Monetary Policy Report

	Frequency	Accountable for Report	Explicit Targeting Horizon	Inflation Forecast
Australia	4/year	Bank as a whole	No	Yes
Brazil	4/year	Monetary Policy C'ttee	After Target Deviation	Yes
Canada	2 +2 year	Executive Board	6-8 quarters	Yes
Chile	3/year	Executive Board	8 quarters	Yes
Colombia	2/year	Executive Board	No	Yes
Czech Republic	4/year	Executive Board	No	Yes
Ghana	4-6 year	Bank as a whole	No	Yes
Hungary	4/year	Staff	No	Yes
Iceland	4/year	Bank as a whole	After Target Deviation	Yes
Israel	2/year	Executive Board & Staff	After Target Deviation	Yes
Mexico	4/year	Bank as a whole	No	Yes
New Zealand	4/year	Governor	6-8 quarters	Yes
Norway	3/year	Governor & Executive Board	4-12 quarters	Yes
Peru	3/year	Bank as a whole	No	Yes
Philippines	4/year	Monetary policy C'ttee	After Target Deviation	Yes
Poland	4/year	Staff	No	Yes
Republic of Korea	4/year	Monetary policy C'ttee	No	Yes
South Africa	4/year	Staff	No	Yes
Sweden	4/year	Executive Board	4-8 quarters	Yes
Thailand	4/year	Monetary policy C'ttee	No	Yes
United Kingdom	4/year	Monetary policy C'ttee	After Target Deviation	Yes

Sources: Horska (2004), Truman (2003) and Heikensten (1999)

The Bank of Ghana's communication strategy includes a press conference after the MPC meetings, press releases and publication of detailed monetary reports covering all the sectors of the economy after every MPC meeting. The reports published every two months include:

a.   Global economic outlook and Ghana's external sector developments.

b.   Fiscal developments.

c.   Monetary and financial developments.

d.   Financial stability reports.

e.   Real sector developments (including the composite indicator of economic index, business and consumer confidence surveys);

f.   Inflation outlook and developments.

This information is also available on the Bank of Ghana's website. A major difference however is that, except for Ghana, all countries implementing inflation targeting appear to publish their inflation forecasts in the monetary policy reports usually expected to anchor the public's inflation expectations. As well, limited lectures are delivered by MPC members and staff on the current policy regime.

Table 5.5 Accountability

	Hearing in Parliament	*Open Letter or Report when off target*
Australia	Yes	No
Brazil	No	Yes
Canada	Yes	No
Chile	Yes	No
Colombia	Yes	No
Czech Republic	Yes	No
Ghana	No	No
Hungary	Yes	No
Iceland	No	Yes
Israel	Yes	Yes
Mexico	Yes	No
New Zealand	Yes	Yes
Norway	Yes	Yes
Peru	No	No
Philippines	Yes	Yes
Poland	Yes	Yes
Republic of Korea	Yes	No
South Africa	No	No
Sweden	Yes	Yes
Thailand	No	No
United Kingdom	Yes	Yes

Sources: Horska (2004), Truman (2003) and Heikensten (1999)

The inflation targeting framework thus improves the accountability of the Bank of Ghana because it provides an explicit and publicly known benchmark that must be reached over a specific time frame. Unlike in other countries, the Governor of the Bank of Ghana does not currently write an open letter or report when the target is missed (Table 5.5). In communicating with the public (particularly at the press conferences) the Governor and Chairman of the MPC explains the possibilities and progress being made to achieve the target or factors that may result in the target being missed.

From the foregoing, it is clear that the practical elements of implementation of inflation targeting in Ghana are similar to practices in other inflation targeting countries. Some differences however exist; notable among them is the publishing of forecasts.

Practical experience with inflation targeting in Ghana

The adoption of inflation targeting in Ghana, very much like the case in most emerging market economies, engineered a significant disinflation process between 2001 and 2007 (Figure 5.5) with the lowest average inflation and low volatility since the 1970s. There were however or a few short periods of inflation jumps in Ghana in the first quarters of 2003 and 2005. The reason for these jumps was the strong external oil price shocks as well as the realignment at the onset of and subsequent implementation of deregulation in administered domestic pricing of petroleum products. There was also an increase in inflation in 2008.

The inflation targeting regime enhanced the transparency of the monetary policy, improved communication strategy with the public and improved the monetary policy framework. The general goal of the new regime to set inflation on a downward path has been achieved even though meeting the announced inflation target has proved to be elusive (Figure 5.6).

Figure 5.5: Ghana: CPI Inflation (1985-2008)

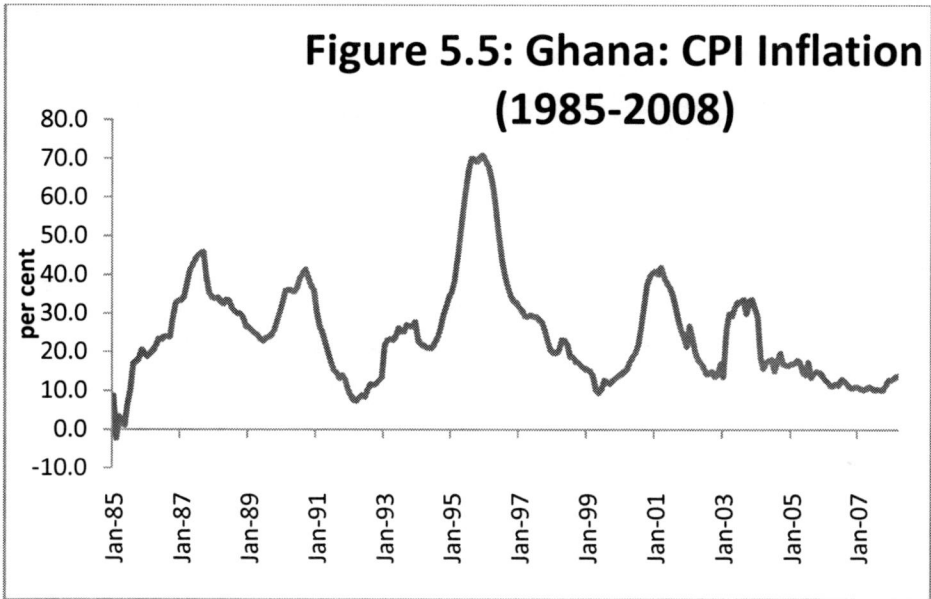

Figure 5.6: Ghana, CPI Inflation (Actuals and targets) 2001 - 2008)

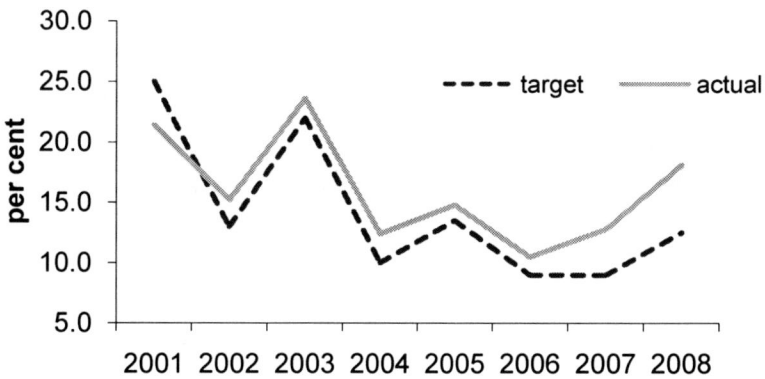

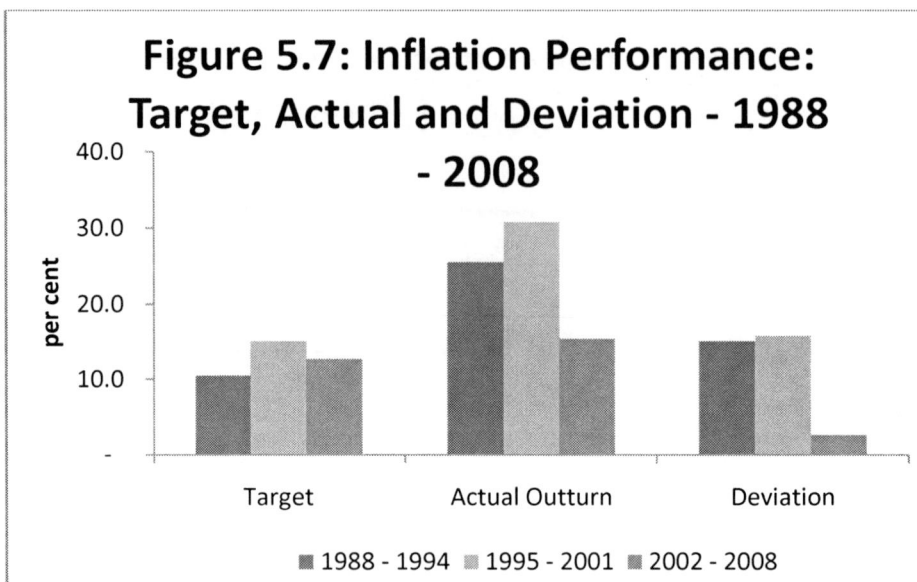

Figure 5.7: Inflation Performance: Target, Actual and Deviation - 1988 - 2008

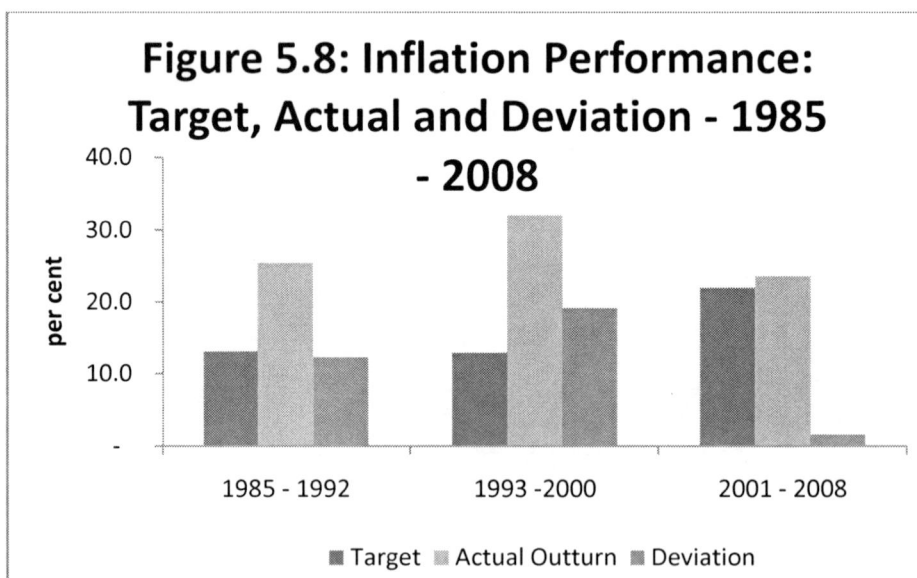

Figure 5.8: Inflation Performance: Target, Actual and Deviation - 1985 - 2008

For example, Ghana attained the single digit inflation target in April and May 2006 when inflation was reduced to 9.9 percent and 9.5 percent respectively. Similarly the Ghana attained single digit inflation in May 1999 when inflation was reduced to 9.4 percent under monetary targeting. However, the deviation of inflation from target since the 1980s has been the lowest under the inflation targeting regime, demonstrating that there has been an increased convergence towards the targets perhaps due to improved credibility with inflation expectations well anchored (Figures 5.7 and 5.8). At the same time there has been significantly reduced volatility in not only inflation, but also real economic variables such as real GDP growth.

The MPC's policy rate decisions (2002-2008)

In this section, an attempt is made to empirically investigate the form of inflation targeting that Bank of Ghana has so far implemented. The MPC since its inauguration held some 30 meetings by December 2008. The ex-post analysis of the policy rate decisions show that the MPC did not change its policy rate some 53 per cent of the time (16 times). Rates were cut in some 30 per cent of the time (9 times). The MPC hiked rates on 5 occasions (or 16.7 per cent of the time) over the period. With inflation expectations firmly anchored over the period, the MPC's rate decisions thus tilted more towards rate cuts than hikes, consequently providing some strong impetus for output growth (figures 5.9 and 5.10).

In this context, how strict was the Bank of Ghana's inflation targeting regime? Figure 5.11 shows that while the while the Bank of Ghana Policy Rate remained positive in real terms for most of the period, it was negative between April 2008 and December 2008, indicating that there was room to tighten monetary policy (i.e. increase interest rates at this time). However, the inflation targeting framework is a forward-looking framework and the policy stance is driven by the underlying forecast for the 24- month horizon.

Figure 5.9: Analysis of MPC rate decisions (November 2002 - May 2008)

number of times

magnitude of rate change (per cent)

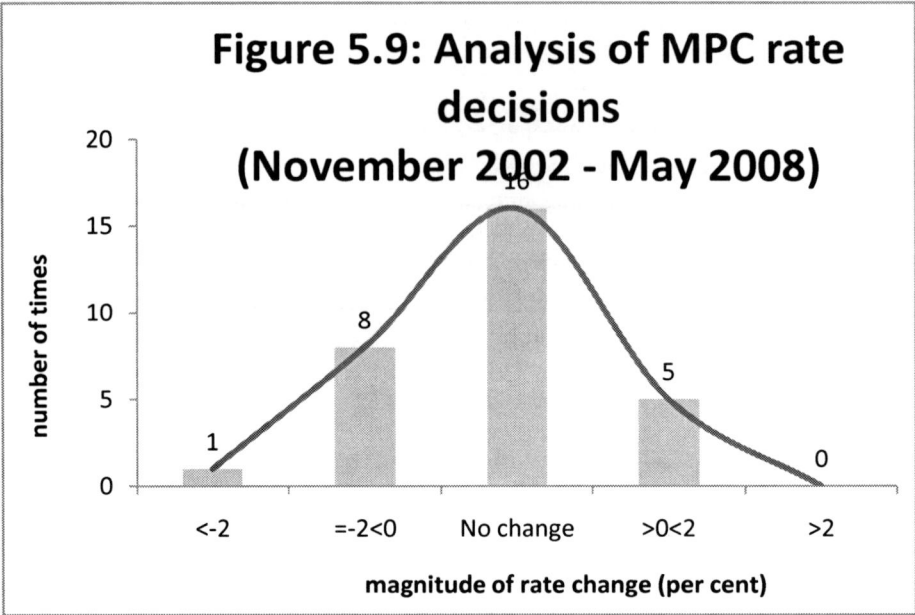

Svensson (2007) argues that there is in practice never a 'strict' inflation targeting but always 'flexible' inflation targeting. Practically, all inflation targeting central banks not only aim at stabilizing inflation around the inflation target but also put some weight on stabilizing the real economy, for instance, implicitly or explicitly stabilizing a measure of resource utilization such as the output gap between actual output and 'potential' output (an application of what economists refer to as the Taylor Rule). Thus, the 'target variables' of the central bank include not only inflation but other variables as well, such as the output gap.

Figure 5.11: Ghana: Policy rate (2002 - 2008)

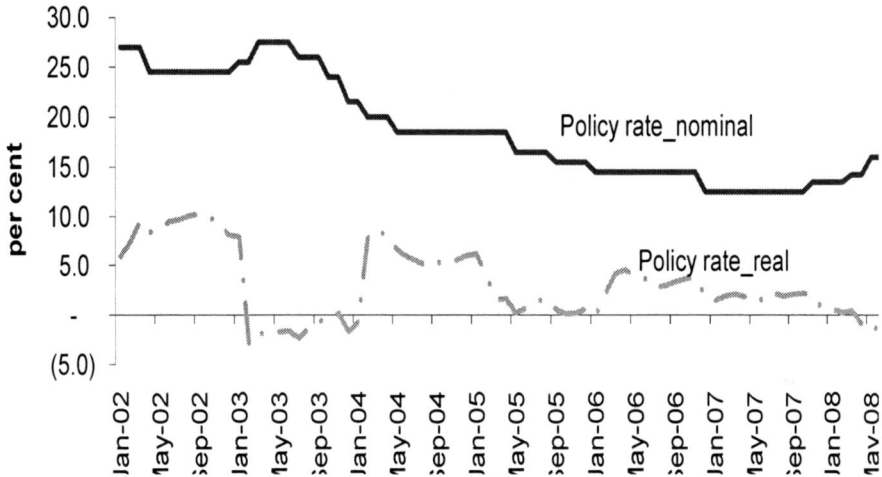

An ex-post assessment of the BOG's inflation targeting framework has found that MPC's interest rate decisions wittingly or unwittingly placed a higher weight of 0.69 placed on output gap, and 0.31 for deviations of estimated inflation from its target[11]. This policy stance was also in the context of a major global economic and financial crisis along with a domestic energy crisis in 2007/2008. The MPC policy stance perhaps, partly explains the sustained growth witnessed in the Ghanaian economy over this period (Figure 5.12) in the midst of a global recession.

---

[11] Bawumia, Amoah and Mumuni (2008)

Figure 5.12: Real GDP Growth

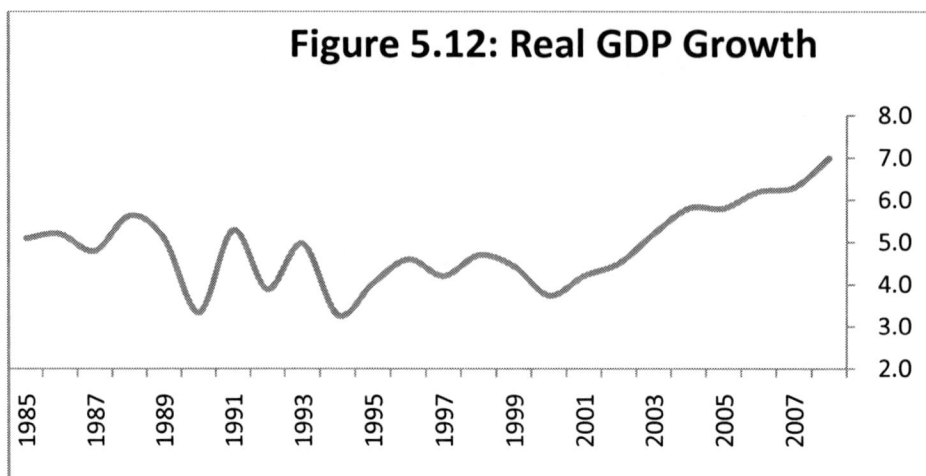

This is contrary to the popular misconception that an inflation targeting central bank does not pay much attention to the real sector of the economy. In fact, the Bank of Ghana's MPC analyzes a lot of data on real sector developments and undertakes surveys of 45 companies covering all sectors of the economy every two months. The object of creating a low inflation environment is to allow sustained economic growth to take place and not low inflation for its own sake.

To address the existing gap in information about developments in the real sector of the economy, the Bank of Ghana introduced a new economic indicator, the Composite Indicator of Economic Activity, to complement its regular surveys of business. The Bank of Ghana's Composite Indicator of Economic Activity measures real sector activity including output of selected key enterprises, industrial electricity consumption, domestic VAT, port activity, imports, exports, and employment contributions.

The Bank of England is also facing similar challenges with its monetary policy in the context of a global recession.

Figure 5.13 shows that the Bank of England real Policy Rate has been negative since September 2008. The inflation rate at May 2010 turned in at 3.4 percent (with an inflation target of 2.0 percent) while the policy rate was 0.5 percent. For an inflation targeting central bank facing economic recession, the Bank of England's policy stance has weighed more towards the output gap than the inflation gap, with a concern more about the risk to output than the risk to prices.

Figure 5.13 Bank of England Real and Nominal Policy Rate (2001-May 2010)

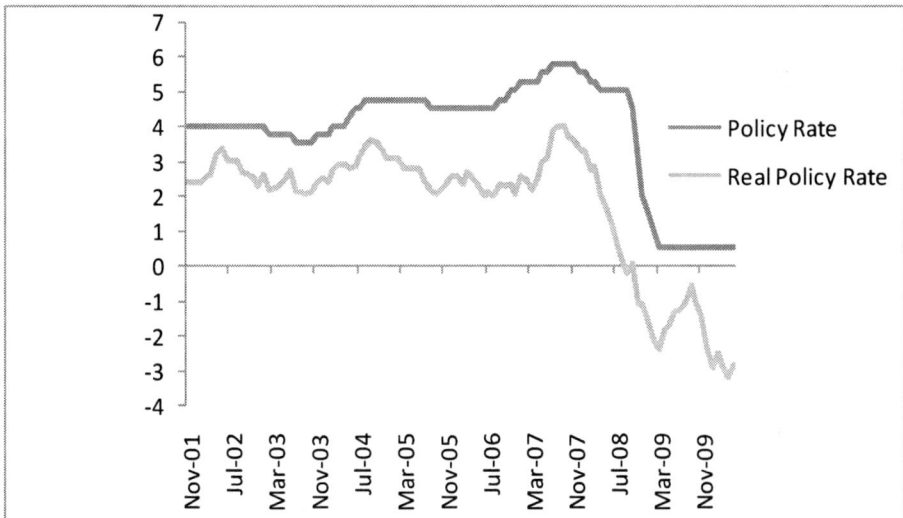

Not only is the real policy rate negative, the Bank of England has also injected some GBP 200 billion into the economy under its quantitative easing programme to stimulate the economy. The Bank of England took the view that it was not going to try reducing inflation further at the risk of choking off growth in the economy and increasing unemployment. That is not generally a difficult task compared to maintaining price stability in a growing economy.

This policy stance by the Bank of England is however increasingly creating disagreements amongst members of its MPC with some like Adam Posen arguing that the risk to the recovery calls for the continued maintenance of the current stance (as at July 2010) while others like Andrew Sentance worried about the risk to inflation and arguing for policy tightening (U.K. Daily Telegraph, July 21, 2010). The arguments here are no different from those that the Bank of Ghana faced.

In practice, the inflation targeting framework at the Bank of Ghana is somewhat different from that at the Bank of England because the latter does not have responsibility for financial stability (which is the responsibility of the Financial Services Authority (FSA). At the Bank of Ghana, the framework envisages monetary policy and financial stability as essentially two sides of the same coin and therefore the analysis of financial stability implications of monetary policy decisions are an integral part of the MPC process. A separate Monetary Policy and Financial Stability Department was therefore set up to provide the required analytical input into these areas. Furthermore, this provided the Bank of Ghana with additional tools like reserve requirements and open market operations together with the interest rate variable. As it turns out, the new U.K. Chancellor of the Exchequer (David Osborne) has decided to return the remit for financial stability to the Bank of England.

MONEY MARKET/MONETARY POLICY REFORMS

To enhance the inflation targeting framework, the Bank of Ghana introduced a number of policy reforms to its monetary policy framework in July 2005. The reforms were aimed at:

- increasing the efficiency of the transmission of monetary policy.
- gradually moving towards a separation between Bank of Ghana open market operations (OMO) and funding the Public Sector Borrowing Requirements (PSBR).
- enhancing the development of the secondary market.
- Enhancing the transparency and competitiveness of the interbank money market and making it the primary money market for the banking system.

In the money market:

- The BOG announced that the Prime Rate (the Monetary Policy Rate) will continue to signal the direction of short-term interest rates and act as a reference rate for some facilities, such as the repo.

- Overnight Repo and reverse repo facilities will now be available, in addition to existing facilities, at the BOG Prime Rate and reverse repo rate respectively. This will provide the BOG a presence on the interbank market and increase its ability to influence rates on this market.

- The new framework also aims at encouraging banks to use the interbank market as their primary source of liquidity and therefore has in-built incentives to ensure that recourse to the central bank is not the first choice of banks. To accomplish this, the BOG'' new framework widens the existing interest rate corridor for its money market operations from 1.0 percent to 3.0 percent.

- Reverse repos will be undertaken at 2.0 percentage points below the prime rate rather than the 1.0 percent under the existing framework. This will achieve the objective of ensuring that the reverse repo rate is below the interbank market rate. In this situation, banks should find it more attractive to lend to other banks than to the central bank.

- Furthermore, to encourage banks to deal with each other in squaring up their liquidity positions in meeting reserve requirements, the new BOG framework provides that on the final day of the maintenance period for reserve requirements, fine-tuning repos will be available at 1.0 percent above the BOG Prime rate.

- Transparency on the interbank market would be enhanced through the provision of information on interbank market transactions and quotations via a Reuters screen available to all banks on a real time basis.

- Periodic auctions will be held for purposes of Open Market Operations (OMO) by the Bank of Ghana, separate from the auction for the Public Sector Borrowing Requirement (PSBR) of Government. In the meantime, the current auction for the PBBR and OMO will continue.

Reserve Requirements*:*

The Bank of Ghana also announced major changes on its liquid reserve requirements for banks. At the time, banks were required to hold 9.0 percent of their eligible deposits as primary reserves at the central bank. In addition, banks were also required to hold 35.0 percent of their eligible deposits as secondary reserves, in the form of treasury bills and medium term government securities.

The high level of reserve requirements is the legacy of high fiscal deficits and the need for the government to have a captive market to finance these deficits. The economic landscape had however changed the new fiscal/monetary policy framework resulted in a disinflation process that had taken hold. In balancing the stability of the economy with the efficiency of the market, the BOG's new policy framework contains the following changes to reserve requirements:

- The primary reserve requirement will continue to be 9.0 percent.

- The secondary reserve requirement was reduced from 35.0 percent to 15.0 percent, initially and abolished a year later.

- The requirement that Banks hold 15.0 percent of deposits in the form of medium term securities was abolished.

Crucial among the reforms were in the area of the Bank of Ghana's operational framework in the money market.

Bank of Ghana's Operational Monetary Policy Framework

Under the new operational monetary policy framework, the Bank aims at consciously steering the short-term (overnight) interest rates within an interest rate band (or interest rate corridor). Reverse repo rate (i.e. at the repo/prime rate minus 200 basis points) defines the lower limit of the band while its newly introduced fine-tuning operations (conducted at the repo/prime rate plus 100 basis points) define the upper limit.

As part of the reforms and in order to create incentives for banks to deal among themselves in the interbank market, the Bank widened the interest rate corridor to 300 basis points from 100 basis points. In addition, to provide the BOG a presence on the interbank market and increase its ability to influence rates on this market, overnight repo and reverse repo facilities were introduced alongside the then existing facilities, at the BOG Prime Rate and reverse repo rate respectively.

In general, commercial banks operate under conditions of uncertainty, and may not know in advance on which side of the market the central bank will eventually stand. In equilibrium however, given arbitrage considerations, the level of the overnight market interest rate is expected to be equal to a weighted average of the rates on its lending and deposit facilities (i.e. within the interest rate corridor).

Steering the short term overnight rate within the corridor

The framework for operations in the money market is based on a weekly reserve averaging mechanism. This is intended, aside from the conventional reasons of customer 'liquidity insurance' and of prudential considerations, also to serve as a buffer of liquidity to absorb the day-to-day shocks of liquidity supply and thus help stabilize money market interest rates. To ensure a smooth functioning of the payment system, banks are in addition required to maintain non-negative balances with BOG by the close of each business day i.e. before the payment system closes[12].

As noted earlier, the operational framework of BoG is geared towards steering the short-term interbank overnight rate within the interest rate corridor. The corridor is currently set at a spread of 300 basis points intended to make the BOG only a marginal actor, but with greater incentives for banks to deal amongst themselves. In steering the overnight interest rate, BOG uses a combination of instruments from its armory of monetary policy instruments. In general, depending on the liquidity situation in the market (i.e. the actual reserve money position vis-a-vis a programmed target) OMOs are conducted to either withdraw or inject liquidity.

Open market operations (OMOs)

Weekly auctions of government securities constitute the principal instrument used in withdrawing excess liquidity from the system. The auctions fulfill two objectives. The first is to meet the government's financing needs including, importantly, rolling over maturing securities issued at previous auctions. The second is to conduct Bank of Ghana's open market operations (OMO's) in order to hit a weekly reserve money (RM) target.

In practice, the bank on a weekly basis (every Friday) forecasts how much liquidity will have to be withdrawn or injected into the system in the coming week and on the basis of the forecasts, conducts the auctions using the Dutch Auction System.

Since the above forecasts are made for a whole week, in practice, it is possible that tensions could arise from the day-to-day liquidity needs of the market. To deal with these, the Bank also conducts repos (at the prime rate) and reverse (lower bound of the corridor) in order to meet the short term liquidity needs of the market (figure 5.14). In addition, the bank may from time to time decide,

---

[12]   BoG's payments system is on Real time Gross Settlement (RTGS) basis .

depending on the liquidity situation, conduct OMOs by issuing its on bills (currently the maturity of these bills ranges from two weeks to two months). These are issued on a standard auction basis with rates that are market determined.

Fig 5.14: **G's operational framework**

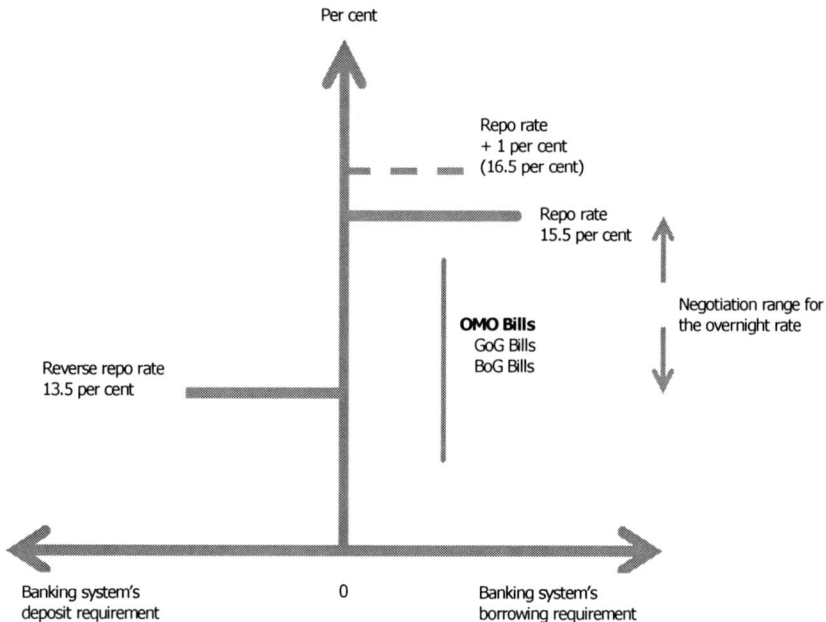

Per cent

Repo rate
+ 1 per cent
(16.5 per cent)

Repo rate
15.5 per cent

Negotiation range for
the overnight rate

OMO Bills
GoG Bills
BoG Bills

Reverse repo rate
13.5 per cent

Banking system's
deposit requirement

0

Banking system's
borrowing requirement

Interest rate levels as at 30th December, 2005

Finally, another novel feature of the current framework is the introduction of a fine-tuning window at the end of the weekly maintenance period. Fine-tuning lending operations are conducted to allow the system to square up. However, in order to allow banks to participate more in the interbank market as well as the regular OMOs, these operations are conducted at 100 basis points above the repo/prime rate (Figure 5.14 – Bank of Ghana's Operational Framework).

The current operational framework of the Bank of Ghana is therefore highly market based. The framework is geared towards steering short-term interbank overnight rates within the interest rate corridor.

CHAPTER 6

FINANCIAL SECTOR REFORM: 2001-2008

The financial sector reform programme (FINSAP), which was implemented between 1988 and 1999 achieved a great deal, including the liberalization of interest rates, abolition of directed credit, restructuring of financially distressed banks, strengthening of the regulatory and supervisory framework, privatization of state owned banks, promotion of non-bank financial institutions, liberalization of the foreign exchange market, establishment of forex bureaux, and the beginnings of a capital market with the establishment of the Ghana stock exchange in 1990.

By 2001, a number of constraints still remained in the financial sector, including high nominal interest rate spreads, low financial intermediation, crowding out of the private sector in the credit market, cash dominated payment system, large unbanked population, the absence of a credit information system, a complex foreign exchange regime, and the absence of a clear legal framework that addressed the rights and responsibilities of borrowers and lenders. There was also a need to fashion a legislative framework that would allow Ghana to position herself as an international financial center within the sub-region.

These issues led to the launch of a new wave of home grown reforms, some of which were later placed under the banner of the Financial Sector Strategic Plan (FINSSP) in 2003. The stated objectives of FINSSP were; to make the financial sector the preferred source of finance for domestic companies, promote efficient savings mobilization, establish Ghana as the financial gateway to the Economic Community of West African States (ECOWAS) region, enhance the competitiveness of Ghana's financial institutions; ensure a stronger but also "user-friendly" regulatory regime, and achieve a diversified domestic financial sector within a competitive environment.

REFORMING THE LEGAL FRAMEWORK – 2001-2008

The 2001-2008 period saw a wide range of legal reforms comprehensively affecting the financial sector. These reforms were meant to build on the earlier reforms of the 1980s and 1990s under FINSAP, address remaining bottlenecks and to better position Ghana's financial sector to drive Ghana's agenda of accelerated growth. Among the laws that were passed in this period were the Bank of Ghana Act 2002, The Banking Act 2004, Payments System Act 2003, Long Term Savings Act 2004, Venture Capital Trust Fund Act 2004, Foreign Exchange Act 2006, Central Securities Depository Act 2007, Banking Amendment Act 2007, Credit Reporting Act 2007, Borrowers and Lenders Act 2008, Non-Bank Financial Institutions Act 2008, Home Mortgage Finance Act 2008.

Bank of Ghana Act, 2002

The Bank of Ghana Act of 2002 was a landmark legislation which re-established the independence of the Bank of Ghana. It would be recalled that the Bank of Ghana Ordinance of 1957 which established the Bank provided it with statutory and operational independence. This independence was however taken away from the central bank with the passage of the Bank of Ghana Act 1963 (as was discussed earlier). After 45 years of government interference in the operations of the central bank which was largely characterized by fiscal dominance, and with the economic crisis of 2000 still fresh, Parliament passed the Bank of Ghana Act of 2002 which once again enshrined into law the independence of the Bank of Ghana.

Section 3(1) of the Bank of Ghana Act 2002 specifies that **"the primary objective of the Bank is to maintain stability in the general level of prices".** The Act further states that , " (2) without prejudice to subsection (1) the Bank shall support the general economic policy of government and promote economic growth and effective operation of banking and credit systems in the country, **independent of instructions from the Government or any other authority**" This provision has made the Bank of Ghana (on paper at least) one of the most independent central banks in the world.

The Bank of Ghana Act 2002 has refocused the central bank on the major task of inflation control and away from the developmental activities which characterized the Bank of Ghana's operations in the past. Other provisions of the Act include the following:

- a Monetary Policy Committee will be responsible for formulating monetary policy, which should bring transparency to the central bank's operations and its communications with the public

- Government borrowing from the central bank in any year shall be limited to 10 percent of its revenue, which ties the hands of government and the central bank in a way that is much stricter than the 20 percent ceiling which prevails in the CFA zone countries, for example.

The statutory mandate of the central bank was rooted in a resurgence of public interest in economic policy and a heightened aversion for inflation and awareness of how much stability, in a growing economy, contributes to raising the standard of living of its people. The prevailing concern was that instability and weaknesses in the regulatory framework had accounted for the poor performance of the private sector.

The independence of the Bank of Ghana under the Bank of Ghana Act also provided the Bank with the freedom to pursue policies in the interest of the financial sector without having to wait on approval from the Government or any other authority. This was a major breath of fresh air for the bank. There are however legitimate questions about the extent to which the Bank of Ghana

Act demands accountability from the Bank to Parliament for example as is the case with the Bank of England or the Federal Reserve.

Universal Banking

Financial sector policy conducted through the licensing of banks sought to serve multiple objectives other than the fundamental goal of debt and equity intermediation, these were (a) to develop specialized segments of banking and financial services notably merchant banking, development banking, retail banking, mortgage banking, and rural-based banking and finance institutions.

In 2003, the Bank of Ghana introduced the concept of Universal Banking to replace the increasingly fragmented banking system. Universal Banking, which involves the removal of restrictions on banking activity, was introduced to allow banks to choose the type of banking services they would like to offer in line with their capital, risk appetite and business orientation. It removes for instance, the monopoly that was given to commercial banks in the area of retail banking. It creates room for diversification of the range of financial services that a bank can provide. It allows merchant banks for example to compete for retail deposits. This process was expected to lead to branch network expansion, increasing banking penetration, and also competition for deposits at the retail level. The introduction of Universal Banking was basically a recognition that the financial system had to become integrated and thus the old divisions between commercial banks, development banks and merchant banks had become anachronistic. Universal banking therefore, leveled the playing field and opened the financial sector to competition and the entry of new banks.

The Bank of Ghana at the same time recognized that for banks to adequately perform their roles as universal banks, it was important that they were adequately capitalized to take on additional risk. The Bank of Ghana therefore raised the minimum capital requirement for banks from ¢25 billion (US$3.3 million) for Ghanaian banks ¢25 billion (US$3.3 million) for Ghanaian banks,

¢50 billion (US$6.7 million) for foreign banks, ¢50 billion (US$6.7 million) for foreign banks, to ¢70 billion ($7.2 million) in 2003.

Along with universal banking, the central bank also adopted an open but selective licensing policy, which allowed the entry of new banks. The addition of new banks was expected to encourage faster modernization of banking operations and efficiency of the financial system in order to support the growth and diversification of the financial service industry. Competition was also expected to positively affect the tariffs banks charge for their products and services, lower lending rates in line with credit risks, and make credit accessible to all sectors in the economy. While the entry of new banks would increase competition, the Bank of Ghana also recognized that excessive numbers within the system could dilute the franchise value of banks and increase instability. Entry therefore had to be selective, well-managed, and paced over time and clear exit rules and prudential supervision vigorously enforced to safeguard systemic stability.

The Banking Act 2004 and Banking Amendment Act 2007

The Banking Act 2004, Act 673, was passed by Parliament to bring the banking law up to date with international standards as well as strengthen the operational independence of the Bank of Ghana in its role as a regulatory authority and to ensure greater transparency in the regulatory framework. The Act was however amended by the Banking Amendment Act 2007 as part of the legal framework to support Ghana as an International Financial Services Centre (IFSC), a world-class hub to facilitate the delivery of a wide range of cross-border financial services to clients in other countries in the mould of Mauritius, Singapore or London.

Taken together, the Banking Act 2004 and the Banking Amendment Act 2007 have resulted in fundamental changes in the regulatory framework for banking in Ghana.

Licensing

The Bank of Ghana now issues three types of banking license; Class1 License, Class II License and a General License.

A Class 1 license allows a bank to conduct universal, development, or merchant banking business as existing banks currently do. All existing banks are therefore designated as Class I banks. A Class II banking license restricts the clients of the bank to non-residents. Class II banking business is conducted in a currency other than the Ghana cedi. A bank with a Class II banking license may accept deposits and make loans or offer other financial services only to non-residents. The domestic economy is expected to benefit from the direct foreign investment, employment, fees and taxes and skills transfer. A General Banking License allows the bank to combine both Class I and Class II activities.

Capital Adequacy

Holders of General and Class I banking licenses are required to maintain a minimum capital adequacy ratio of 10.0 per cent. The capital adequacy ratio for a class II license holder on the other hand will be set by the bank of Ghana for each bank separately depending on the financial resources available to the Bank in question and the nature, scale and risks of the banks' operations.

Minimum Capital Requirements

The Banking Amendment Act 2007 established minimum capital requirements for Class I and General License banks at ¢70 billion (the equivalent of some $7.0 million) while that for Class II banks was to be determined by the Bank of Ghana from time to time.

In February 2008, the Bank of Ghana set a new minimum capital requirement for obtaining a Class 1 banking license (universal banking) at GH¢60 million (the equivalent of some $60.0 million at the time). Existing banks were required to attain a minimum capitalization of GH¢ 60 million by December 31st 2009. Ghanaian-owned banks were however given a longer time period to meet the new minimum capital requirement. Under the directive, banks with local majority share ownership will have to attain a capitalization of at least GH¢ 25 million by the end of 2010 and GH¢60 million by 2012. The capitalization requirement constitutes part of the Bank of Ghana's strategy to deepen the financial sector and support Ghana's drive for accelerated growth of the economy.

Long Term Savings Scheme Act, 2004

One of the factors inhibiting capital market development and the availability of medium to long term loans from financial institutions in Ghana is the dearth of long term savings. While the history of macroeconomic instability and high inflation has contributed to this outcome, the absence of incentives for voluntary long term savings is a major obstacle. It is as a result of this that the Long Term Savings Scheme Act, 2004 was passed by Parliament to provide for the operation of tax incentive based voluntary savings plans for retirement, education, home ownership, all purpose, disability or death. Between 10%-17.5% of contributions by employers to various savings schemes are tax deductable by the contributor. A Long Term Savings Scheme Agency was established under the Act to administer the scheme.

Venture Capital Trust Fund Act 2004

The Venture Capital Trust Fund Act, 2004 established a Venture Capital Trust Fund to provide financial resources for the development and promotion of venture capital financing for Small and Medium scale enterprises (SMEs) in specified sectors of the economy. Funding for the Trust Fund was to come from a number of sources, including 25% of the National Reconstruction Levy from the 2003 financial year, budgetary allocations by government, grants, fees, and investment income.

Any venture capital financing company is eligible to apply for funds provided it:

(i)   is incorporated in Ghana as a limited liability company under the companies code (1963),

(ii)   has as its sole authorized business, the business of assisting the development of small businesses by making equity investments and providing managerial expertise in which it has made or proposes to make an eligible investment

(iii)   Is managed by an investment advisor who is licensed by the securities and exchange commission and is in good standing

(iv)   Has met minimum capital requirements,

(v)   Has in place adequate governance, internal control, and monitoring procedures for the selection and monitoring of investment projects

(vi)   Meets any other conditions specified by the Board.

Payment System Act 2003

One area in the financial sector which needed major reform was the payment and settlement system. It was therefore important to put in place the legal underpinning to support these reforms and move the payments and settlement system into the 21st century.

A Payment System Act was passed by Parliament in 2003 to provide for the establishment, operation, and supervision of electronic and other payment, clearing and settlement systems. The Act also provided for the rights and responsibilities of transacting and intermediating parties.

The Payment Systems Act 2003 was a response to the need to develop non-cash payment products and clearing systems in order to reduce the over-dependence on cash payments in the economy.

The Act gives the Bank of Ghana the power to establish, operate and supervise the payment and settlement system. Section 1 stipulates that

> *"the Bank of Ghana may establish, operate or supervise funds payment, funds transfer, clearing and settlement systems subject to such rules as it may publish, and designate any other payment, funds transfer, clearing and settlement system operating in the country which the bank considers to be in the public interest for the Bank to supervise under this Act"*

Participants in the payments and settlement system are expected to play by the agreed rules of the system. The Act states that a transfer made in accordance with the rules, without prejudice to any remedies that may exist to recover an equivalent amount in case of fraud, mistake or similar factors is irrevocable once executed. The discharge of settlement obligations between institutions participating in the system is made through entries in the accounts of the settlement bank and such an entry is final and irrevocable.

Foreign Exchange Act, 2006

One of the key reforms in the legal framework was the review of the basic laws governing foreign exchange transactions and the subsequent passage of the Foreign Exchange Act in 2006 to replace the Exchange Control Act of 1961. A number of key issues drove this reform.

The first was the need for Ghana to rationalize its foreign exchange system to make its economy more efficient within an integrated global financial system, which has been experiencing constant capital flows.

Secondly, when the foreign exchange regime in Ghana was liberalized by policy in the mid 1980s, this was not accompanied by a corresponding reform of the existing relevant statutes. This therefore created a situation where the policy direction on foreign exchange transactions was diametrically opposed to statutory law.

Thirdly, Ghana is seeking to establish itself as an International Financial Centre within the West African sub-region. This calls for a reform of all laws that can facilitate such a project.

Fourthly, as a member of the West African Monetary Zone, Ghana had an obligation to liberalize its capital account transactions as a precondition for entry into the common currency arrangement.

The Foreign Exchange Act, 2006 signaled an open and liberal exchange and payments system for Ghana. Unlike the Exchange Control Act of 1961, which prohibited all foreign exchange dealings and transactions unless permitted by the Minister and the Bank of Ghana, the philosophy of the Foreign Exchange Act of 2006 is to permit all foreign exchange transactions unless otherwise prohibited by the BOG.

For current account transactions, the Foreign Exchange Act requires the payments in foreign currency to or from Ghana between residents and non-residents to be made through a bank. Furthermore, payments for merchandise exports from Ghana are required to be made through the bank of the non-resident exporter to the exporter's bank in Ghana. This provision is to allow the Bank of Ghana to monitor Ghana's export proceeds. Under the Foreign Exchange Act, an exporter who fails to repatriate proceeds from merchandise exports through an external bank commits an offence. Exporters are however free to utilize the proceeds of their exports as they deem fit with the exception of cocoa and gold where there are surrender requirements.

In the area of capital account transactions, while the Exchange Control Act placed restrictions on the issuance and transfer of securities as well as external loans contracted between residents and non residents, the Foreign Exchange Acts liberalized the inflows of foreign exchange into Ghana for foreign direct investment purposes. Also, loans contracted by residents will no longer require Bank of Ghana approval. However, there are restrictions on short term money market investments, with non-residents allowed to invest in instruments of a tenor of three years or more provided these instruments are held for at least two years.

Broadly, with the passage of the Foreign Exchange Act of 2006, there is a shift in emphasis away from controls embodied in the Exchange Control Act to an increased focus on monitoring foreign exchange transactions. In this regard, and consistent with international best practice, banks are required to submit reports on all underlying transactions related to transactions in foreign exchange to the Bank of Ghana.

Anti-Money Laundering Act, 2008

The Anti-Money Laundering Act was passed in 2008 to reinforce existing mechanisms for monitoring terrorist finances and money laundering within the global financial system. This was especially important as Ghana seeks to position itself as an International financial services centre. In this regard, it was important that the necessary safeguards be put in place.

The Act provides for the establishment of a Financial Intelligence Centre (FIC) to assist in the identification of proceeds of unlawful activities and the combat of money laundering activities. The transfer of currency physically of electronically will be subject to the Bank of Ghana regulations consistent with the Foreign Exchange Act, 2006.

The Act also provides that when an individual or institution becomes aware or a transaction involving money laundering or the financing of terrorism, such an individual or institution is required to submit a suspicious transaction report to the FIC within twenty four hours of becoming aware of the transaction.

Under the Act, the Financial Intelligence Centre may freeze a transaction or a bank account to prevent suspected money laundering but is required to go to court within seven days for the freeze to either be upheld or denied.

Credit Reporting Act, 2008

A major constraint to accessing credit has been the existence of asymmetric information in the credit markets. Lenders generally cannot be certain about the credit worthiness of borrowers with the absence of credit information. To address this problem, the Credit Reporting Act was passed by Parliament in 2007. The purpose of the Credit Reporting Act (Act 726) is to provide a legal and regulatory framework for credit reporting in Ghana. The availability of credit information is generally accepted to be crucial for the development and maintenance of an effective financial sector. Borrowers tend to have a natural incentive not to reveal negative information about themselves. The lack of a credit information system therefore increases the risks of lending, and causes financial institutions to provide less credit. A credit reporting system in Ghana would provide timely, accurate, and up – to - date information on the debt profile and repayment history of borrowers and would lead to a number of benefits, including:

(a)   The reduction of information asymmetry between borrowers and lenders.

(b)   Enabling financial institutions to make informed decisions about the allocation of credit.

(c)   Reducing default probabilities of borrowers as they seek to meet their obligations in a timely manner.

(d)   Improving access to credit facilities by small and medium-sized businesses.

(e)   Enabling the Central Bank to monitor systematic risks on an aggregate basis; and ultimately.

(f)   Promoting financial stability and efficient allocation of resources in the Ghanaian economy.

This Credit Reporting Act is designed to promote the orderly development of a credit reporting system for Ghana and to promote public trust in credit bureau operations. Specifically, the Act provides for the licensing of private credit bureaus (and gives the Bank of Ghana the authority to set up a public credit bureau), regulates the activities of credit bureaus, establishes guiding principles for the conduct of the credit reporting system, and provides for credit data submission, data management and protection, and dissemination. It seeks to strike a balance between the rights of borrowers on the one hand, and the need to share credit information effectively, on the other.

The Bank of Ghana is the regulatory authority for the Credit Reporting Act and the first credit reference bureau in Ghana was licensed in 2008.

Borrowers and Lenders Act, 2008

The Borrowers and Lenders Act, 2008 (Act 773) was enacted to address a major gap in the financial sector, the absence of a legal framework governing the rights and responsibilities of borrowers and lenders. Stakeholder meetings convened by the Bank of Ghana to address this issue revealed very deep suspicions of each of the parties. Borrowers felt rather powerless in dealing with lenders (the banks). High interest rates, hidden charges, non-disclosure of pertinent information, unfair denial of access to credit, and discrimination were some of their complaints. The lenders on the other hand complained about high default rates, difficulty of enforcing collateral through the courts, customers pledging the same collateral to more than one bank, and the misapplication of funds.

.

The Borrowers and Lenders Act, 2008 provides the legal framework for credit, improves the standard of disclosure of information by borrowers and lenders, and promotes a consistent enforcement framework relating to credit.

Home Mortgage Finance Act, 2008

The Home Mortgage finance Act, 2008 (Act 770) was passed to clarify and rationalize the regulatory framework for home mortgages so as to deepen the development of the home mortgage market. In this regard, this Act takes precedence over the Mortgages Act, 1972 where there is a conflict between the two.

The Act covers inter alia the requirements for a mortgage; disclosure requirements for the mortgagor and mortgagee, use of the loan, registration of mortgages, default and remedies, and sale of mortgaged properties in case of default. It is a borrowers and lenders law specifically for the home mortgage market.

Non-Bank Financial Institutions (NBFI) Act, 2008

The Financial Institutions (Non-Banking) Law 1993 (PNDCL 328) was promulgated in 1993 to provide a prudential regulatory framework for nine categories of institutions designated as non-bank financial institutions. These were Discount Houses, Finance Houses, Acceptance Houses, Building societies, Leasing and Hire Purchasing Companies, Venture Capital Funding Companies, Mortgage Financing Companies, Savings and Loans Companies, and Credit Unions. The Bank of Ghana subsequently issued the Non Bank Financial Institutions (Bank of Ghana) Business Rules for Deposit Taking Institutions and the Non-Bank Financial Institutions (Bank of Ghana) Business Rules for Non-Deposit Taking Institutions in 2000, to provide detailed prudential rules for NBFIs. While PNDCL 328 regulated certain Micro Finance Institutions (MFIs) such as savings and loans companies and credit unions, a good number of MFIs including NGOs and some informal operators such as *Susu* collectors remain outside the scope of prudential regulation with potential system risks.

Ghana's Financial Sector Strategic Plan (FINSSP) identified the need to review the existing NBFI and MFI regulatory framework to ensure that they meet current challenges of the market. FINSSP recommended the revision of PNDCL 328 to remove ambiguities in the objectives of regulation and to liberalize the regime for the development of NBFIs. It also envisaged the progressive deregulation of non-deposit taking NBFIs and the establishment of consistency in the regulation of deposit-taking NBFIs and banks.

The Non-Bank Financial Institutions Act, 2008 (Act 774) has a number of key provisions, including;

(i) Non-Bank Financial Services are defined under the Act as leasing, money lending, money transfer, mortgage finance, non-deposit taking microfinance services, and credit unions. Discount houses, Acceptance houses, and building societies are to be phased out and converted into other licensed NBFIs under the Act.

(ii) The NBFI Act 2008 defines a deposit taking NBFI as one that "offers debt securities to the public and is in the business, directly or indirectly, of lending money or providing other financial services".

(iii) Deposit-taking NBFIs would now be regulated as closely as possible to banks in view of the fact that they pose similar risks to the financial system. The NBFI Act 774 provides that Savings and Loans Companies, Finance Houses, and deposit-taking microfinance institutions will now be regulated under the Banking Act 2004 (Act 673).

(iv) Non-deposit taking NBFIs such as leasing/hire purchase companies, finance houses, mortgage finance companies are to be brought under a lower tier prudential regulatory regime, with a view to a progressive de-regulation of non-deposit taking NBFIs and MFIs.

(v) The Money Lenders Ordinance 1941 (Cap 176) under which money lending licenses could be issued by police stations has been repealed under the NBFI Act 774.

The Act also seeks to promote self-regulation of NBFIs and Microfinance Institutions through strong industry associations or networks such as the existing Ghana Micro Finance Network (GHAMFIN) and the *Susu* Collectors Association.

Risk Based Supervision

All G20 countries have recently committed to adopt the Basel II Capital Framework by 2011. This will make the Basel II framework the operational one in the supervision and regulation of financial systems across the globe. Many African central banks have also expressed the intention to adopt the Basel II framework in due course.

As part of the overall preparation toward the adoption of the Basel II capital framework, the Bank of Ghana adopted the risk based supervision framework in 2007. Risk based supervision is a structured process aimed at identifying the most critical risks that face each bank and through a focused review by the supervisor to assess the bank's management of those risks and the bank's financial vulnerability to potential adverse experience. It involves the continuous monitoring and evaluation of the risk profiles of banks in relation to their business strategies and exposures. This assessment is facilitated by the construction of a risk matrix for each bank, and therefore creates the room for focused supervision in relation to available resources.

Electronic Financial Analysis and Surveillance System (eFASS)

With the increasing size and complexity of Ghana's banking industry, it also became necessary to automate certain aspects of the banking supervision process to enable the Bank of Ghana adopt a more risk-focused, qualitative approach to Supervision. In this regard, the Bank of Ghana implemented the Electronic Financial Analysis and Surveillance System (eFASS) in 2007. The system serves as a decision support system for the Bank by facilitating submissions online and by processing returns and providing users with a vast range of analytical reports and ratios. The preparation of returns by the financial system has also been largely automated, minimizing the human intervention in the preparation of the returns as well as the burden on the institution. The eFASS system has also automated the more routine aspects of surveillance by identifying breaches in statutory regulations and automatically computing penalties. The system helps the Bank of Ghana more easily identify problem institutions through its early warning system reports.

Stress Testing the Banking System

As part of its early warning system the Bank of Ghana also introduced rigorous stress testing of financial institutions and the banking system as a whole in 2006. The results of the stress tests are regularly presented as part of the financial stability report during the Bank of Ghana's Monetary Policy Committee meetings.

ISO 27001 Certification for the Bank of Ghana

Following a major upgrade of the Bank of Ghana's Information Technology systems to meet international standards, the Bank applied for and secured the ISO/IEC 27001 certification (in March 2009), which is the world's highest accreditation for information protection and security. The ISO certification demonstrates that the Bank of Ghana has addressed, implemented and controlled the security of the bank's information, and that Bank of Ghana's management information and systems are secure to ensure the integrity of data sent out as well as data received, significantly limiting security and privacy breaches.

By this certification, the Bank of Ghana became the first central bank in Africa to obtain this certification and joins a small group of central banks including Federal Reserve Bank of New York, Reserve Bank of India, Bank of Indonesia, and Bank of Taiwan that have attained this status.

Insurance Act of 2006 (Act 724)

To create a more vibrant insurance industry and to bring the insurance law in the country in tune with the International Association of Insurance Supervisor's (IAIS) core principles on insurance supervision, the Insurance Act 2006 (Act 724) was enacted. The Act gives the National Insurance Commission (NIC) wider oversight powers, including conducting on-site inspections of insurance companies and insurance intermediaries. Under the old law, PNDCL 227 of 1989, the NIC was allowed to carry out an investigation into the affairs of an insurer, but only in case of a breach of the law or regulations. The Act also contains provisions on good corporate governance and related issues such as the need for independent board members and a 'fit and proper person' test.

The Insurance Act 2006 also removed the monopoly of the State Insurance Company (SIC) over all the insurances of government businesses. Furthermore, under the old Insurance law, the Ghana Re-Insurance Organization received 20 percent of premiums received in the industry, apparently to check capital flight. The new Act removed such compulsory cessions to create room for competition in the insurance industry.

The Capital requirements for insurers and insurance intermediaries under the old law were inadequate as they had been eroded by inflation. The old law did not also enable capital requirements to be easily adjusted to take account of inflation. Under the new Act, there is greater flexibility for the NIC in setting the minimum capital requirements and solvency margin.

Pension Reforms: National Pension Act, 2008

The Pension Ordinance No.42 (CAP 30) was established in 1950 as a Pension Scheme for public servants in the Gold Coast. The Social Security Act 1965 (ACT 279) was subsequently enacted to create a contributory Social Security Fund for payment of superannuation, invalidity, survivor and other Pension Benefits for workers. In 1972, The Social Security Decree (N.R.C.D. 127) repealed ACT 279 and established SSNIT to administer a Social Security Fund for Ghana. The Social Security Act, 1991 (PNDC Law 247), was also promulgated to transform the 1972 Scheme from Provident Fund to a defined benefit scheme. The pension system however, still excluded the vast majority of Ghanaian workers.

One of the most important financial sector reforms introduced between 2001 and 2008 was in the area of Pension Reform. To address the deficiencies in the pension system, including the fact that no formal arrangement existed to cater for the retirement needs of workers in the informal sector (about 80 percent of the working population) President Kufuor established a Presidential Commission on Pensions (Chaired by Mr. T.A. Bediako) in 2004 to examine and make recommendations for the reform of the pension system in Ghana.

The recommendations of the Commission formed part of the Government White Paper and a National Pensions Bill which was enacted in 2008. The main provisions of the Act are as follows:

- The creation of a new Contributory three-tier pension system comprising two mandatory schemes and a voluntary scheme,

- the phasing out of the CAP 30 scheme on grounds of its unsustainability,.

- decentralization of public sector pension management and the restructuring of the Social Security and National Insurance Trust (SSNIT) by overhauling its governance, management and administrative structures,

- establishment of a National Pensions Regulatory Authority to regulate both public and private pension schemes in the country;

- pension coverage for the informal sector and

- the unification of pensions within 5 years of the coming into effect of the Authority.

The Three-Tier Pension Scheme

The first tier, the basic national social security scheme, shall be mandatory for all employees in both the private and public sectors; (payment of only monthly pensions and related benefits such as survivors benefit).

The second tier occupational (or work-based) pension scheme, is mandatory for all employees but will be privately managed, and designed primarily to give contributors higher lump sum benefits than presently available under the SSNIT or Cap 30 pension schemes;

The third tier is a voluntary provident fund and personal pension scheme, supported by tax incentives to provide additional funds for workers who want to make voluntary contributions to enhance their pension benefits as well as workers in the informal sector. Under this tier, informal sector workers can elect to contribute any amount they can afford on monthly or regular basis.

The new Pension scheme would also be a source of increased national savings and availability of long term funds for economic development.

Treasury Single Account (TSA) - Reforming the Management of Government's Cash Balances

To minimize Government borrowing costs or maximize interest-bearing deposits, operating cash balances should be kept to a minimum. In Ghana, Government Ministries, Department and Agencies (MDAs) often accumulate idle balances in their bank accounts. These idle balances increase the borrowing needs of the government, which must borrow to finance the payments of some agencies, even if other agencies have excess cash. Therefore, despite a positive balance with the Bank of Ghana, the government in the past had to borrow on many occasions from the financial markets.

The Treasury Single Account (TSA) allows a centralization of all government cash balances. The TSA is an account or set of linked accounts through which the government transacts all payments. It operates on the simple principle that all government cash belongs to government.

Under the Treasury Single Account arrangement:

(i)   line ministries hold accounts at the Bank of Ghana, which are subsidiary accounts of the Government's account,

(ii)   spending agencies under the line ministries hold accounts either at the Bank of Ghana or, for banking convenience, with commercial banks; in both cases, the accounts must be authorized by the Treasury (Ministry of Finance/Controller and Accountant General),

(iii)   spending agencies' accounts are zero-balance accounts, with money being transferred to these accounts as specific approved payments are made,

(iv)   spending agencies' accounts are automatically swept at the end of each day,

(v)   The central bank consolidates the government position at the end of each day including balances in all the government accounts.

The work to establish the TSA involved the Ministry of Finance and Economic Planning, the Controller and Accountant General Department, and the Bank of Ghana. It was made possible because of the significant improvement that had taken place in the payment system infrastructure and the IT system of the Bank of Ghana.

The implementation of the Treasury Single Account was announced in the March 2009 budget.

Reforms of Rural Banking

The regulatory framework for the governance and supervision of the rural banks was reformed with the passage of the Association of Rural Banks

(ARB) Apex Bank Regulations, 2006 (L.I. 1825). This framework specifies the core functions of the ARB Apex Bank and provides for the ARB Apex Bank to perform a role similar to a "central bank" for the rural banks subject to the overall supervisory authority of the Bank of Ghana. L.I. 1825 also provides detailed guidelines on the relationship between the BOG and ARB Apex, ARB Apex Bank and the rural and community banks, Association of Rural Banks, Government, microfinance institutions, etc.

The Bank of Ghana also introduced a number of rural banking reforms in February 2008 covering the ownership structure and governance, minimum reserve requirements, secondary reserve requirements, and loan ratification.

Ownership Structure and Governance of Rural Banks

Rural and Community Banks (RCBs) were established from inception as community-owned banks with members of the community as shareholders. Individual and corporate shareholding was therefore limited and decision making was based on a one-shareholder one-vote principle. In this regard even an individual or corporate entity that owned 30% of the shares was entitled to the same vote as one with 0.001% of the shares. This model (at least in theory) generated widespread participation of the rural community in the affairs of the bank. In practice however, this model was also at the same time limiting the ability of rural banks to raise capital as well as impacting negatively on the governance of the rural banks. Shareholders saw their purchase of shares, not as an investment but as a social contribution and hardly took much of an interest in the day-to-day running of the bank. Under this model, many rural banks were unable to raise the capital requirement of GH¢50,000 (the equivalent of some $50,000) by the end of 2007.

After consultation with stakeholders, the Bank of Ghana issued new directives from July 1, 2008 as follows:

- Corporate ownership of RCBs would be restricted to 50% of the total shares (as presently applies)..

- Financial institutions are not allowed to hold shares in rural banks.

- Individual ownership would be restricted to 30% of the total shares (as presently applies)

- Family ownership (related individuals) should cumulatively be restricted to 40% of the total shares held.

- Shares of rural banks should always be available for purchase by the public.

- Decision making by shareholders should be in accordance with section 50(1) of the Company's Code, 1963, Act 179 which enjoins shareholders to take decisions through *polling* (i.e. voting should represent the quantum of shares held).

Minimum Capital Requirements for Rural Banks

The new minimum capital requirement for rural banks was increased to GH¢ 150,000 and existing RCBs were required to grow their stated capital to GH¢150,000.

Secondary Reserve Requirements

Following the abolition of secondary reserve requirements (SRRs) for banks, SRRs were also abolished for rural banks. However to provide the rural banks with an additional incentive to computerize, the abolition of secondary reserve requirements for rural banks only applied to those rural banks that complied with the directive to put their financial data in the format (as specified by ARB Apex Bank) in readiness for the implementation of the computerization/Wide Area Network project under the Millennium Challenge Account (MCA).

Loan Ratification

From July 2008, Bank of Ghana approval for loans above GH¢ 2,000 was no longer required. Rural banks were rather required to submit to the Bank of Ghana returns on loans granted on a monthly basis.

These reforms together with the establishment of the common e-zwich platform were implemented to reinvigorate the rural banks and also level the playing field to enable them compete with other financial institutions (specially the banks) that were increasingly entering the rural areas.

The legal and regulatory reforms enacted between 2002 and 2008 were far reaching and comprehensive. While it will take some time for the impact of these reforms to play out, one cannot ignore the significance of these reforms. Building upon the earlier FINSAP reforms, these reforms have provided the financial sector a form for further deepening.

Other financial sector reforms, including payment system reform and redenomination of the currency are discussed in the following chapters.

CHAPTER 7

PAYMENTS AND SETTLEMENT SYSTEM REFORM IN GHANA

A dynamic growth-oriented financial system must be underpinned by an efficient payment and settlement system. Ghana is still essentially a cash-based economy with embedded high transaction costs. It is therefore important that the financial system moves towards more efficient payment methods like cheques and electronic cards. With the passage of the Payments System Act, 2003, the Bank of Ghana embarked on a major reform of Ghana's payments and settlement system. The Bank undertook reforms in the legal, institutional, and infrastructure framework of the payments system to make the Ghanaian financial system modern and competitive.

One of the major constraints for the development of an efficient domestic capital market has been the absence of the requisite payment and settlement system infrastructure. Two critical components of this infrastructure are the Real Time Gross Settlement System (RTGS) and the Central Securities Depository (CSD). In the area of payments system infrastructure, The Bank of Ghana introduced the Real Time Gross Settlement System (RTGS) in 2002 (the first in West Africa) for high value interbank settlements. The RTGS has created an enabling environment for safe, sound, secure, and timely payments. It has also reduced systemic, payments and settlement risks as payment orders are settled almost instantaneously.

The absence of a CSD was a major barrier to capital market development. With issuer of securities maintaining its own ownership register and each purchaser issued with a physical certificate of title it is difficult for trades to take place as registers of ownership as well as proofs of title are diffused. This is why it was important to have a modern CSD. The Bank of Ghana established a Central Securities Depository System in 2004 as part of measures to support the bond market.

The CSD will make it possible for records of ownership of individual securities to be maintained centrally as well as at the respective primary dealers. This should reduce the risks to investors that arise from possible poor record-keeping or any dealer malfeasance.

The Central Securities Depository would enable securities to be held and processed electronically by book entry and therefore make it easier to trade in securities. For example, it will enable an investor to rediscount a security with a dealer other than the one through which the security was first purchased, and transfer that security to any dealer willing to pay the highest price for that security. The CSD represents an important step in developing a secondary and liquid market for government debt instruments and other securities and it should put a hard-wire around the capital market infrastructure to improve security and investor confidence.

Parliament passed the Central Securities Depository Act in 2007 to underpin capital market development in Ghana. The Act provides the legal basis for dematerialization (i.e. the elimination of physical certificates or documents of title that represent ownership of securities so that securities exist only as accounting records). The Ghana Stock Exchange established a Central Securities depository for the equity market in 2008.

Codeline Cheque Clearing

There were 11 cheque clearing houses in Ghana distributed across all the regions (in each Regional capital plus Hohoe in the Volta region). Each served as a local clearing area and the clearing cycle for a cheque was normally 3 days. The other cheques are inter-zonal and had a 6-9 day clearing cycle depending on distance. While the clearing system in Accra was automated and centralized, it still involved the physical movement of cheques. The 10 clearing houses outside of Accra on the other hand undertook manual processing.

In reforming the cheque payments system, the Bank of Ghana set a goal of implementing a system that would allow cheque clearing the next working day anywhere in Ghana (rural or urban). To accomplish this, the Bank of Ghana implemented the Codeline Cheque Clearing (CCC) system. This system is an online processing system which has improved the processing time of cheques in Ghana to within a day. The major difference is that the CCC automated system undertakes capture, processing and storage of check images rather than the handling of physical cheques as was done previously.

Automated Clearing House

In addition to the Codeline Cheque Clearing, the Bank of Ghana also initiated the establishment of an Automated Clearing House (ACH). The Automated Clearing House is an electronic clearing system that will enable files of payment instructions to be exchanged among banks. The payments may be credits, debits and direct debits. The files will be processed and netted to arrive at the net position of each bank. Until now, direct debits on accounts of individuals or firms have not been possible in Ghana because of the absence of an Automated Clearing House. It is expected that this will enhance both credit delivery, loan recovery, bills settlements and reduce cash-based transactions. The ACH is expected to commence operations in 2010.

Banking the Unbanked – The e-zwich Common Platform

Economics of Banking the Unbanked

Banks can only lend out the savings of their depositors or what they borrow from the money market. If there are no savings (or placements) by depositors there can be no loans. The price of loans (interest rates) like that of any other good or service is fundamentally determined by demand and supply. When the demand for loans increases relative to supply (savings), the price (the interest rate) will rise. In this sense one should expect that in an economy where savings in the financial system are low for whatever reason, market determined interest rates would be higher.

The importance of increasing the supply of savings in the financial system through making financial services available to the population has long been recognized by the developed economies. For example, by 1772, Scotland (a country one-third the size of Ghana) had established a nationwide banking system. By this time 31 banks were operating in Scotland with branches and agencies covering most of the country making Scotland the first country in the world to establish an almost nationwide system of branch banking. One of the first savings banks in Europe was established in Hamburg in 1778. By 1836 there were 280 savings banks in Germany, and by 1850 they had reached 1,200 savings banks. By 1913, they numbered 3,133 with total assets more than double those of the commercial banks. By 1914, the number of rural credit co-operatives in Germany reached 17,000. The Friendly Society Act was enacted in England in 1793 to encourage savings by the poor. The Savings Bank movement however, started around 1810 with the Rothwell Savings Bank established by Henry Duncan as a bank for the poor widely imitated not only in Britain but also France and Holland. The evolution of the banking system in many European countries saw the rapid spread of banks including savings banks and rural banks targeted at the poor (Davies, 1996). Wide access to financial services in the developed economies has therefore increased the supply of savings and reduced the cost of borrowing. In the UK for example, some 95 percent of the population has access to a bank account (House of Commons Treasury Committee, 2006).

To improve domestic resource mobilization, there are the usual recommendations for governments to improve the efficiency of tax collections, through reform of the public financial management system, automation of tax administration, stemming capital flight etc. However at the heart of the problem of tax collection in developing countries is the highly informal nature of many economies, underpinned and supported by the predominance of cash transactions as a result of financial exclusion. Unfortunately, many developing countries have not made the link between financial exclusion on the one hand and the difficulty of collecting taxes on the other. One of the quickest ways to the formalization of the economy and therefore to increase the tax net is to bank the unbanked.

If undertaken on a comprehensive scale, financial resources locked up in non-financial assets would be brought into the banking system for intermediation and this could be a significant source of resources (representing potentially 3-5 times what is being currently intermediated in the financial system).

In Ghana, after 50 years of independence and more than two decades of financial sector reform, over 70.0 percent of the population still has no bank account and therefore no access to payment instruments other than cash for transactions since most alternative payment instruments are bank-based. This means that the level of savings in the financial system is low relative to potential. A major reason why interest rates on loans continue to be high in many developing countries like Ghana is that financial savings are too low, inter alia. In such an environment, it is likely to be the case that even after the central bank reduces its policy rate, commercial banks may not respond in tandem and lending rates will continue to be high.

The banking system from its colonial heritage has evolved and developed in such a way that it has excluded the majority of the population from the financial system. This situation has arisen because the traditional payment systems offered by the major banking institutions do not address the key requirements of the unbanked population. These include inter alia:

- the difficulty in opening bank accounts –paper work, utility bills etc,
- the need to have basic literacy, administration and record keeping abilities and English-language capacity to operate a bank account,
- many people find banking halls intimidating,
- the high costs associated with maintaining a bank account relative to customers' income levels,
- the requirement of significant infrastructure (including ATM's and communications systems) to settle transactions "on-line", which are often unavailable in rural areas and informal sector,
- security concerns relating to protection against fraudulent transactions.

Most of the payment system infrastructure which has been developed in Ghana has its origin in the developed world which has a completely different environment. So for example, when a bank introduces a debit card as an alternative to cash, virtually the entire rural population is excluded because there is either no electricity, limited telecommunications infrastructure, no bank, no ATM or no point of sale offering VISA or MasterCard services.

Payment and settlement system development in Ghana as in many other developing countries has therefore largely focused on access by the tiny banked segment of the population. Banks have developed products like ATM networks and debit cards, which are largely limited to their own customers or members of their own network. This path of payment system development over the last fifty years has resulted in the exclusion of the vast majority of the population from access to financial services.

The nature of payment system development has also increased the cost of banking in Ghana because banks end up with a small customer base over which to spread the cost of their operations. Their fees and interest rates would therefore be higher than banks in other jurisdictions with a much larger customer base. Banks have over the years not made much of an effort to bank the unbanked because the history of macroeconomic instability provided them with a very lucrative and zero risk customer, the Government. This, along with high fees and interest rates, yielded very good returns on investment for banks.

The banks have also been very reluctant to co-operate on technology which has meant that over the years, very expensive investments have had to be amortized over a small customer base. One area of glaring omission in payments system development was the absence of a common platform that ensures interoperability across different bank networks or switches. A common platform ensures that a customer of one bank is able to use the ATM or point of sale of any other bank.

The problem of cooperation as has been the experience in other countries, has been around the issue of who owns the network? If a few banks own it, other banks are reluctant to participate. Attempts by the banks to establish a common platform in Ghana failed.

With very little progress having been made on this front over the years, the Bank of Ghana convened stakeholders meetings in 2006. The meetings sought to chart a way forward in payment system development for the Ghanaian banking system. From the experience of other countries, the Bank of Ghana realized the importance of achieving consensus rather than imposing a solution. The process was as follows:

A stakeholders meeting was held to brainstorm on the way forward for payment system development in Ghana to allow the banking of the unbanked. There was a consensus that a common platform was needed amongst the banks in Ghana. However, it was also recognized that a common platform, while necessary, is not sufficient to address the problem of the unbanked if that platform is not accessible to people in the rural or informal sectors. What was needed was a payment system designed with the needs of the unbanked at the center and not at the periphery as currently exists. The banking system needed a payment system that is accessible, has low transaction costs, has limited infrastructure needs, able to work in the rural and informal sector areas, secure, and simple to use. In sum, the banking system needed a payment system that was inclusive of the majority of the population in terms of access to financial services.

A technical committee with representation from the Ghana Association of Bankers, Bank of Ghana, and the private sector, was subsequently set up to draft request for proposals for common payments platform with the most potential to promote financial inclusion and bank the unbanked. The technical committee recommended the establishment of a national switch (or common platform) which would be accessible online as well as offline and provide a fully integrated payment switching and settlement system for all banks, rural banks and savings and loans companies, Susu and other microfinance operators. The Switch would also be suitable for multiple applications and services, meeting the requirements of the banked and the un-banked in terms of accessibility, low transaction costs, limited infrastructure needs, personal safety, security, convenience; and simplicity.

Furthermore, the committee also recommended the introduction of a smart card (based on biometric identification) payment system, which is compatible with the domestic switch and that, can be used nationally. The system was required to be able to work in any rural part of Ghana as well as in the urban areas (with or without electricity) and accessible to both the literate and the illiterate, most of whom were reluctant to even visit the premises of a bank.

It was also critical that the system was not just for use in the payments for goods and services (i.e. not just another debit card) but had multiple applications that would allow consumers to access a full range of banking services like savings accounts on which interest could be paid, accessing loans, making and receiving money transfers, paying utility bills, insurance premiums, school fees, receiving wages, etc. without anyone having to step into a traditional bank branch.

It was also recommended that the system introduced should ultimately have an interface with international card schemes such as VISA, MasterCard, Europay, Diners, American Express etc. and be able to settle transactions with local and international issuers and acquirers.

On the basis of these recommendations submitted by the Technical Committee, the Request for Proposals was drafted. After reviewing all the proposals and visiting all the countries of the respective providers, the Technical Committee (comprising the Ghana Association of Bankers, Bank of Ghana, and the private sector) recommended the Universal Electronic Payments System (UEPS) as the payments platform that best met Ghana's requirements.

The entire process of choosing the common platform which was named the *e-zwich* platform, and biometric smartcard (the *e-zwich smartcard*) was therefore consultative, open and transparent. All the banks were involved through the Ghana Association of Bankers. It was therefore not the case of the central bank imposing a solution or consumer product on the banking system. Once the e-zwich platform was chosen as the solution to the intractable problem of achieving interoperability while providing a vehicle for banking the unbanked, the central bank moved to implement the solution, again in consultation with the banks.

The Bank of Ghana explained these principles to representatives of some of the major international card operators when they expressed concern that Ghana should allow "market forces" to dictate the development of the payment system. The Bank of Ghana explained that this process of choosing a common platform was market driven. What the Bank of Ghana did as a central bank was to bring stakeholders together to define Ghana's needs as far as payment system development was concerned. After a consensus was reached, the Bank of Ghana advertised in the open market for a supplier of the solution and the international card operators, like other providers, were free to compete. The one major challenge the international card operators had was that their cards could not meet the Bank of Ghana's requirement that of being able to work offline[13], in rural areas without electricity, etc. and they therefore saw the central bank's facilitation of the process as a threat to their existing comparative advantage which basically ruled out the savings and loans, rural banks and the majority of the population from access to the technology.

The e-zwich payment platform was formally launched by the Bank of Ghana on April 28, 2008.

---

[13] i.e without a telephone connection to a central system. This was to cater for the reality of the state of telecommunications infrastructure in Ghana..

Advantages of the e-zwich Payments Platform

The e-zwich system has a number of advantages, including the following:

• The system requires little numeracy due to its biometric features; and it can work both on-line and off-line. This unique feature of the e-zwich makes it an efficient vehicle to promote financial inclusion, particularly targeting the unbanked segments of the population who at the moment do not benefit from the various services in the financial sector. To promote financial inclusion, all rural banks as well savings and loans companies andl commercial banks will have access to the common e-zwich platform. In a sense, the e-zwich platform has leveled the technological playing field and allows the rural banks and microfinance institutions equal access to the technology that the commercial banks have in this area.

• With the deployment of the e-zwich point of sale devices at merchants, post offices, fuel stations, etc, banking services can be provided nationwide. Money transfers can be received and made from these merchant outlets and salaries can be received without stepping into bank branches.

• One of the critical considerations in the choice of a biometric-based smartcard system was that of security. With the experience of card fraud in most of the developed economies as cards are swiped or Personal Information Numbers (PIN) numbers stolen, the whole process of moving to electronic payments can be jeopardized if the public lose confidence in the system because of fraud. A biometric-based system basically eliminates this risk. With e-zwich, transactions are authenticated using the finger print of the cardholder. This feature eliminates the problem of identity theft that prevails in many countries where card transactions are usually authenticated through PINs. With the new payment system Ghana has leapfrogged the existing technology in use in many advanced countries. Indeed, the banks in the advanced countries would also have moved to the biometric-based card system but for the huge investment they have already made in existing systems. The first biometric ATM in Europe was only installed in Poland in July 2010 to much publicity. Biometric technology became particularly popular in Japan after the passing of legislation in 2006 that made banks liable for withdrawals by criminals using stolen or counterfeit bank cards. As a result there are now over 80,000 biometric ATMs in Japan, currently used by more than 15 million customers.

• There is also the issue of the ease of opening a bank account. Opening a traditional bank account is a very cumbersome process. An e-zwich smartcard on the other hand is much easier to obtain. All that is required are your fingerprints to get the smartcard (no utility bills etc. required). Also, the e-zwich smartcard contains both a current account and savings account wallet. Holders can undertake transactions such as paying for goods and services, money transfer, cash withdrawals, third-party bill payments, and receiving salaries or pensions at any e-zwich point of sale terminal in the country. This means that people can undertake basic financial transactions at shops and petrol stations, post offices, etc.

• With e-zwich implementation in the public sector, ghost names and the corruption associated with the practice of ghost workers should become a thing of the past. With government workers being paid through an e-zwich card it is not possible to have a "ghost worker" since a "ghost" cannot have a finger print. Workers would also find it convenient because they can access their salaries without going to a bank. It would also increasingly result in a formalization of the economy and allow greater revenue collection by the tax authorities.

• The e-zwich card can also be used as the National ID and Voters ID Card as well as Driving License, NHIS (an all in one card) similar to cards in Malaysia for example. The Malaysian card incorporates a national identity card, driving license, passport information and e-cash on the same card. The problem of fraudulent voting or multiple registrations of voters will be eliminated if for example, the Electoral Commission issued voters ID was based on the e-zwich card (since no single individual can have more than one set of finger prints). For Ghana, the infrastructure is already available (and the investment has already been made) therefore, it will be very easy to implement these suggestions at much lower cost to government. The e-zwich card is able to handle more than 100 separate applications (apart from being a payments and savings vehicle) on the card and is therefore not just another debit card.

The e-zwich platform and smartcard represent a major transformation of the payment system in Ghana and is the first of its kind in the world in terms of system-wide application. Other attempts to reach the unbanked thus far, e.g. M-PESA in Kenya and Wizzit in South Africa, are based on designing separate systems and technologies for the unbanked. There is therefore a dual system, one for the banked, and the other for the unbanked. Ghana's approach is however different because the e-zwich system is a common platform designed for both the banked and the unbanked.

There are many competing technologies for banking the unbanked and while it is important to bring the best experiences and practices to bear, one cannot help but notice a sense of "we know what is best for you" attitude by some donors involved in the push for certain payment system technologies to be adopted by African and other developing countries in the name of banking the poor. Ultimately, African countries should decide for themselves what technology best suits their needs and there should not be a one-size fits-all approach. There should be no requirement that African or other developing countries adopt systems simply because they are "cheaper". When Ghana opted for the e-zwich system, comments made included "this is too sophisticated for an African country", "why don't you adopt a cheaper alternative?" While cost is always important, systems should be adopted because they are the best for the needs of the country in the long run. Why must Africa or the developing world always be saddled with second or third-best solutions? Why are these technologies okay for the Japanese but not so for the African?

In this regard, the approach that has been adopted by the Bank of Ghana represents a paradigm shift. With the e-zwich common platform, a holistic system has been put in place to serve both the banked and the unbanked.

There is not only a common platform for financial institutions; there is also a common platform for their customers. This is the first such systemic approach to resolving the problem of banking the unbanked in the world. It has been implemented in the face of intense lobbying from powerful interest groups and their surrogates who would rather have the status quo ante which provides them with a virtual monopoly at the expense of the unbanked.

It is expected that if the e-zwich payments platform is adequately supported, within the next five to ten years a major transformation from a cash-based to an electronic card based payment system should take place in Ghana. The move from cash to electronic payments involves behavioral change which takes time. Even in the most advanced economies like the United States, the transition was very long. Experience from other countries like Malaysia and Singapore in this area shows that unless a country is willing to wait at least another 200 years to get there, the transformation from cash to predominantly electronic payments requires the active support and participation of government, the central bank and the private sector. The transition from cash to electronic payments is qualitatively similar to the transition from driving on the left to driving on the right hand side of the road in the 1970s. It didn't just happen. It had to be made to happen. For Ghana, thanks to the efforts of the Bank of Ghana and the banks, the infrastructure required for this transition is already in place and no new money has to be spent on that to make it happen.

Ghana Interbank Payments and Settlement System (GHIPSS)

In putting together such a comprehensive payments and settlement system infrastructure the issue of management and protection of such major investments has become important. It is for this reason that the Bank of Ghana decided in consultation with the banks, to bring all the various aspects of the payments system infrastructure (the national switch, smartcard, cheque clearing, central securities depository, real time gross settlement, and automated clearing house) under a single entity, the Ghana Interbank Payments and Settlement System (GHIPSS) a limited liability company to allow more efficient management and oversight. All banks are members of GHIPSS either directly or through member banks.

A country's payment and settlement system is the central nervous system of its financial sector. Ultimately the payments system of any country is one that the regulatory authorities should pay close attention to otherwise haphazard and unregulated development can serve to undermine the financial system in the long run. Any country can be destabilized if its payment and settlement system is destabilized. It is because of this potential systemic risk that the Bank of Ghana decided that banking services (including branchless banking services) should be provided by licensed financial institutions.

Improving the Rural Payments System

Some 60.0 percent of Ghana's population lives in rural areas. Similarly, over 60 percent of the poor are rural dwellers. Any effort to make the payment system more inclusive must therefore, pay attention to the rural financial system. The Bank of Ghana therefore set about integrating the 126 rural banks effectively into the national payments system. This was part of Ghana's proposal under the Millennium Challenge Account (MCA) Compact with the U.S. Government. With support from the MCA , all 126 rural banks and their branches will be computerized and provided with a standard banking software (which the rural banks have chosen).

In addition, all 126 rural banks and their branches will also be linked through a Wide Area Network (WAN) using satellite (VSAT) infrastructure. The linking up of rural banks through a Wide Area Network will allow the rural banks to operate on a common payments platform with a switch connected to the existing bank switches and would essentially mainstream the rural banks into the national payments system.

The computerization of the rural banks with a standard software along with the VSAT-based WAN should lower their operating costs. It would also reduce errors and fraud within the banks as an audit trail can be traced for all transactions. Supervision of the rural banks would also be a lot less time-consuming and costly under a computerized and networked environment. Rural bank data is currently not part of the Bank of Ghana monetary survey due to the long delays in the submission of data. The computerization and net working of rural banks should allow more timely data submission and a more comprehensive and timely assessment of monetary and financial sector developments. Furthermore, Banks can also quickly process loan and payment requests and thus reduce the waiting time for their customers.

The comprehensive reform of the payments system infrastructure, including the Real Time Gross Settlement System, Codeline Cheque Clearing, Automated Clearing House, and the national e-zwich common platform, e-zwich biometric smartcard, along with mobile phone banking, has positioned Ghana as the country with probably the most advanced payment system infrastructure in sub-Saharan Africa (outside of South Africa). The task now is for financial institutions and policy makers to leverage this infrastructure for the benefit of the wider population.

CHAPTER 8

REDENOMINATION OF THE CEDI

One of the major reforms undertaken by the Bank of Ghana was the redenomination of the cedi. The announcement of the redenomination exercise took place at the Annual Bankers Dinner in Accra on November 25, 2006. The Governor, Dr. Paul Acquah took everyone by surprise.

Rationale for Redenomination:

The rationale for redenomination was manifest in the quantum of notes required for every day transactions. The legacy of the previous episodes of high inflation had been the rapid increases in the numerical values of prices (moving into millions, billions and trillions depending on the context) as well as foreign currency exchange in local currency terms. This imposed the burden and cost of a high note regime on the economy.

Ghanaians became accustomed to carrying cash for everyday transactions in black polythene bags. At the market or petrol station for example, one could easily observe the inefficiency when it came to counting money, by both the buyer and the seller. Most of the time each party counted at least two times because of the sheer volume of notes being counted for a transaction worth the equivalent of $50. The highest denomination of the currency at the time was ¢20000 (the equivalent of some $2.00 at the time). Considering the average daily time spent in counting money per transaction, it became very clear that the economy was losing productivity from the high note regime.

The prevailing note regime placed a significant deadweight burden on the economy. This was in several forms such as the high transactions costs at the cashiers, general inconvenience and high risks involved in carrying loads of currency for transaction purposes, increasing difficulties in maintaining bookkeeping and statistical records and ensuring compatibility with data processing software, and the strain on the payments system, particularly the

ATMs as we were moving into a new era of interoperability under a common payments platform.

Conditions for Successful Re-denomination

Historical analyses suggest that re-denominations are successful in an environment of macroeconomic stability, i.e. declining inflation, stable exchange rate, fiscal prudence, and well-anchored expectations of policy credibility. And, the benefits are incalculable. However, when implemented under high inflation and unstable macroeconomic environment, the benefits have been elusive, and credibility lost.

In the years preceding the redenomination, macroeconomic stability had taken root; inflation was falling; interest rates falling; the currency was stable; the cedi's role as a store of value had been restored, and the country had built a good cushion of external reserves, under a policy of commitment to fiscal and monetary prudence. Inflation recorded single digit levels in 2006 (April (9.9 percent) and May (9.5 percent)) and hovered around 10.1 percent through to October 2007. Economic stabilization and other reforms were underpinned by fiscal policies anchored on domestic debt reduction with the benefit of external debt relief and multilateral debt cancellation. The cedi exchange rate was relatively stable over a period of about 24 months, fluctuating within a narrow band against the three major currencies. Figure 8.1 provides a diagrammatic representation of the macroeconomic stability that had been attained in terms of levels and volatility of variables like inflation, interest and exchange rates. These created the appropriate conditions for the re-denomination exercise in Ghana.

Furthermore, the Governor noted in his speech that redenomination was not taking place in a vacuum. The macroeconomic environment had changed and the context was different. A significant reform of the financial sector had taken place, and redenomination, by stripping the prices and values of the numbers that the force of inflation had embedded in them, was "putting a

hard-wire around all these economic changes and measures and lifting the
dead weight burden the existing note regime placed on the economy".

Figure 8.1. Trends in Macroeconomic Indicators

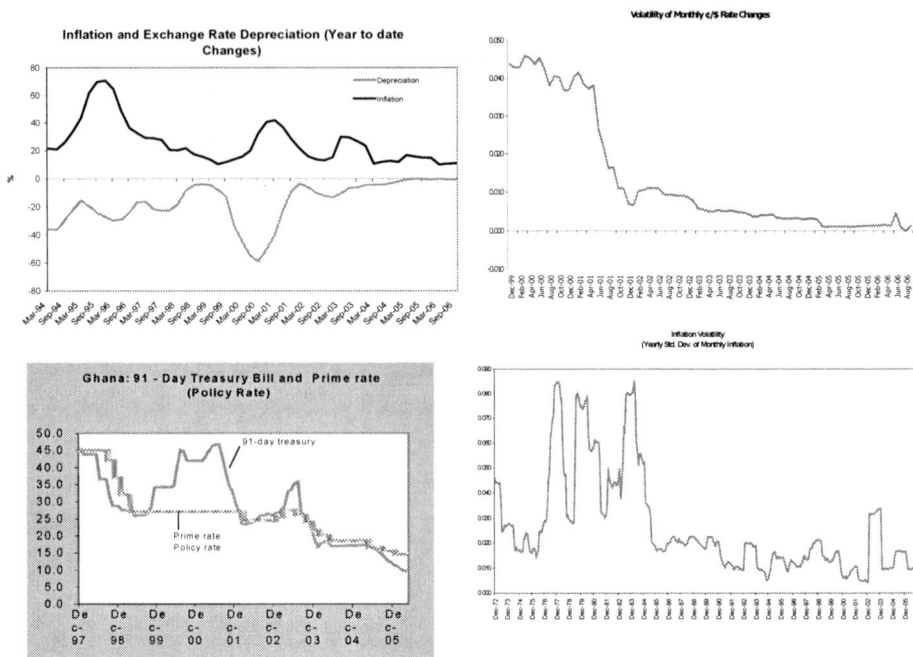

The re-denomination freed the economy to do business in the most efficient
way, based on the cedi as a means of exchange and as a store of value for all,
both within and outside the banking system. A sound monetary unit is
indispensable for growth and prosperity, and for the quest to become an
emerging market economy and a nation of a middle-income status. However,
the re-denomination demands a continued commitment to financial stability, a
dedication to preserve the values of the currency unit as a monetary standard,
to maintain its value in terms of the quantity or basket of goods and services.

Re-denomination

The re-denomination set the old cedi at *¢10,000=GH¢1=100Gp*. The name of new currency was the Ghana Cedi (GH¢), with the sub unit of as the Ghana Pesewa (Gp). This was to distinguish the old and new cedis which were circulating in parallel. There was considerable discussion about whether to eliminate three zeros or four zeros (as was done). The analysis based on survey data at the time however supported the elimination of four zeros. The denominations were determined to set a note-coin boundary that was reflective of the pricing system in the economy at that time, with an added aim of also providing a psychological boost to the re-introduction of the coin culture in Ghana[14]. The series of notes and coins introduced were as follows:

- o Notes: GH¢1, GH¢5, GH¢10, GH¢20 and GH¢50.
- o Coins: 1Gp, 5Gp, 10Gp, 20Gp, 50Gp and GH¢1.

The redenomination was taking place on the 50th anniversary of Ghana's independence and it was decided to use the portrait of the six leaders of the United Gold Coast (UGCC), the leading political party in the then Gold Coast who initiated the fight for an independent Ghana. They are Dr. Ebenezer Ako-Adjei, Dr. Kwame Nkrumah, Dr. Joseph Boakye Danquah, Edward Akufo-Addo, Emmanuel Odarkwei Obetsebi-Lamptey, and William Ofori-Atta. They were collectively known as the "Big Six". They symbolized unity and the great potential for the country if the country was united. There was a question about whether they should be featured individually but it was decided that the Big Six together are greater than the sum of their individual parts.

---

[14] The years of high inflation rendered coins worthless and this has resulted in a general preference of notes over coins. It will take some time and continued macroeconomic stability to change this attitude as these same Ghanaians tend to use coins without hesitation when they visit other countries with a longer history of macroeconomic stability.

The Bank also decided to use the picture of the Supreme Court on one of the currencies. However, when the photographers presented the picture of the court building, it included the busts of three high court judges who were murdered along with an army officer on 30th June 1982. In line with the spirit of promoting national unity, the Bank of Ghana decided not to use this picture as it was bound to evoke painful memories of a time past when the judiciary was under threat. It was not a positive and unifying image for the country. In the interest of national unity, the Bank of Ghana therefore decided to use the picture of the Supreme Court without the busts of the three murdered judges on the new currency (GH¢20).

The new currency notes and coins were planned for introduction by July 2007. Both the old and new cedi banknotes and coins were physically in circulation for a period of at least 6 months and both the old and new notes and coins had the same external value. The old cedi notes and coins were withdrawn from circulation starting from July 2007. This starting date was chosen to allow for familiarization before the cocoa season begun in October 2007. While the old notes and coins seized to be legal tenders after the first six (6) months, unlike previous such exercises, there was no deadline for the exchange of currency and the Bank of Ghana undertook to exchange the old currencies anytime they were presented (even 100 years down the road). This exchange can take place at the Bank of Ghana or any commercial and rural bank. This was critical to the almost seamless run of the entire exercise.

Old notes and coins were withdrawn through deposits of notes and coins in the course of banking transactions as well as the voluntary exchange of the old notes and coins outside the banking system for new notes and coins. Within the first six (6) months, about 90 percent of the old notes and coins had been withdrawn. To facilitate conversion from old to new notes and coins, prices were quoted in both new and old notes and coins at the same time during the transition period and after.

It was important to explain the redenomination exercise in simple terms and to assure the general public that no one would be short-changed as a result of the exercise as had happened in previous such exercises. After some deliberation, the Governor came up with the message which was to captivate the nation and become the mantra for the exercise: *"The Value is the Same, There is no Change in Value"* which proved to be very popular amongst the public.

On July 1 2007, the redenomination of the cedi was successfully ushered in, considering the scale of the exercise that had been undertaken. It was however not an easy exercise and not without risk. It stretched the Bank of Ghana to its limits. When the Governor announced the exercise, there were many politicians in the ruling government who were genuinely worried about the implications for the government if the exercise was botched up. The opposition parties were also very skeptical about the exercise thinking it would be too costly but also worried that it could be used as a means to funnel money to the ruling party to finance the upcoming general election. With both sides of the political divide apprehensive, the Bank of Ghana had little room for error but remained steadfast. The Bank was confident that the exercise could be successfully executed.

A coherent and comprehensive programme of the logistics and implementation of activities associated with the distribution of new and withdrawal of old currency notes and coins was put in place along with a comprehensive public education programme with the sole objective of ensuring that the new notes and coins were available on demand on the first day of the re-denomination exercise.

Public Education Programme

Public education was considered a critical component of the success of the exercise. A comprehensive publicity programme was developed for various media which was evaluated and reviewed on a regular basis. A Committee was set up to steer the organization and management of the public education programme. The Committee planned and executed a multi-media education campaign that ensured total accessibility to all the various segments of society country wide.

The Communication Strategy

The campaign strategy derived from the Timeline of activities was in four (4) Phases and had the following as main features:-

Phase 1 of the communication strategy, which was implemented from December 2006 to January 2007, was to create awareness about the re-denomination and explain its rationale and timing. This was implemented through Radio jingles on 52 stations and Advertising Strips in 23 newspapers as well as "TV mentions". During this phase, outreach programmes were also undertaken to several institutions and associations to educate them on the re-denomination exercise. Pamphlets on Frequently Asked Questions (FAQs) were also circulated as advertising inserts in the newspapers. These pamphlets were widely circulated to the banks, institutions, associations, etc. The first phase sought to create awareness on the basic messages of the re-denomination.

Phase II of the Education Campaign which covered the period February 1 to March 31, 2007 had the following objectives:

1. Deepen awareness about the re-denomination and give assurances about the maintenance of the value. "The value is the same".
2. Create awareness about the equivalents and emphasize the exchangeability of the two currencies in transactions during the transition period.
3. Create awareness about the time frame for the simultaneous circulation and the change.
4. Assure the public that they have all the time to change their money and that the entire exercise will be conducted under conditions of normalcy, devoid of any panic.

5.   Dual Pricing – prices to be quoted in both currencies during the transition period.

The tempo of the campaign was intensified through Phase III in order to keep the public well informed about the exercise until the posters and other educational materials on the currency were received following which the public education campaign would be taken to a higher level. Conversion Charts were introduced to guide the public on the conversions of the old to the new currencies.

During this period the new currency was also unveiled. This Phase of the Education campaign covered the period April 1 to June 30 2007 and had the following objectives:

1. Intensify the campaign by further consolidating the messages in the previous phases.
2. Create familiarity with the images of the new currency and educate the public on main features.
3. Emphasize the re-denomination procedure.
4. Allay the fears of the public through further assurances (This would not be like those of the past).
5. Address queries from review of Phase I and II.
6. Unveil the new currency.

Phase III covered the most critical period prior to the roll-out date and several messages were delivered through various media of communication. However, these were phased to ensure that the public was not saturated with the messages which included the following:-

- Knowing the features of the new currency
- Parallel circulation for at least six (6) months.
- Dual Pricing – retailers were to price goods and services in old and new currencies with effect from May 1, 2007.
- The change would be at no cost.
- Both currencies would be exchangeable.

- Old currency would cease to be legal tender after December 2007
- After December 31, unchanged old notes and coins could still be changed at the Banks and Savings and Loans Companies.
- Monies should only be changed at the Banks and Savings and Loans Companies.
- Monies should never be changed through middlemen.
- Reassurances to address concerns raised in Phases I and II.

Technical guidelines on dual pricing, banking transactions and accounting systems were issued by the Bank. This became an important message in the public education campaign particularly the outreach programmes.

Phase IV of the Education Campaign covered the period July 1, 2007 to January 31, 2008 and focused on managing any transition challenges. The new currency was launched during this phase. It had the following objectives:-

1. Further educate the public on the security features of the new currency.
2. Intensify education on keeping the cedi clean
3. Inculcate in the public the culture of using coins (Emphasize its convenience for transactions and pricing).
4. Deepen the understanding of the conversions.
5. Address queries and concerns that may arise during the period.
6. Launch the new currency.

Logistics Programme

A comprehensive logistics programme was put in place after the Bank had put together a Logistics Committee. The Committee took into account the Bank's own storage capacity around which a comprehensive allotment and distribution programme was put in place with the sole objective of making sure that on the day of the re-denomination every bank teller and rural and savings and loans company will have the new notes in place and this would be done in a "business as usual mode".

A joint task force involving all the security services (particularly the Military and Police), and the Bank of Ghana and logistics firms, was put in place to ensure adequate security before, during and after the introduction of the re-denomination exercise.

Benefits of the Redenomination Exercise

The benefits of redenomination are significant and include:

- Convenience.
- Reduction in cost and overall risks of carrying large volumes of notes.
- Efficiency in payments systems, in particular, ATMs.
- Simplification of accounting records and the ease of expressing monetary values.
- Significant reduction in transactions volume.
- Promoting tourists expenditures.
- Restoration of confidence in the currency
- Finally, there are significant gains in cost of banknote production. These savings were generated because the redenomination meant that for example, one GH¢50 note replaced the cost of printing one hundred ¢5000 old notes.

If a money value were placed on all these benefits, it is clear that the redenomination exercise not only saved money beyond the currency printing costs but it will generate additional savings and benefits to the economy for years to come.

The Integrity of the Redenomination Exercise

The Bank of Ghana's currency operations follow laid-down procedures and security arrangements that involve a number of officials comprising currency officers, the Bank's Security Personnel, Internal Audit, and Banking Department Staff, Armed Guards (from the Ghana Armed Forces), Escort Security (from the Ghana Police Service) and in case of currency incineration, a representative of the Controller and Accountant General's Department. All these parties have individual and collective responsibility to protect the integrity of these currency operations. All currency transactions are audited by both the Bank's Internal Audit Department and the External Auditors on a regular basis. These procedures which are standard operating procedures at the Bank of Ghana preserved the integrity of the redenomination exercise.

CHAPTER 9

GHANA'S DEBUT SOVEREIGN BOND ISSUE

History was made in 2007 when Ghana issued its debut $750 million Sovereign Bond on the international capital markets, the only Sub-Saharan African country other than South Africa, and joined only Egypt, Morocco and South Africa on the entire continent to do so. The bond issue was successful and was four times oversubscribed. It was also awarded the Emerging Market deal of the year 2007, and with it Ghana was formally transformed from a HIPC country to a "frontier" emerging market economy that signaled a graduation from IMF/World Bank supported (financed) economic management policies and programmes (at least that is what was thought at the time).

What was more remarkable was that Ghana was a HIPC Country just a year before and therefore became the first post-HIPC country to access the International Capital Markets. Furthermore, the Ghana Bond was four times oversubscribed as bids totaled some $3.2 billon at a time when headwinds of the international financial crisis were very strong. This success was a testament to the remarkable transformation that had taken place in the Ghanaian economy and a vote of confidence by the international capital markets in the future of Ghana's economy. Of course, the decision to access the international capital market did not just happen in 2007. It was a culmination of sustained progress made since 2003, and a critical component of the government's objective of moving the economy from stability to growth.

Rationale for Accessing the Capital Markets: Moving Away from Aid Dependency

After the perceived humiliation of having to adopt the HIPC initiative, and its exposure of how dependent the economy was on aid, there was a consensus that for Ghana to develop, it had to move away from aid dependency which does not appear to have served the country well, especially looking at the growth performance of the economy between 1960 and 2000 (Table 9.1).

Until the mid-1960s, aid flows were relatively unimportant in Ghana. Overseas Development Assistance (ODA) per capita (1987 constant dollars) in 1960 amounted to $1.44, rising to $8.55 by 1964. This reflects the fact that the Nkrumah government inherited a sizeable amount of foreign reserves from the colonial government and thus needed very little by way of external aid at this time. Real GDP growth was positive during this period, with a declining trend from an average of 3.8% between 1960 and 1963 to 1.3% by 1965 and –1.27% in per capita terms. Aid inflows increased in the second-half of the 1960s averaging around $19.00 per capita for 1965-1969. Aid per capita increased from $8.55 in 1964 to $20.88 by 1966 and $24.28 by 1969.

As a share of GDP, ODA to Ghana in this period was higher than that for Sub-Saharan Africa (SSA) and low-income developing countries. After the overthrow of the Nkrumah government in 1966, the NLC government, confronting a large accumulated debt burden left by the Nkrumah government, signed an agreement with the IMF to devalue the cedi and cut public expenditures. There was increased programme aid as a result to support the balance of payments. As Table 9.1 shows however, real output growth declined in 1966 by 5% as a result of the effects of the coup d'état. By 1969 however, output growth had increased in real terms to 5.5% with real per capita income growing by 3.5%.

The 1972-83 period was a decade of consistent poor economic performance. It should be noted that this period was one of sustained deterioration in the economy under six "different" governments. By no means did these governments pursue the same policies.

Table 9.1. Official Development Assistance, External Debt and Real GDP Growth in Ghana (1960-2000)

YEAR	ODA PER CAPITA (1987 US$)	Total External Debt $ Million	Real GDP (1987) Growth	Real per Capita GDP Growth
1960	1.44			
1961	1.40		3.3	0.72
1962	2.72		4.0	1.3
1963	7.93		4.3	1.6
1964	8.55		2.1	-0.47
1965	18.73		1.3	-1.2
1966	20.88		-5.1	-7.1
1967	17.03		2.6	0.56
1968	18.83		0.3	-1.7
1969	24.28		5.5	3.4
1970	19.10	431	9.2	7.5
1971	17.40	434	5.3	2.2
1972	16.79	519	-3.0	-5.9
1973	10.05	576	2.8	0.15
1974	7.43	591	7.0	4.6
1975	22.56	705	-14.3	-16.5
1976	10.76	743	-3.5	-5.4
1977	14.16	797	1.8	0.28
1978	16.17	1335	9.3	7.9
1979	20.93	1328	-1.6	-3.3
1980	20.48	1,407	0.55	-1.6
1981	13.67	1,978	-2.9	-5.6
1982	12.57	1981	-6.7	-9.7
1983	9.35	2109	-4.5	-7.8
1984	17.22	1957	8.3	4.8
1985	15.22	2,226	4.9	1.3
1986	27.89	2,726	4.9	1.4
1987	30.21	3,262	4.5	1.1
1988	39.32	3,048	5.3	2.1
1989	45.18	3,296	4.8	1.6
1990	33.11	3,486	3.0	-0.02
1991	49.79	3,802	5.1	2.0
1992	33.91	3,968	3.5	0.62
1993	32.75	4,679	4.6	2.1
1994	27.83	5,022	3.6	0.96
1995	33.54	5,074	4.3	1.7
1996	34.8	5,346	4.9	2.3
1997	38.0	5,651	4.2	1.6
1998	45.61	5,921	4.6	2.1
1999	37.12	6,001	4.3	1.8
2000	28.12	6,148	3.7	0.65

Sources: Younger and Harrigan (2000), Bank Of Ghana Annual Reports, Ghana Statistical Service, IMF

However, for the most part, the policies of this period emphasized import substitution, underpinned by a restrictive foreign exchange regime, quantitative restrictions upon imports and price controls, with the state playing a major role as producer. At the time of the overthrow of the Busia government in 1972, ODA per capita (1987 constant dollars) was $16.79. ODA per capita declined to $7.43 by 1974 under the Military regime of Colonel I. K. Acheampong. This was in response to Colonel Acheampong's decision to repudiate some of Ghana's commercial debts on the grounds that they were contracted irregularly.

Aid flows, however, increased in the second half of the decade reaching $20.93 per capita by 1979. The aid was largely in the form of multilateral loans rather than grants[15]. This led to an increase in the total external debt from $895m in 1975 to $1,407m by 1980. Ghana faced difficulties servicing the debt by the end of the 1970s. In 1979, arrears on payments of short-term loans amounted to $432m and the international financial institutions began to refuse credit. The balance of payments crisis led to a depletion of gross official reserves and an accumulation of payments arrears, reaching $577m by 1982. Growth performance in the 1970s was mixed. The lowest growth of - 14% was experienced in 1975, coinciding with the oil-supply shock as well as a policy reversal from a market-oriented stance to an inward looking protectionist regime. The period of turbulence, however, also had positive growth episodes, with the highest peak rate reaching 9% in 1970 and 1978. Between 1979 and 1982, economic growth was decidedly negative, averaging –3.0% per annum. Aid flows in this period also declined sharply from $20.93 per capita in 1979 to $9.35 by 1983.

Between 1984 and 2000 Ghana's SAP involved a liberalization of the exchange rate (devaluation) and trade regime, privatization of state enterprises, financial sector reform, and a tightening of the budget. The

---

[15] Multilateral loans are loans from multilateral institutions like the IMF, World Bank and African Development Bank)

persistence with which Ghana tackled the SAP in the 1980s made it a darling amongst the donor community. ODA per capita increased from $9.35 in 1983 to $45.18 by 1989. Much of the support was in the form of non-concessional loans[16]. As Younger and Harrigan (2000) note most of the reforms under Ghana's SAP would not have been possible without the external support provided by the donors. Public spending was also increased with grants to support the budget increasing from 0.55% of domestic revenues in 1983 to 10.23% by 1991.

Notwithstanding this considerable amount of aid received in the 1984-2000 period, the economy still ended up as a HIPC economy at the end of 2000. Against this background and experience of Ghana's economy with aid, the government was determined to reduce Ghana's dependency on aid by diversifying financing sources, including developing the domestic capital market and accessing the international capital market,

Going for Growth

After adopting the HIPC Initiative, there was a consensus amongst policy makers of the NPP government that Ghana's economy should be able to stand on its own two feet and move away from HPIC and donor dependence in the shortest possible time.

At the Consultative Group (CG) meeting between Ghana and its development Partners in June 2007, it was noted that Ghana had experienced steady and increasing real GDP growth in recent years, moving from 3.7 percent in 2000 to 6.2 percent in 2006. In addition, there was a significant decrease in poverty, with the headcount falling from 51.7 percent in 1991-2 to 28.5 percent in 2005-6. However, Ghana needed to grow faster if it was at the minimum to attain the Millennium Development Goals. The medium-term framework which underpinned Ghana's Growth and Poverty Reduction Strategy (GPRS) II envisaged a growth rate of 6.0 percent. This level of growth was however

---

[16] i.e. loans at market interest rates

not adequate to allow for the attainment of the MDGs. It was estimated that a minimum of 8.0 percent GDP growth is required in the medium term to achieve the MDGs consistent with the objectives of. GPRS II.

While continuing to maintain macroeconomic stability and strengthening the investment climate, it was time for the Government of Ghana to focus on investments that would address the constraints to accelerated growth. Infrastructure bottlenecks represent a critical constraint to growth in Ghana. A relatively long period of steady growth with very little investment in infrastructure elevated the infrastructure bottlenecks in 2006. A combination of high demand for ,and low supply of electricity following inadequate rainfall and under capacity production of the hydro-electric power plant (Akosombo Dam). led to power rationing and disrupted production. It was important to undertake critical investments in the energy sector. Consequently, investments in power, transport, water supply, and ICT were top priorities. These were joined by investments in health and education to provide the levels of human capital that will be critical for Ghana to move towards middle income status.

While all the donors agreed on the critical need for the investment priorities set by the Ghana Government, when it came to the mobilization of resources to finance these investments, this consensus did not find ready translation into dollars and cents (Table 9.2).

There was an annual financing gap between $2.5-$3.5 billion that needed to be raised from private investors and public sources (domestic and international). It was not clear where this would come from. After the CG meeting, the Government of Ghana was even more convinced about the case for accessing the international capital markets to begin the process of filling some of this gap which could also accelerate investments from the private sector.

Table 9.2. Financing Gaps from Sector Priorities (US$ million)

	2007	2007	2008	2008	2009	2009
Sector	**Cost**	**Gap**	**Cost**	**Gap**	**Cost**	**Gap**
Education	492.2	163.0	532.5	401.0	488.8	350.1
Energy	900.0	400.0	900.0	400.0	900.0	400.0
ICT	222.7	212.7	222.7	212.7	222.7	212.7
Health	258.3	224.6	258.3	224.6	258.3	224.6
Urban Water	224.4	37.9	224.4	37.9	224.4	37.9
Rural Water	12.1	1.6	12.1	1.6	18.1	4.1
Rail/maritime	279.3	279.3	279.3	279.3	279.3	279.3
Roads	487.1	486.0	487.1	486.0	487.1	486.0
Agriculture	628.2	532.2	628.2	532.2	628.2	532.2
Totals	**3504.2**	**2337.4**	**3544.5**	**2575.4**	**3506.8**	**2527.0**

Source: Consultative Group Meeting, June 2007

Donors and the IMF in particular were hesitant about this policy stance of accessing the international capital markets. First, they were worried that Ghana would begin a new cycle of unsustainable debt accumulation. Secondly, Ghana may set an example for all other HIPC countries that after obtaining debt relief may pursue this path. This was however at the same time that Ghana was being described by the Fund as a "mature stabilizer" and their arguments against Ghana's strategy did not appear consistent with their own assessment of the performance of the Ghanaian economy.

Benchmark for the Private Sector

Another reason for accessing the international capital market was to set a benchmark for Ghana sovereign risk which could be used by the Ghanaian corporate sector to borrow on the international capital market. This is the same reason why a country like Russia with hundreds of billions of dollars in foreign exchange reserves (and therefore one could argue that it does not need the money) has recently issued a sovereign bond.

Inadequacy of Concessional Resources

Concessional financing[17] is normally preferable if available. However, concessional financing is generally directed at social sectors (health and education) which have low economic returns but high social returns. Capital market financing was to be directed at growth critical investments which have high economic returns given that concessional financing is not sufficient to meet Ghana's investment requirements. Furthermore there are significant delays in obtaining concessional funding (usually 2-4 yrs for infrastructure).

Moving Away from Donor Dependency and Conditionality

The access to international capital market financing was also seen as an opportunity for Ghana to pursue its own development priorities without the usual donor conditionality attached. Donor conditionality came in direct forms (e.g. the meeting of performance criteria set by lenders like the IMF) and in indirect forms in terms of leverage exercised by donor country governments on policy choices in Ghana. Notwithstanding that the capital markets are probably more ruthless in punishing bad policies than any donor institutions, there appeared to be an air of the attainment of "freedom" in the move to the capital market. Furthermore, there was the argument that when one priced in the delays involved in accessing donor funds and the conditionality attached, the real price of these funds were actually not concessional.

---

[17] i.e. loans at below market interest rates

Accessing the International Capital Markets – The Process

In preparation for accessing the international capital market, Ghana submitted itself to the sovereign credit rating process in 2005. The strategy of seeking a sovereign credit rating was also to subject the Ghanaian economy to greater market scrutiny and surveillance and thus enhance accountability and transparency. Following the first ratings assessment, a B+ rating was assigned by Standard and Poors and a "B Positive Outlook" assigned by Fitch Ratings. Though not investment grade, they were nonetheless testaments to the track record that Ghana was forging at the time and as far as we were concerned, it represented a good starting point to build on. These ratings put Ghana at par (in terms of sovereign credit risk) with countries like Turkey and Indonesia.

A Capital Market Committee (CMC)[18] was formed (with membership from the Ministry of Finance and the Bank of Ghana, including Dr. Sam Mensah, Dr. Ernest Addison, Mr. Kwabena Oku-Afari, Mr. Mark Starr, Dr. Maxwell Opoku-Afari, Mr. Francis Andoh, Ms Yvonne Quansah, Ms Nelly Apo, Mr. Edward Abrokwah and Dr. Mahamudu Bawumia) to prepare Ghana for a historic sovereign bond issue on the international capital markets. The CMC recommended the issue of a 10-year bond. Government selected Citibank and UBS on the basis of competitive tender as Co-Lead Managers for the Bond. Ecobank Development Corporation, Databank and New World (Ghana) were co-managers.

The Ghana Sovereign Bond Deal was announced on the markets on September 14th and the Government of Ghana team led by the Minister of Finance and the Governor of the Bank of Ghana embarked on a six-day investor road show in the United States (New-Port Beach, Los Angeles, New York, and Boston) and Europe (London, Frankfurt/ Munich and Zurich). The team basically had to tell Ghana's story and convince these sceptical investors that they should bet on Ghana by investing in the bond.

---

[18] This was an ad-hoc Committee for the specific task of the sovereign bond issue.

171

Investors were very tough and rigorous in their questioning of the Ghana team. They were primarily concerned about the emerging fiscal and current account deficits in the projections for 2007 and 2008. The Ghana team explained that the deficits were driven largely the outcome of many non-recurring expenditures relating to the 2008 Africa Cup of Nations (including four Stadia) Ghana's 50th Anniversary Celebrations, Non-Realization of Divestiture Proceeds, and Emergency Power Generation associated with the Energy Crisis, and the expenditure of the proceeds from the Sovereign bond which would increase the deficit in the interim by 3.5% of GDP other things being equal. It was expected that Government would return to the path of fiscal consolidation subsequently. Furthermore, investors were comforted by Ghana's debt sustainability numbers which showed quite clearly that Ghana's borrowing on the international capital market would not impair its ability to service its debt notwithstanding the 2006-2008 increase in the deficit. Indeed a 2008 joint IMF/World Bank Assessment of Ghana's debt sustainability following the sovereign bond issue (Table 9.4) reinforces this view.

However, on a lighter side, Ghana's performance during the 2006 FIFA world cup finals in Germany appears to have put Ghana on the global platform and in most cases during the road show, it became the ice-breaker for the rather more mundane economic management discussions.

Ghana's total public debt as a percentage of GDP (including the sovereign bond) at the end of 2007 was 49.8 percent (Table 9.3). For the first time the 2008 Ghana Government budget also put a ceiling on the total public debt to GDP at 60 percent, consistent with ECOWAS guidelines and the same level as pertains in the European Union.

Table 9.3. Ghana: Total Government Debt
($m unless stated otherwise)

	2003	*2004*	*2005*	*2006*	*2007*
External Debt	7,549	6,448	6,348	2,177	3,587
Multilateral Institutions	5,058	5,287	5,565	1,327	1,710
Bilateral	2,223	922	602	732	956
Commercial	268	239	180	118	920
Domestic Debt	1,540	1,868	1,997	3,133	3,969
Total Debt	9,089	8,315	8,345	5,311	7,556
Memo Items					
Total Debt/GDP %	119.1	93.7	77.8	41.7	49.8
External Debt/GDP %	99.0	72.6	59.2	17.1	23.7
Domestic Debt/GDP %	20.2	21.0	18.6	24.6	26.2

Source: Bank of Ghana, Ministry of Finance and Economic Planning

The debt/GDP ratio rose to some 50.1 percent by the end of 2008, down from 156% in 2000 and 119% in 2003. Even though Ghana's debt/GDP was still high compared to some emerging market countries, it was within comfortable range by international comparisons.

Furthermore, the burden of Ghana's debt by the end of 2007/2008 was very manageable. At the end of 2008, Ghana spent only 4.3% of its export revenue on debt service compared to 27.5 % between 1993 and 2000. The joint IMF/World Bank debt sustainability analysis in 2008 underscores this fact. Table 9.4 shows that by the end of 2008 all the debt indicators for Ghana were significantly below the debt sustainability thresholds.

Ghana's recent discovery of oil also strengthened the debt sustainability outlook. The IMF/World Bank debt sustainability oil-exporting scenario (Table 9.4) further reinforces the sustainability of Ghana's debt. What is interesting about this data and the underlying debt sustainability estimates is that at the time of the sovereign bond issue an IMF technical assistance mission had discovered the GDP had been significantly underestimated by as much as 50%! This meant that Ghana's debt/GDP and deficit/GDP numbers would look even better than they were looking in 2007.

By the time the bids for Ghana's debut sovereign bond closed, it was clear that investors had bought into Ghana's future prospects. The bond was oversubscribed by four times to the tune of $3.3 billion and the order book was much diversified with high quality investors (158) across the globe.

Table 9.4. External Debt Sustainability Indicators Under Alternative Scenarios

	Thresholds	*2008*	*2018*	*2028*
		Baseline	Scenario	
NPV of Debt to GDP ratio	50	20	35	40
NPV of Debt to exports ratio	200	45	109	150
Debt service to exports ratio	25	3	11	23
		Low GDP	Growth	Scenario
NPV of Debt to GDP ratio		20	38	56
NPV of Debt to exports ratio		45	122	185
Debt service to exports ratio		3	12	29
		Oil	Exporting	Scenario
NPV of Debt to GDP ratio		20	22	9
NPV of Debt to exports ratio		45	69	34
Debt service to exports ratio		3	9	7

Source: IMF/World Bank DSA (2008)

Pricing of the Bond

Ghana's debut bond closed at a coupon rate of 8.5% (387 bps spread over US Treasuries). There was concern that this was steep. For a first time issuer (a HIPC country just a year before) with a B+ credit rating in tough market conditions (the credit crunch was taking hold), one can argue that it was a fair price for what Ghana was getting in return. Ghana achieved inter alia:

175

- A very positive high profile deal, Emerging Market Deal of the Year!
- A buoyant liquid sovereign benchmark which can be used by Ghana's corporate sector.
- A lot of goodwill and reputation from investors which should have made subsequent issuance easier.
- A strong diversified global investor base.

A few months after Ghana's debut bond, Gabon (an oil producing country with a large buffer of oil reserves) issued a $1 billion 10-year bond at 8.2% even though the notes were rated BB- by Fitch and Standard and Poors.

Table 9.5. Ten Year Bond Yields: Selected Countries
(28, April 2010)

Country	S&P Credit Rating Foreign Currency LT	Yield
Australia	AAA	5.72%
Germany	AAA	3.02%
Portugal	BB+	6.37%
Brazil	BBB-	12.69%
Mexico	BBB	7.38%
Greece	A-	11.53%
Ghana	B+	6.38%

Source: Financial Times

April, 2010 market pricing for other sovereign bonds puts the Ghana issue in perspective. Table 9.5 shows the coupon yields on Ten Year Bonds of a few selected countries. It is worth noting the vast difference in ratings between countries like Brazil (BBB-), Australia (AAA) and Ghana (B+). Yet the coupon for Brazil's 10 year paper is 12.69%, Australia's 5.72% while Ghana's yield is 6.38%, similar to the yield on Portugal's 10 year bond.

Use of Sovereign Bond Proceeds

With the realization of the capital market proceeds, there was a general mood of optimism and satisfaction for the attainment of this historic feat. The Capital Market Committee however quickly turned its attention to the issue of the use of bond proceeds as the committee had spent some time in putting together a strategy for the use of funds.

In preparation for the international capital market, the first task of the CMC was to identify a portfolio of projects which were viable for capital market financing. As part of this process, the MDAs presented projects in various sectors totaling over $8 billion. These projects formed the basis for discussion with donor partners at the Consultative Group (CG) meeting in 2007.

The CMC quickly came to the conclusion that while many projects were desirable, not all would meet the criteria for access to capital market (commercial) financing[19]. In particular, projects selected for capital market financing preferably had to:

- Be commercially viable in their own right.
- Yield a high enough economic rate of return to service the underlying debt.
- Be growth catalytic by removing critical bottlenecks in the economy.

---

[19] Concessional funding was to be sought for projects like the Bui Dam, Water and other roads

Debt Sustainability Analyses (DSA) was conducted using these assumptions to assure Government of the sustainability of Ghana's debt after accessing the markets for projects of this nature.

Part of Ghana's strategy in accessing the international capital market was also to leverage the funds to allow for private public partnerships in the execution of some projects. The energy and road sectors were identified as the sectors with projects that would meet the above criteria. In the prospectus for the Sovereign Bond, Ghana indicated the use of proceeds as for investment in infrastructure (mainly but not limited to) the energy and road sectors.

To maintain discipline over the use of proceeds, the Committee considered the following guidelines:

- Funds provided to MDAs for projects should be in the form of loans with a supporting cash flow from the MDAs indicating how such loans would be repaid.

- An escrow account should be immediately set up at the Bank of Ghana into which such repayments would be deposited. These funds can be used pay the interest and principal on the sovereign bond.

- If an MDA is unable to show how such funds allocated to it from the sovereign bond proceeds can be amortized, Government should consider alternative investments.
- For projects selected, there needs to be an independent verification of the cost estimates presented by the MDAs for various projects.

- To reduce the carry cost of the loan, payments on projects should only be made on invoices submitted

- Clear and monitorable performance benchmarks should be set for each MDA.

- A monthly report should be submitted by each MDA on the use of proceeds.

- Private sector participation should be immediately solicited for some key projects to allow a leveraging of funds.

To monitor and transparently track the use of proceeds, a dedicated sovereign bond proceeds account was established at the Bank of Ghana into which all sovereign bond proceeds were lodged and out of which all related expenditures were to be made.

As it turned out, by the end of 2008 the proceeds the proceeds of Ghana's debut sovereign bond were spent mainly on the energy and road sectors. The 2009 Government of Ghana Budget Statement indeed notes that "*An immense proportion (76 per cent) of the Sovereign Bond proceeds was earmarked under the Government of Ghana (GoG) 2008 Supplementary Budget to cover capital expenditures for VRA, GRIDCO, ECG and Bui Power Authority (BPA)*".

One of the implications of opting for a sovereign credit rating and subsequently issuing a bond on the international capital market is that it established Ghana as a "frontier emerging market economy" and as a result there is increased market scrutiny of Ghana's economic policies by investors and other stakeholders. In this regard, policy makers have to be particularly sensitive about pronouncements that are made about the economy, which if not guarded, may do damage to investor perceptions and undermine their attempts at growing the economy. The door to the international capital market has been opened and subsequent access by Government or the private sector should be much easier if properly managed.

CHAPTER 10

MACROECONOMIC PERFORMANCE UNDER THE INFLATION TARGETING REGIME: 2001-2008

The fiscal and monetary policy framework put together in the context of GPRS I and GPRS II resulted in significant improvements in the economy, especially between 2001 and 2007 (Table 10.1).

Figure 10.1. Inflation and Monetary Growth (2000-2008)

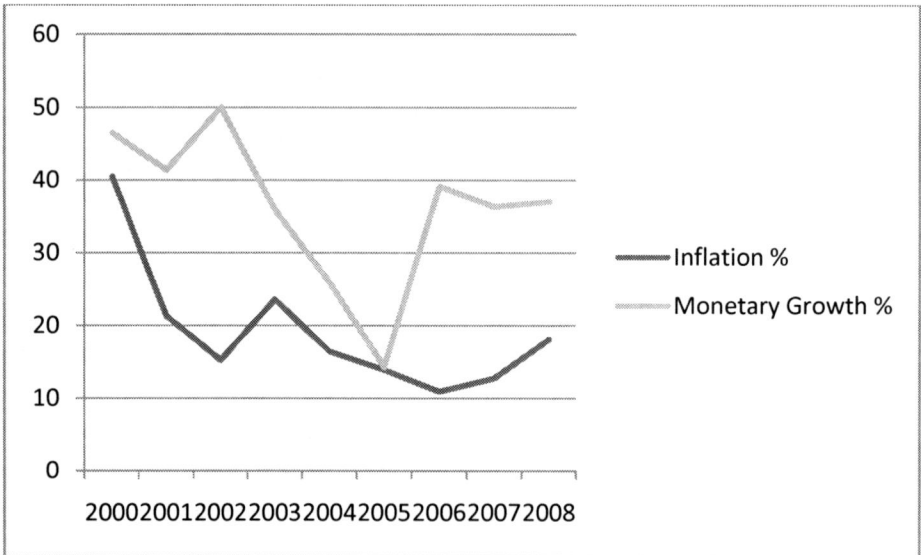

By the end of the first term of the Government in 2004 (an election year) a good measure and a track record of macroeconomic stability had been established. There was sustained disinflation, reduced exchange rate volatility and inflationary expectations.

Headline inflation declined from a peak of 41.5 percent in March 2001 to 16.4 percent in December 2004 and decreased further to 10.9 percent in 2006, before increasing to 12.7 percent in 2007 and 18.1 percent in 2008 (Figure 10.1).

Exchange rate stability also returned to the foreign exchange market. The exchange rate depreciation vis-à-vis the US dollar was 4.5 percent over the year 2003, and 2.2 percent for the year 2004, 0.9 percent in 2005, 1.1 percent in 2006 and 4.8 percent in 2007. Between 2004 and 2007, the cedi depreciated by an average of 2.25 percent against the U.S. dollar. Placed in the context of the historic instability of the cedi and the 2000 experience of some 50.0 percent depreciation, this level of stability of the cedi was remarkable.

This stability in the nominal exchange rate, with declining inflation resulted in a real appreciation of the cedi by 17.0 percent between 2004 and 2007. There were concerns expressed in some quarters at this time about whether the stability of the nominal exchange rate was not making exports uncompetitive. The empirical evidence did not support this view however. Issoifov and Loukoianova (2007)[20] for example show that the real appreciation of the cedi that was taking place was a restoration of the cedi towards its equilibrium value following the real depreciation in 2000, concluding that on the basis of the fundamentals, the *real effective equilibrium exchange rate in 2006 was close to its equilibrium level*".

For many analysts the surprising development was the fact that Ghana was not experiencing a nominal appreciation of the cedi under these circumstances. Fitch Ratings captured this sentiment in their 2007 Sovereign credit ratings report on Ghana, noting that:

"It is all the more remarkable that the nominal exchange rate should have remained so stable since 2004, notwithstanding a series of balance of

---

[20] "Estimation of a Behavioural Equilibrium Exchange Rate Model for Ghana" IMF Working Paper, WP/07/155. Washington D.C.

payments surpluses. While the case for building international reserves is a legitimate one, the real effective exchange rate against the USD has appreciated by 17% since 2004. Admittedly, non-traditional exports continue to prosper, eliminating concerns about competitiveness, but greater nominal appreciation could assist the BOG in its quest for single digit inflation"

What these independent assessments show is that the cedi exchange rate was being driven by the fundamentals and not by any artificial intervention by the central bank. In fact, by 2007 the Bank of Ghana was being advised by analysts to allow the nominal exchange rate to appreciate through selling more foreign exchange on the market rather than building its foreign exchange reserves. Given that almost 100 percent of cocoa export proceeds are surrendered to the Bank of Ghana, the Bank provides these proceeds to support import demand (i.e. balance of payments support) and this can sometimes be confused with market intervention to maintain an unsustainable exchange rate. The Bank of Ghana policy during this period was to focus on inflation and allow the exchange rate to be determined by the fundamentals and the market.

That said, in an economy that seeks to be export driven, it is very important that policy makers continuously keep an eye on the real exchange rate lest a real appreciation makes Ghana's exports uncompetitive. There was however a 20.1 percent nominal depreciation of the cedi exchange rate in 2008 (Table 10.1).

Gross official reserves increased from US$233.4 million in 2000 to some US$1.7 billion by 2004, an unprecedented sum, for the economy at the time, and equivalent to about 3.3 months of import cover, compared to less than one month cover in 2000. By 2007 Gross international reserves had reached $2.83 billion (2.7 months of imports), before declining to $2.03 billion by the end of 2008 (2.2 months of imports) – Table 10.1.

The current account deficit, after decreasing from 10.16 percent of GDP in 2000 to 1.3 percent of GDP in 2003, increased to 16.7 percent of GDP in

2007 and 24.2 percent of GDP by 2008 (Table 10.1). However, the overall balance of payments was in surplus between 2001 and 2007 (except for the deficit of $10.5 million recorded in 2004).

Table 10.1 Selected Macroeconomic Indicators. 2000-2008

	2000	2001	2002	2003	2004	2005	2006	2007	2008
Real GDP %	3.7	4.2	4.5	5.2	5.7	5.8	6.4	6.3	7.3
Inflation %	40.5	21.3	15.2	23.6	16.4	13.9	10.9	12.7	18.1
Broad Money %	46.5	41.4	50	35.8	25.9	14.3	39.1	36.3	37
Reserve Money %	52.6	31.3	42.6	28.2	18.5	11.2	32.3	30.6	34.1
Ex. Rate Depreciation	49.8	3.7	13.2	17.3	2.2	0.9	1.1	4.8	20.1
91-Day T-Bill Rate	38	27	26.6	19.6	17.1	11.8	9.6	10.6	24.7
Gross Reserves ($m)	233.4	364.8	640.4	1425.6	1732.4	1894.9	2269.8	2838.7	2036
Months of Import Cover	0.84	1.2	2.2	3.2	3.3	3.5	3	2.7	2.2
Overall Balance ($m)	-116	8.6	39.8	558.3	-10.5	84.3	415.1	413.1	-940
External Debt ($m)	6021	6025	6131	7548	6447	6347	2172	3590	3871
Debt Service/Exports	28.1	16.4	10.1	4.9	7.2	7.7	4.5	4.6	4.3
Budget Deficit/GDP %	8.6	7.7	4.9	3.2	3.2	2	7.8	8.1	14.5
External Debt/GDP %	158.3	115.9	105.9	101	73.1	59.6	17.2	24.9	27
Debt Service/GDP %	14.1	5.9	3.5	1.7	2.2	2	1.3	1.3	0.4
Ext. Debt Service ($m)	544.8	306.6	204	126	194.9	215.2	166.7	192.5	52.2
Curr. Acc. Bal/GDP %	10.1	10.7	4.3	1.3	9.7	12.6	13.1	16.1	24.2

Interest rates were also on the decline. The 91- day Treasury bill interest rate had declined from 38.0 percent in 2000 to 17.0 per cent by the end of 2004, 9.6 percent by the end of 2006 and 10.6 percent by 2007, reflecting reduced government borrowing and inflation expectations (Figure 10.2).

Figure 10.2. 91- Day T Bill Rate (2000-2008)

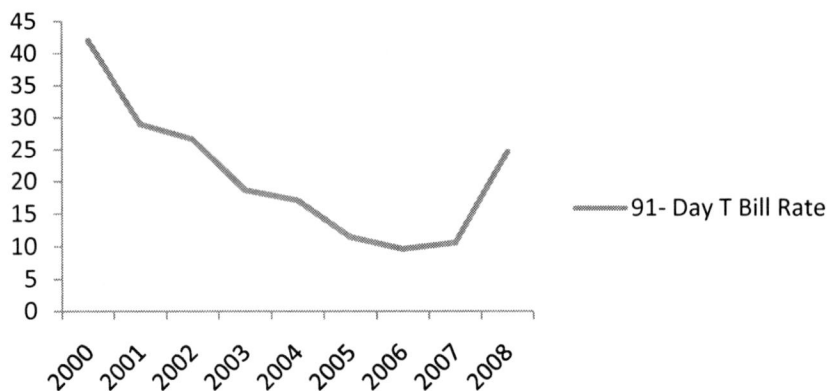

On the money market, high inflation alongside strong inflation expectations of the earlier periods had resulted in a shift in preferences towards short-dated government securities. As of end-2001, the share of the short-dated securities (including the 91-days and 182-days Treasury bills) in the outstanding stock of government securities was 83.0 per cent. This eased subsequently to 20.7 per cent by 2007 as inflation expectations remained well-anchored over the period. The year 2008 however, saw some reversal of the earlier trend as the disinflation process came under some stress. Thus market demand for the securities shifted significantly towards the short-dated instruments, ending the year at 45.7 per cent. It is important to note that the earlier shifts away from short-dated instruments had allowed for the introduction of long-dated instruments (securities with maturities up to 5 years) on to the market (Figure 10.3). These instruments gained substantial patronage and the significant extension of the maturity profile of outstanding government securities and led to the introduction of a benchmark yield curve.

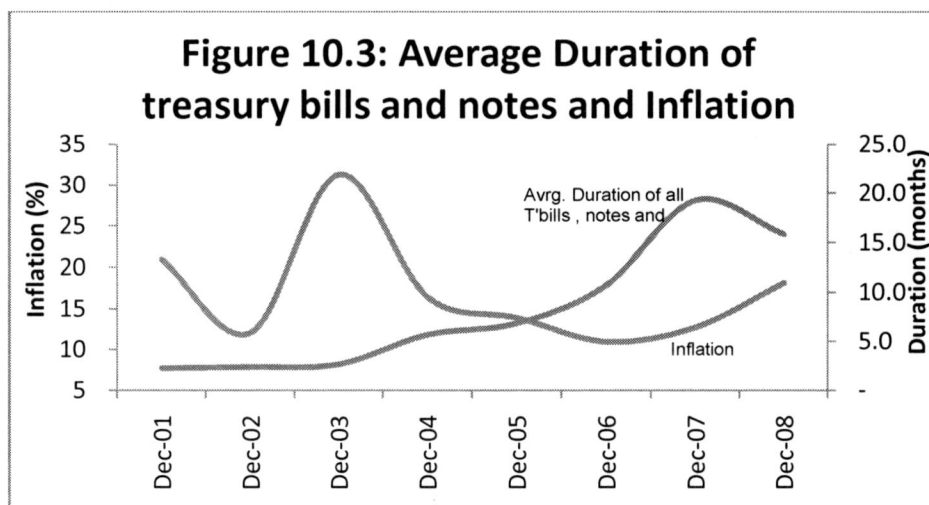

Figure 10.3: Average Duration of treasury bills and notes and Inflation

Avrg. Duration of all T'bills , notes and

Inflation

By 2008 however, the increase in inflation meant that the long-dated securities had began to lose their attractiveness and the average duration of treasury bills and notes began to decline even though the duration was still 50.0 percent longer than in 2006 and four times longer than in 2000.

Government finances also improved between 2001 and 2005. The government budget balance as a percentage of GDP declined from 8.6 percent of GDP in 2000 to 2.0 percent of GDP by 2005, before increasing to 7.8 percent of GDP in 2007 and 14.5 percent of GDP in 2008. The fiscal slippage in 2008 was the result of government subsidies of utilities, election year wage increases, and increased capital investment from proceeds of Ghana's sovereign bond largely to deal with an energy crisis (Table 10.1).

The stabilization in most of the macroeconomic indicators between 2001 and 2007 was achieved by strictly limiting the central government's borrowing requirements (PSBR). On the monetary side, open market operations shifted the financing of the budget deficit from bank to non-bank sources. The Government's fiscal policy strategy from 2001 was underpinned by a debt reduction path aimed at ensuring the availability of enough financial resources into the economy for the private sector to access for increased economic activity.

Figure 10.4. Bank Deposits and Bank Credit to Private sector (% of GDP)

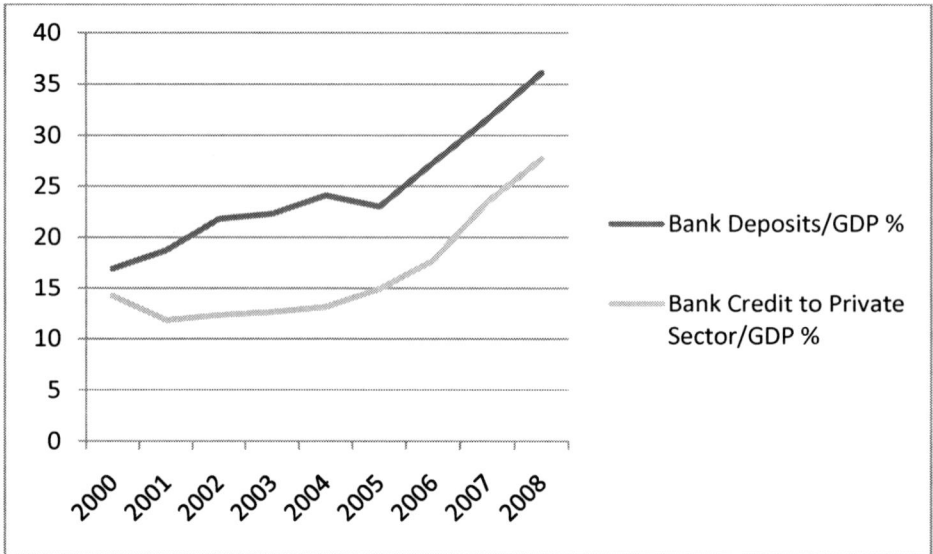

These developments resulted in a crowding-in of the private sector as bank lending to the private sector increased together with bank deposits. Bank deposits as a percentage of GDP increased from 16.9 percent in 2000 to 36.1 percent by 2008 while credit to the private sector increased from 14.2 percent of GDP to 27.7 percent of GDP over the same period (Figure 10.4).

As macroeconomic stabilization took hold, economic growth increased. GDP growth increased from 3.7 percent in 2001 to 5.7 percent in 2004, 5.8 percent by 2005, and 6.3 percent in 2007.

With this track record of economic performance, the World Bank's Country Performance and Institutional Assessment (CPIA) index (which ranks countries according to the quality of their policies and institutional arrangements) ranked Ghana 5th among all 75 low-income countries, second in Sub-Saharan Africa and above several middle-income countries in 2007. Between 2001 and 2007, this index went from 3.4 to 4.0 (the highest score for the index).

By 2005, Ghana had built a track record of good governance, growth and poverty reduction underpinned by macroeconomic stability that made the country eligible for HIPC debt relief.

HIPC Debt Relief

At the end of 2000, Ghana's total external debt amounted to $6.2 billion. $4.6 billion of this debt was owed to multilateral institutions (mainly the World Bank, IMF and African Development Bank) and $1.47 billion constituted bilateral debt. HIPC debt relief was provided on the following terms:

- The debt relief only applies to debt incurred before June 20, 1999 (the cut-off date). This implies that all debts contracted since this date is not subject to HIPC Relief.

- The debt relief provided by the multilateral institutions is in terms of a reduction in debt service obligations and not a reduction in the stock of debt itself. The relief provided spans a period of some 20 years, i.e. through to 2023 and totaling some $2.2 billion in nominal terms.

- The Paris club creditors (mainly bilateral official creditors) have provided a stock cancellation of $1.78bn of debt along with a reduction of debt service. This has reduced the total stock of bilateral debt from $2.1bn in 2003 to the current level of $380 million.

THE G-8 DEBT RELIEF

In July 2005, the world's richest countries - the G8- agreed to write off the some $40bn debt owed by 18 mainly African countries. The key elements of the G-8 debt relief package, known as the Multilateral Debt Relief Initiative (MDRI) of debt cancellation are:

- 100 percent, irrevocable stock debt cancellation of outstanding obligations of completion point HIPCs to the IMF, World Bank and African Development Bank contracted prior to January 1, 2005.
- Debt relief should be additional to previously committed assistance, with the additional assistance provided through IDA and the AfDF allocated to recipient countries on the basis of country performance. Good governance, accountability and transparency are described as crucial to realising the benefits of additional debt cancellation.

- All countries receiving the relief must be current with their repayment obligations to the International financial institutions. In addition, countries must not have experienced serious lapses, including in governance, such that their "IMF programmes" would be at risk.

Ghana qualified for inclusion in the list of beneficiary countries on the basis of a per capita income of $380 (the cut-off income). The relief was effective January, 2006. Debt Relief under G-8 Initiative for Ghana amounted to $4.2 billion in nominal terms, comprised approximately of: IDA ($3,482.9million), IMF ($274.6 million), and AfDB ($445.5 million).

After reaching the completion point of the enhanced HIPC initiative and also qualifying for the Multilateral Debt Relief Initiative (MDRI), Ghana's external debt was significantly reduced. From a level of 156 percent of GDP in 2000, Ghana's external debt declined to 27 percent of GDP in 2008.

Ghana's success at obtaining debt relief did not happen by chance however. It was the result of a deliberate policy of sound and sometimes very difficult macroeconomic policy choices (like the deregulation of the petroleum sector) and the manifestation of these policy decisions into a strong track record of macroeconomic performance (Table 10.1). During some of the difficult periods in the progress towards reaching the HIPC Completion Point, the economic team had to rely on the personal intervention of President John Agyekum Kufuor (who was held in high esteem and had built many personal relationships with the G-8 leaders). He leveraged these contacts to Ghana's benefit when it mattered most, just as he did later when Ghana was selected as the beneficiary of the U.S. Government's $547 million Millennium Challenge Account (MCA) Compact. Ultimately however, what made the difference was Ghana's track record of economic performance and good governance.

Ghana's overall debt profile was significantly improved with the debt burden well within the threshold of sustainability. Ghana's external debt (thanks to HIPC relief) had declined from some $6.1 billion in 2000 to $3.87 billion by 2008 (including the sovereign bond of $750 million issued in 2007). Furthermore, the debt service/exports ratio, i.e. the proportion of exports used to service Ghana's debts declined from 28.0 percent in 2000 to 4.3 percent by 2008 (Table 10.1).

The 2007-2009 Global Financial Crisis

In what started as a localized crisis in the United States, the credit/financial contagion of 2007, compounded by historically high oil prices (reaching $147 per barrel with predictions of $200/barrel) and rising food prices, spread to the real economy of most economies and resulted in a strongly synchronized global economic contraction with many economists drawing parallels with the Great Depression.

The global financial crisis of 2007-2009 occurred against the background of significantly improved growth and macroeconomic performance by African countries as a group over the last decade. GDP growth rates had steadily increased (averaging 6.0% over the last five years), inflation was on the decline in many countries before the fuel and food price crisis in 2008, and external reserve positions had also improved. These developments were underpinned by structural policy reforms, favorable terms of trade and debt relief. In 2007 for example, the average annual GDP growth rate in Africa was 6.1%. While impressive when compared to the negative growth rates recorded in the 1980s, this was still below the 7% p.a. growth rate required to reduce poverty by half by 2015.

The global financial crisis could therefore not have come at a more inopportune time for the African continent as many countries were just finding their feet and gaining some traction after decades of economic stagnation and macroeconomic instability. Initially, the conventional wisdom was that African countries were unlikely to be hard hit or at worst have only minimal impact of the effects of the crisis because low-income countries are generally less exposed to the financial contagion than emerging markets, as their financial institutions are not strongly integrated into the global financial system, and because the complex structured financial instruments at the heart of the crisis are rarely used in poor countries.

The evidence thus far however suggests that the global financial crisis after all, had significant ramifications for Africa (AfDB, 2009):

There has been a significant slowdown in economic growth on the African continent with the onset of the financial crisis. AfDB forecast a growth rate of

2.3 percent for 2009 (from 5.7% in 2008) which implies that per capita income will contract for the continent as a whole for the first time since 1994.

Export revenues have declined following the downturn in global demand and falling commodity prices. Exports from Africa are estimated to decline by $250 billion in 2009 with Nigeria and Angola accounting for one-third of the export decline, driven by oil export revenues. On the other hand the oil import bill for oil importing countries increased significantly. This decline in export revenues and the increase in the import bill resulted in a deterioration of the external positions of several countries with widening current account deficits and declining international reserves. The current account balance for Africa was projected to decline from a surplus of 2.7 percent of GDP in 2008 to a projected deficit of 5.3 percent of GDP in 2009, a worsening by 8% of GDP in one year (AfDB, 2009)

The global financial, energy and food crisis also coincided with a number of domestic factors in Ghana:

- A fiftieth anniversary of independence celebrations in 2007.
- The hosting of the African Cup of nations in 2008 which required the building and rehabilitation of four stadia.
- The country was hit with a major energy crisis in 2007 as a result of low water levels (as a result of low rainfall) at the hydroelectric Akosombo Dam , the country's primary source of energy supply. Emergency power supply was contracted which proved to be very expensive given the very high oil prices.
- The discovery of oil in commercial quantities in 2007 after several decades of trying
- Excessive fiscal expenditure in the run-up to the 2008 Presidential and Parliamentary elections.

In the midst of the global crisis, domestic energy problems and rising food prices and forthcoming elections, the NPP Government was unable to bite the bullet and allow full-cost recovery in petroleum and electricity prices. This was politically difficult as the assessment was that the populace, supported by loud complaints from the opposition parties, was not in the mood to accept price increases at that time. There was also an economic argument that as the world was heading towards a recession, what was needed was countercyclical policies and therefore aggregate demand needed to be increased in the interim (the fiscal stimulus argument). The budget would then be balanced when the crisis was over.

This policy stance combined with the global economic crisis, had adverse economic consequences. The Ghanaian economy, which was one that seemed to have all the prerequisites for a successful take off (good governance, sound economic management, institutions, etc.), suffered a setback with inflation increasing from 10.9 percent at the end of 2006 to 18.1 percent at the end of 2008 and the exchange rate depreciating by 20.1 percent in 2008, compared with 1.1 percent in 2006, a budget deficit of 14.5 percent of GDP and a current account deficit of 24.2 percent of GDP (Table 10.1).

Ghana's economic situation in 2008 was however not unique. The financial crisis resulted in a deterioration of the fiscal stance of virtually all African countries, with the projected budget deficit for the continent as a whole of 5.8 percent of GDP in 2009 (from a surplus of 2.8 percent of GDP in 2008), a worsening by 8.6% of GDP on average. Fiscal deficits for instance worsened not only because of the plunge in export revenues but also because of the need to increase social spending and safety nets and to provide the fiscal stimulus required to mitigate the worst consequences of the financial crisis. Botswana, for example, the historical example of prudent fiscal management on the continent and famous for perennial budget surpluses, recorded a projected budget deficit of some 13% of GDP in 2009 as government attempted to stimulate the economy in the face of a decline in diamond-based export revenues. The worsening fiscal stance was not limited only to African countries. Many industrialized countries experienced significantly increased deficits in the context of the global financial crisis. For example, the U.S. government budget deficit for 2009 reached a record 13.5% of GDP following President Obama's fiscal stimulus plan.

On the whole however, notwithstanding the impact of the global financial crisis and the domestically induced fiscal stimulus, Ghana recorded a relatively strong economic performance on several fronts during the 2001-2008 inflation targeting period. An assessment of the performance of the Ghanaian economy in the 2001/2-2008 period is contained in the Letter of Intent and Memorandum of Economic and Financial Policies (MEFP) submitted to the International Monetary Fund by the Ghana Government in June 2009 as part of the process of obtaining an IMF loan. The MEFP states as follows:

"Recent economic and social achievements

Real GDP growth increased steadily from 3.7 percent in 2000 to 7.3 percent in 2008. This growth was fostered by significant debt relief which provided the country with fiscal space to embark on critical infrastructure investments, particularly in the energy and road sectors, as well as targeted social spending, all under the Ghana Poverty Reduction Strategy (GPRS). The combination of higher output growth, declining inflation, and improved social spending under the GPRS framework contributed significantly to lower poverty levels. The national incidence of poverty declined from 39.5 percent in 1998/99 to 28.5 percent in 2005/06. At this rate, Ghana is poised to achieve the Millennium Development Goal (MDG) of halving extreme poverty ahead of 2015.

In the education sector, gross enrolment ratios have increased. A major initiative for improved enrolment ratios was the abolition of mandatory school fees for basic education and the introduction of capitation grants in the 2005–06 academic years.

In the health sector, there have been progressive improvements in the delivery of a number of important outputs. Most notable are: increase in life expectancy from 55 years in 2003 to 57.9 years in 2006; the introduction of a pre-paid National Health Insurance Scheme in 2004; and the introduction of free maternal care for expectant mothers. These, together, have put healthcare within the reach of the poor and vulnerable groups.

Gender disparities are gradually declining in some areas of service provision, such as in primary education, where the country has almost achieved gender parity. Recent estimates suggest that gross enrolment ratios have been higher for girls than for boys putting Ghana on track to achieve MDG 3 (gender parity in primary enrolment).

The improved macroeconomic environment during the period paved the way for Ghana to make a debut on the international capital markets in October 2007, raising US$750 million as additional capital targeted at infrastructural development for growth, especially in the key area of energy.

In the financial sector, important structural and institutional reforms have also been undertaken recently. In particular, a comprehensive legal and regulatory framework and strengthened risked-based prudential supervision policies have been put in place to further deepen the financial sector and safeguard the safety and soundness of the financial system.

Macroeconomic stress during 2007–08

In spite of the progress in the macroeconomic and structural areas, the economy has come under severe stress since 2006. The macroeconomic situation deteriorated sharply on the back of both domestic and external shocks. In 2006–07, Ghana suffered a severe energy crisis as a result of severe drought, leading to a significant shift from a predominant hydro to thermal power generation at a time of rising crude oil prices, with adverse impacts on the economy.

The global food and fuel price increases in 2007–08 adversely impacted most sub-Saharan African countries, including Ghana. In the context of these global shocks and the 2008 elections, public sector spending increased substantially, raising the fiscal deficit from 7.5 percent of GDP in 2006 to

14.5 percent of GDP in 2008. Contributing to the strong fiscal expansion were high energy-related subsidies, increased infrastructure investment, higher wages and salaries, and a rise in social mitigation expenditures to dampen the effects of the global price shocks.

The global financial crisis has contributed to further balance of payments pressures. While export proceeds have not, thus far, been significantly impacted, private remittances are slowing, there has been some outflow of portfolio investments, and the outlook for foreign direct investment is not encouraging. Official access to global market financing is now extremely limited. This has reinforced the urgency of macroeconomic adjustment and efforts to identify new external financing from development partners.

Strong public spending growth combined with rapid credit expansion and rising oil import costs contributed to a widening of the external current account deficit from 9.9 percent of GDP in 2006 to 19.3 percent of GDP in 2008. In 2008, the overall balance of payments recorded a deficit of US$941 million compared with a surplus of US$413 million in 2007 (inclusive of the balances on sovereign bond proceeds). The 2008 deficit was mainly financed by a drawdown of reserves, leading to a decline in the stock of gross international reserves, by US$800 million to US$2,036 million at the end of 2008, equivalent to 2.2 months of import cover.

Real GDP growth for 2008 remained strong at an estimated 7.3 percent, up from 5.7 percent in 2007. The pass through from higher global commodity price shocks, combined with fiscal expansion, resulted in a rise in headline inflation from 12.7 percent in December 2007 to 18.1 per cent by end-2008. The Bank of Ghana responded by increasing the prime rate by a cumulative 350 basis points in 2008, ending the year at 17 percent ".

The 2001-2008 period also saw a significant increase in social spending aimed at protecting the poor and vulnerable in society. This was reflected in initiatives such as the:

- National Youth Employment Programme –providing opportunities and jobs for the youth to get a start in the job market

- The School Feeding Programme to provide food to pupils in basic schools
- Capitation Grant to make education affordable and accessible
- The National Health Insurance Scheme (NHIS) to provide accessible healthcare to the population. The NHIS provides free healthcare for children below 18 and the elderly over the age of 70 and HIV positive individuals now receive highly subsidized anti-retroviral medicines.
- Free maternal care for all pregnant women under the NHIS.
- Introduction of a Metro Mass Transit transport service for urban to provide subsidized transport for commuters and a free bus ride for basic school pupils in Ghana.
- Introduction of the Livelihood Empowerment Against Poverty (LEAP) programme under which welfare grants are paid to the extreme poor.

These public interventions were made possible by the significant growth in the size of the economy and the attendant increase in tax revenue, fiscal space provided by debt relief, as well as donor support. However, one cannot help but notice the irony of the "free-market" oriented NPP government implementing policies that were to some extent more social democratic in orientation on the one hand, and the "social democratic" government of the PNDC/NDC on the other hand adopting a free market approach in the management of the economy under IMF guidance. One can only hope that this is the beginning of the forging of a "Ghanaian Consensus" on the management of the economy across the political divide.

CHAPTER 11

TWO MONETARY POLICY REGIMES, TWO EXTERNAL SHOCKS AND TWO MACROECONOMIC OUTCOMES (1993-2008)

The years 1993-2000 and 2001-2008 make interesting comparison because the two periods were characterized by two distinct monetary policy regimes. The monetary policy framework in 1993-2000 was one of Monetary targeting while that for 2001/2-2008 was one of Inflation Targeting. Furthermore, Ghana's economy was hit by external shocks in the form of declining commodity terms of trade in 1999/2000 and 2007/2008. The period also spans the tenure of office of two governments, the NDC and the NPP in Ghana's democratic setting. How did the economy react in the face of the external shocks under the two monetary policy regimes?

External Shocks and the Monetary Policy Regime (1993-2008)

Ghana's major exports and imports are gold, cocoa and oil. The movements in the international prices of these key commodities determine to a large extent, the commodity terms of trade. The developments in the prices of these commodities between 1993 and 2008 were as follows:

Cocoa Prices:

On average, cocoa prices followed a declining path between 1997 and 2008. Cocoa prices generally averaged £1,512.1 per m/tonne (LIFFE) for the 4-year period (1997 – 2000) against an average of £1,108.4 per m/tonne (LIFFE) for the 4-year period 2001 – 2004. Cocoa prices on average similarly softened to an average of £1,031.5 per m/tonne (LIFFE) for 2005 – 2008 (Table 11.2).

Gold Prices:

On average, gold prices followed a rising path between 1997 and 2008. Gold prices firmed-up from average of US$295.7 per fine ounce over the 4-year period (1997 – 2000) to an average of US$337.3 per fine ounce for the 4-year period 2001 – 2004. Gold prices similarly remained strong on average at US$652.0 per fine ounce for the period during 2005 – 2008 (Table 11.2).

Crude Oil Prices:

On average, crude oil prices followed a rising trend during 1997-2008. Crude oil prices rose to from average of US$19.5 per barrel (Brent) over the 4-year period (1997 – 2000) to an average of US$28.7 per barrel (Brent) for the 4-year period 2001 – 2004. Crude oil prices surged to US$73.4 per barrel (Brent) on average for the period 2005 – 2008 with increased upside volatility (Table 11.1).

Table 11.1 Average Commodity Prices and Terms of Trade Index

	Avg. Monthly Cocoa prices (£per m/tone (LIFFE)	Avg. Monthly Gold prices (US$/ fine ounce) MID	Avg. Monthly Crude oil prices ($/bbl) BRENT	Avg. monthly Terms of Trade Index Jan 02 =100)
1997-2000	1,512.1	295.7	19.5	173.1
2001-2004	1,108.4	337.3	28.7	85.5
2005-2008	1,031.5	652.0	73.4	37.3

Source: Bank of Ghana

Summary of trends in Commodity Prices:

The general trends in the above commodity prices show that while the weighted average index of export prices remained broadly unchanged, the crude oil price index firmed-up significantly with strong upside volatility. The terms of trade (TOT) consequently deteriorated significantly, recovering somewhat in the last quarter of 2008 (Figures 11.1 and 11.2).

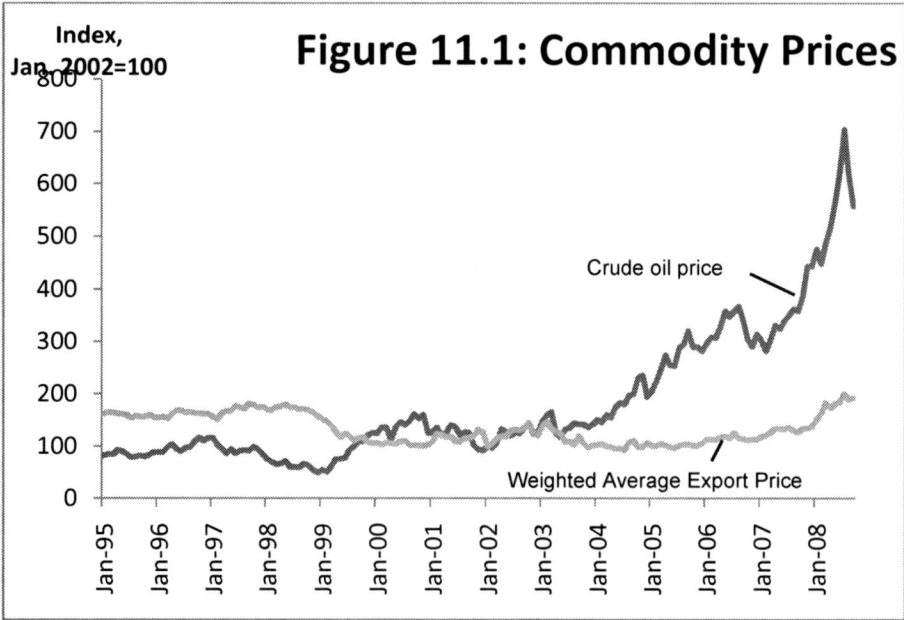

Figure 11.1: Commodity Prices

Table 11.2 shows that the core terms of trade improved significantly from an index value of 175.4 in 1995 to 326.0 by 1998 driven by increasing world prices for cocoa and declining prices for oil. There was however a sharp decline in the terms of trade in 1999 and 2000 with the core index declining from 326.0 in 1998 to 82.3 in 2000. The core terms of trade improved in 2001 to reach a value of 136.9 but steadily declined thereafter to reach a value of 30.8 by 2007, driven by a record increase in oil prices before increasing to 71.9 by the end of 2008.

Figure 11.2: Ghana: Core Terms of trade (1995 - 2008)

Index
Jan 2002=100

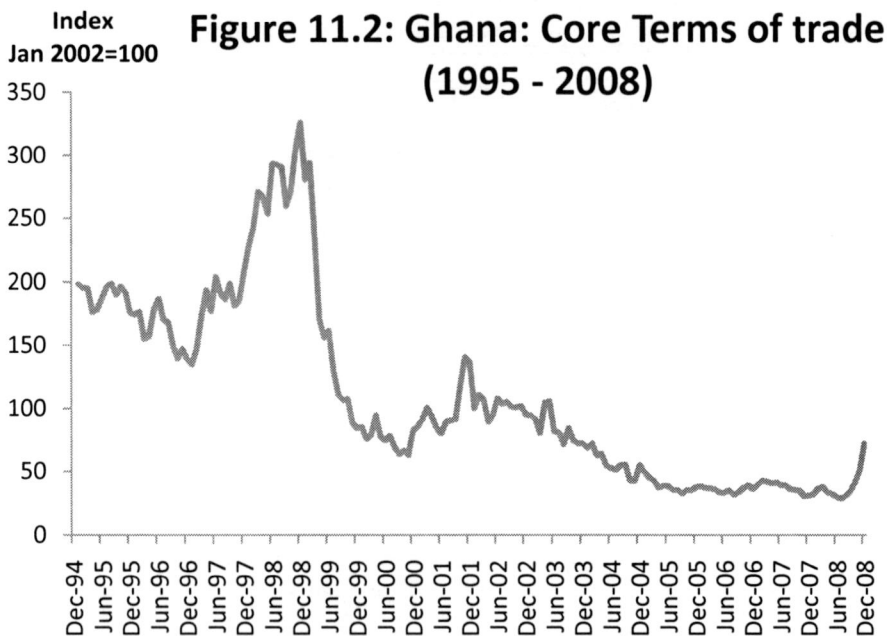

1999/2000 and 2007/2008 were thus years during which the economy experienced significant terms of trade shocks. How did the economy react to these external shocks under the two monetary policy regimes?

Table 11.2. Commodity Price Index and Core Terms of Trade 1995-2008

	Oil price Index	Weighted Average Export Price Index	Core Terms of Trade Weighted Index. (Jan 2002=100)
Dec. 1995	88.6	155.4	175.4
Dec. 1996	116.0	161.3	139.1
Dec. 1997	84.3	175.2	207.8
Dec. 1998	48.3	157.5	326.0
Dec. 1999	125.6	105.9	84.3
Dec. 2000	124.7	102.6	82.3
Dec. 2001	91.7	125.6	136.9
Dec. 2002	125.8	119.6	95.0
Dec. 2003	141.4	101.5	71.8
Dec. 2004	193.7	106.2	54.8
Dec. 2005	281.5	105.6	37.5
Dec. 2006	314.2	112.4	35.8
Dec. 2007	443.6	136.7	30.8
Dec. 2008	250.4	180.0	71.9

Source: Bank of Ghana

For each of the two monetary policy regimes, Table 11.3 looks at the entire period (1993-2000 and 2001-2008), the period excluding the external shock (1993-1999 and 2001-2007) and the year of the shock (2000 and 2008).

Average real GDP growth between 1993 and 2000 was some 3.2 percent compared with 5.7 percent during 2001-2008 (2.5 percent higher real growth on average). Excluding the crisis years (2000 and 2008), real GDP growth for 1993-1999 registered 3.1 percent while 2001-2007 registered 5.4 percent. In the crisis years, real GDP growth in 2000 (3.7 percent) declined while that in 2008 (7.3 percent) increased to twice what was recorded in 2000. (Table 11.3)

The 2001/02-2008 period of inflation targeting was also a period of greater price stability than the 1993-2000 period. Headline inflation was in the 1993-2000 period (32.6 percent) was on average twice that for 2001-2008 (16.4 percent). Excluding the crisis periods, the story is the same. It is important to note that the 2008 inflation (the crisis year) was about half the average for 1993-2000 or 1993-1999.

On the public finance front, the average government budget deficit as a percentage of GDP for 1993-2000 was 8.8 percent while that for 2001-2008 was 6.0 percent (2.8 percent of GDP lower). Excluding the crisis years, the budget deficits in the 2001-2007 period (at 5.4 percent of GDP) was 3.3 percent of GDP lower than the 8.7 percent of GDP recorded for the 1993-1999 period (Table 11.3). In the crisis year however, the budget deficit in 2008 at 14.5 percent of GDP was significantly higher) than the deficit in 2000 (8.7 percent of GDP).

On the external front, the 1993-2000 period recorded significantly lower current account deficits as a percentage of GDP (3.0% of GDP lower) compared with the 2001-2008. Excluding the crisis period, the 1993-1999 period current account/GDP was lower than the 2001-2007 period by some 1.0 percent of GDP. However, the accumulation of foreign reserves was much higher during the 2001-2008 period, with an average gross level of $1.6 billion compared with $485 million for the 1993-2000 period. In terms of import cover, the 2001-2008 period was only marginally higher than the 1993-2008 period. However during the crisis years, the level of reserves was in 2008 was some nine times higher than in 2000 and could cover over twice the months of imports (2.2 months) than the level of reserves in 2000 (0.9 months) - (Table 11.3).

Table 11.3. Comparison of Macroeconomic Performance Under Monetary targeting (1993-2000) and Inflation Targeting (2001/2-2008)

	Monetary Targeting			Inflation Targetng		
	1993-2000	1993-1999	2000	2001-2008	2001-2007	2008
Real GDP Growth %	3.2	3.1	3.7	5.7	5.44	7.3
Inflation %	32.6	31.4	40.5	16.4	16.2	18.1
Budget Deficit/GDP %	8.8	8.7	8.7	6.4	5.3	14.5
Curr. Acct Bal/GDP %	-7.3	-7.2	-10.1	-10.3	-8.4	-24.2
Gross Reserves ($m)	485	521	233.4	1650	1595	2036
Ex. Rate Depreciation	26.7	23.4	49.8	7.9	6.1	20.1
91-Day T-Bill	38.7	38.3	38	18.3	17.5	24.7
Debt Service to Exports %	28	27	28.1	7.4	7.9	4.3
External Debt/GDP %	88.8	83.1	156.3	70	65	27
Credit to the Private Sector/GDP %	7.2	6.5	12.6	17.9	16.2	27.7

Source: Bank of Ghana, IMF

The exchange rate of the cedi was also relatively more stable in the 2001-2008 period compared to the 1993-2000 period. The value of the cedi against the US dollar depreciated by an average of 26.7 percent between 1993 and 2000 compared with 7.9 percent (more than four times less) between 2001 and 2008. Excluding the crisis years, the cedi depreciated by some 23.0 percent between 1993 and 1999 compared with some 6.0 percent in the 2001-2007 period. In the crisis years, the cedi depreciated by some 20.0 percent in 2008 compared with some 50.0 percent in 2000. (Table 11.3).

Driven by the better fiscal performance, interest rates were also much lower in the 2001-2008 period compared to 1993-2000. The benchmark 91-day Treasury bill rate for the latter period was 38.7 percent compared with 18.3 percent for the 2001-2008 (less than half the 1993-2000 period). Excluding the crisis period leaves the picture unchanged.

Thanks to debt relief earned as a result of sound policies, the debt burden of the economy was significantly reduced in the 2001-2008 period. External debt/GDP declined from an average of 88.8 percent during 1993-2000 to 27.0 percent by 2008. The proportion of export revenues use to service debts also declined significantly from 28.0 percent during 1993-2000 to 7.4 percent for 2001-2008. By 2008, only 4.3 percent of export revenue was used to service debts compared to some 27.0 percent in 2000 (Table 11.3).

It should be very apparent from the foregoing that in terms of the main macroeconomic indicators of economic growth, inflation, interest rates, exchange rates, foreign exchange reserves, the debt burden, budget deficit and current account deficit, performed much better during the inflation targeting regime (2001-2008) compared to the monetary targeting regime (1993-2000). What is remarkable is that with the notable exception of the current account and fiscal deficits/GDP, the macroeconomic indicators for 2008 (the crisis year under inflation targeting) was much better than the average for 1993-1999 (the non-crisis years under the monetary targeting regime) in terms of GDP growth, inflation, exchange rate depreciation, interest rates, debt service/exports, and external debt/GDP (Table 11.3).

A key difference in the outcomes for the two periods is that inflation expectations were better anchored under the inflation-targeting monetary policy framework for the 2001-2008 period. Furthermore, notwithstanding the significant improvement in the terms of trade (because of favorable commodity prices) over the 1993-1998 period, the fiscal policy stance meant that foreign exchange reserve cover rather than increasing in this boom period, rather saw a decline from 4.1 months of imports in 1994 to 2.1 months of imports by 1998. This left the economy in a very vulnerable state. There is always a temptation by politicians to spend as quickly as the foreign reserves accumulate. When Gross international reserves of the Bank of Ghana increased from some US$230 million in 2000 to reach US$ I.73 billion by 2004, the Bank of Ghana was asked questions about why the it was accumulating foreign exchange reserves when the economy needed money for investment. The explanation was simple.

Why Foreign Exchange Reserves are Important

It would be imprudent economic and fiscal management to use foreign reserves to fund increases in government expenditure, for a number of reasons:

Foreign exchange reserves are held to provide a buffer against adverse shocks to the balance of payments (BOP) and to enhance confidence in the country's economic management and ability to meet its international payment obligations, such as debt servicing, without disruption. Consequently the level of foreign reserves is an important indicator used in the assessment of a country's sovereign credit rating along with the size of central government budget deficit/surplus. The foreign reserves also provide a buffer against delays in disbursements of donor programme aid. This serves to insulate government spending somewhat from the short term volatility in aid disbursements, without which managing the government budget in tune with a stable macro environment would be very difficult.

Furthermore, a significant proportion of the reserves have already been spent to the extent that they were accumulated from issuing cedis to cocoa farmers in exchange for the foreign currency from Cocobod. The foreign reserves accumulated in this manner thus act as a backing for the cedis in circulation. Spending foreign reserves, which have already been spent for all intents and purposes, is bound to be inflationary and destabilizing for the value of the cedi.

Also, some of the factors which contributed to the increase in foreign reserves are not permanent: external terms of trade are cyclical and can decline just as quickly as they rose. Also, Ghana cannot rely on permanently high inflows of donor to support its balance of payments and budget. Consequently, running down the foreign reserves will undermine the country's future capacity to withstand a balance of payments crisis.

Using foreign reserves to fund wage increases or other recurrent expenditures is imprudent because these are not "one off" expenditures: a wage increase granted now has a permanent impact on the level of the government wage bill, increasing the wage bill in subsequent years. Even if foreign reserves were used to fund a wage increase in the current year, they could not be used to fund the impact of the wage increase on next year's and each subsequent year's government wage bill because the foreign reserves would be continuously rundown until they became exhausted. Consequently, increasing the wage bill now could create a fiscal crisis in the future, because the budgetary resources to fund a permanently higher wage bill will not be available unless the government is prepared to further increase the already high tax levels or cut other equally pressing expenditure.

In sum, using foreign exchange reserves to fund increased government expenditure will severely damage the government's credibility for sound economic management. Running down the reserves to fund fiscal deficits is a classic and widely understood cause of balance of payments crises and exchange rate depreciation in developing countries. The private sector, both domestic and foreign, will fear that the government has abandoned prudent fiscal and macroeconomic policies.

As it turned out, the economy was more resilient and was better able to withstand the external and domestic shocks in 2007/2008 relative to 1999/2000 partly because it was on a firmer footing, inflation expectations were better anchored under the inflation targeting monetary policy framework, and the reserve cushion was higher.

CHAPTER 12

IMPACT OF FINANCIAL SECTOR REFORMS ON FINANCIAL SECTOR DEVELOPMENTS (1984-2008)

Ghana's financial sector has seen a remarkable turnaround from the pre-1988 reform period. Two major financial sector reform programmes have been implemented, one driven by the /World Bank the Financial Sector Adjustment Programme (FINSAP) between 1988 and 2000 and the Financial Sector Strategic Plan (FINSSIP) which was largely home grown and with significant input from stakeholders (between 2001 and 2008). Both sets of reform impacted positively on the banking and financial system in many areas.

Table 12.1. Ghana Banking System Indicators (1988-2008)

	1988	1991	1992	1998	2008
Number of Banks	10	12	13	17	24
Of which private	2	-	4	9	21
Number of branches	405	328	---	315	639
Banking System Assets/GDP	21	19	23	26	60.7
Non-Performing Loans/total credit	--	41	---	27	7.7
Asset Concentration					
4 largest banks	81	77	72	55	51.9
Public Sector Share					
Of total assets	79	73	70	37	24.9
Of total capital	-	77	76	34	31.9
Of total deposits	73	71	65	32	22.9
Of total advances	71	70	63	54	30.7
Of non-performing loans	--	--	--	84	29.8
Number of Account Holders:					
Commercial Banks					3,915,788
Rural Banks					2,827,023

Source : Bank of Ghana, IMF

Entry of New Banks

The liberalization of the financial sector under FINSAP resulted in an increase in the number of banks and non-banks in the financial sector with increased private sector participation. In 1988 the Ghanaian banking system comprised 10 banks with 405 branches (Table 12.1).

In 1998, there were 17 Banks in existence made up of 9 commercial banks, 5 merchant banks and 3 development banks. Nine new banks were licensed since 1990 and two banks (BCC and CO-OP) were liquidated in 1993.

	Ownership (percent)		Number of	%Share of
Bank	Ghanaian	Foreign	Branches	Total Assets
Commercial Banks				
Ghana Commercial Bank Ltd.	97	3	134	24.8
SSB Bank Ltd.	46	54	38	9.2
Barclays Bank of Ghana Ltd.	10	90	24	14.5
Standard Chartered Bank	24	76	23	16.1
The Trust Bank Ltd.	39	61	6	2.5
Metropolitan and Allied Bank	53	47	4	0.7
International Commercial Bank	0	100	3	0.6
Stanbic Bank Ghana Ltd.	9	91	1	1.2
Unibank	100	0	1	0.3
Merchant Banks				
Merchant Bank Ghana Ltd.	100	0	5	4.0
Ecobank Ghana Ltd.	6	64	4	7.1
CAL Merchant Bank	34	66	3	2.5
First Atlantic Bank	71	29	2	1.5
Amalgamated Bank	100	0	1	0.6
Development Banks				
Agricultural Development Bank	100	0	39	
National Investment Bank	100	0	11	
Prudential Bank	100	0	5	

Table 12.2 Structure of the Ghanaian Banking Sector, December 2001

Source: Bank of Ghana

Of the seventeen banking institutions in existence at the end of 2001, foreign investors held a majority of the shares in eight commercial banks, and three banks were state-owned; there are nine purely commercial banks, five merchant banks, and three development banks (Table 12.2). By 2009, there were 27 banks with foreign investors holding the majority shares in 13. (Table 12.3)

Table 12.3 Structure of the Ghanaian Banking Sector, December 2009

BANK	Ghanaian Ownership %	Foreign Ownership %	Number of Branches	% of Total Assets
Barclays	0	100	90	10.1
Standard Chartered	28.5	71.5	22	10.8
GCB	100	0	154	13.9
SG-SSB	48.3	51.7	37	4.2
ADB	100	0	53	5.0
NIB	100	0	27	4.0
MBG	100	0	21	4.9
ECO	9.9	90.1	44	9.6
CAL	94.4	4.6	13	3.2
TTB	70.5	29.5	18	2.2
FAMB	100	0	6	2.1
UTB	100	0	10	0.7
PBL	100	0	22	2.4
ICB	0	100	12	1.4
STANBIC	2.1	97.9	21	4.8
AMAL	51	49	12	2.6
UNIBANK	100	0	12	1.6
HFC	67.8	32.2	21	1.8
UBA	36.9	63.1	27	1.9
ZENITH	0	100	17	4.1
GTB	2	98	13	2
FIDELITY	100	0	14	2.6
IBG	25	75	20	3.2
BARODA	0	100	1	0.1
BSIC	0	100	8	0.2
ACCESS	4	96	1	0.6

Source: Bank of Ghana

Assets and Liabilities of the Banking System- 1993-2008

Table 12.4 shows the trends in the assets and liabilities of commercial banks between 1993 and 2008. It can be observed that there was an increase in the total assets of the banking system from 0.31 percent of GDP in 1993 to 0.44 percent of GDP by 2000 (a 42.0 percent increase) before declining to 0.38 percent of GDP in 2001. This was partly due to the economic crisis of 2000 which adversely impacted the ability of many bank customers to service their loans. Since 2001, total assets of the banking system steadily rose to 0.66 percent of GDP (a 73.0 percent increase) by 2008, reflecting a more vibrant banking system following the FINSSIP reforms.

The period between 1993 and 2000 also saw a shift in the composition of bank assets as lending to the private sector increased at the expense of lending to government. The loans/asset ratio increased from 0.16 in 1993 to 0.40 by 2000 while at the same time the ratio of holdings of treasury and Bank of Ghana bill/total assets declined from 0.40 in 1995 to 0.24 in 2000 before increasing to 0.28 in 2001. This trend was reinforced after 2001 with loans to asset ratio increasing from 0.38 in 2001 to 0.52 by 2008 while the Bills/Total Assets ratio declined drastically from 0.32 in 2002 to 0.14 by 2008 (Table 12.4).

Demand deposits as a proportion of total deposits increased from 48.0 percent in 1993 to 66.0 percent by 2000, before falling to 61.0 percent in 2001. By 2008 however, there was a marginal decline to 58.0 percent. Over the same period, savings deposits declined from 40.0 percent of total deposits in 1993 to 21.0 percent by 2001 and further to 15.0 percent by 2008. Time deposits however increased over the reform periods from 12.0 percent of total deposits in 1993 to 16.0 percent of total deposits by 2000 and further to 26.0 percent of total deposits by 2008 (Table 12.4).

Table 12.4. Banking System Balance Sheet Indicators (1993-2008)

	Loans/Total Assets	Bills/Total Assets	Demand Dep/Total Deposits	Savings Dep/Total Deposits	Time Dep/Total Deposits	Total Assets/GDP
1993	0.16	0.38	0.48	0.40	0.12	0.31
1994	0.17	0.32	0.57	0.31	0.12	0.33
1995	0.18	0.40	0.63	0.21	0.16	0.25
1996	0.23	0.27	0.65	0.19	0.16	0.25
1997	0.29	0.31	0.61	0.24	0.15	0.26
1998	0.33	0.35	0.59	0.22	0.19	0.27
1999	0.36	0.31	0.61	0.21	0.18	0.35
2000	0.40	0.24	0.67	0.18	0.16	0.44
2001	0.38	0.28	0.62	0.20	0.18	0.38
2002	0.30	0.32	0.64	0.22	0.13	0.40
2003	0.35	0.28	0.61	0.21	0.16	0.41
2004	0.36	0.28	0.61	0.21	0.14	0.39
2005	0.43	0.27	0.61	0.22	0.17	0.38
2006	0.45	0.23	0.59	0.22	0.19	0.45
2007	0.50	0.18	0.57	0.18	0.25	0.56
2008	0.52	0.14	0.58	0.15	0.56	0.66

Source: Bank of Ghana

Asset Concentration

At the beginning of the reforms in 1988, the banking system concentration was high, with the four largest banks accounting for 81.0 per cent of the assets of the banking system. Banking system concentration was reduced significantly however, with the top four banks accounting for 55.0 percent of assets by 1998 and 51.9 percent by 2008 (Table 12.1).

The dominant influence of the state in the banking system at the onset of FINSAP is evident from the public sector's share of total assets (79.0 percent), total credit (71.0 percent) and total deposits (73.0 percent). The waning public sector influence after the reforms saw the public sector's share of the total assets of the banking system decline to 37.0 percent by 1998 while its share of total credit and total deposits declined to 54.0 percent and 32.0

percent respectively by 1998. By 2008, the public sector's share of total bank assets had further declined to 24.9 percent and its share of bank advances also declined to 30.7 (Table 12.1).

The reform period also saw a closure of bank branches which declined from 415 in 1988 to 315 by 1998 and 300 by December 2002. The closure of bank branches was part of the efforts of banks to rationalize their activities and close unprofitable branches. Even though the banking penetration ratio (one branch per 54,000 inhabitants at the end of 2002) is relatively high, formal banking reaches less than 10 percent of the population and the coverage varies widely. About 35 percent of the branches are in the Greater Accra region even though this region represents less than 13.0 percent of the population, and about half of all bank branches in the interior of the country belonged to the state-owned Ghana Commercial Bank.

Under FINSSIP, there was an expansion of the bank branch network. By the end of 2008, bank branches had more than doubled from 300 in 2002 to 636 (Table 12.1), reflecting the more vibrant banking environment.

Asset Quality

Following the FINSAP reforms, and the restructuring of the balance sheets of problem banks, there was also an improvement in the quality of the assets of the banking industry. At the end of 2000, the proportion of non-performing loans stood at 12.1 percent (declining from 41 percent in 1988). Non-performing loans however increased to 17.4 percent in 2001 following the economic crisis in 2000. By 2008, Non-performing loans (NPLs) had further declined to 7.7 percent (Bank of Ghana, 2009).

Capital Adequacy

The capital adequacy of the banking system also saw significant improvement following the reforms. The average capital adequacy ratio (CAR) for the banking system increased from 10.73 percent in 1996 to 14.74 by 2001, well above the minimum 6.0 percent required by law. However, there were significant differences between banks even though all banks met the minimum CAR. The Capital Adequacy ratio for the banking industry increased further to 15.67 by 2007 but declined to 13.84 at the end of 2008, still well above the minimum requirement of 6.0 percent (Bank of Ghana, 2009).

Savings Mobilization, Interest Rates and Financial Deepening

The liberalization of the financial sector under FINSAP and FINSSIP brought it expectations of increased savings, deposit mobilization, financial deepening and competition in the banking sector.

Savings Mobilization

The data (Table 12.5) shows that the banking sector witnessed a growth in deposits over the immediate post reform period, with deposits of the private sector with the banking system increasing from GH¢14.0 million in 1990 to GH¢427.8 million by 2000. The FINSSIP reform period of 2002-2008 also saw a major increase in deposits as the economy expanded. Total private sector deposits in the banking system increased from GH¢427.8 million in 2000 to GH¢5,713.6 million by 2008. Time deposits similarly increased from GH¢53.8 million in 2000 to GH¢1,246.1 million by 2008.

The increase in total deposits was reflected in all its categories, demand, savings, foreign currency and deposits. Demand deposits of the private sector increased from GH¢ 8.0 million in 1990 to GH¢70.1 million by 2000. Between year 2000 and 2008, private sector demand deposits in the banking system further increased from GH¢70.1 million to GH¢1,686 million. Similarly, savings deposits of the private sector increased from GH¢109.5 million in 2000 to GH¢964.1 million by 2008 and time deposits increased from GH¢53.8 million to GH¢1,246.1 million by 2008 (Table 12.5).

Table 12.5: Liabilities of Deposit Money Banks: 1990 to 2008

	PRIVATE SECTOR DEPOSITS					PUBLIC SECTOR DEPOSITS			
					(Millions of Ghana Cedis)				
	Demand Deposits	Foreign Currency Deposits	Savings Deposits	Time Deposits	Total	Demand Deposits	Savings Deposits	Time Deposits	Total
1990	8.0		5.5	0.5	14.0	4.0	0.1	0.6	4.7
1991	9.8		7.8	1.0	18.6	4.2	0.1	0.8	5.0
1992	10.7		11.5	1.9	24.1	6.8	0.2	2.3	9.2
1993	14.7		13.6	2.4	30.7	8.9	0.1	3.9	12.9
1994	21.5		20.0	3.3	44.9	10.6	0.6	3.4	14.6
1995	23.3		25.8	7.8	56.9	13.8	0.2	6.7	20.6
1996	27.3	51.6	34.9	14.2	127.9	20.9	0.2	7.7	28.8
1997	57.2	72.9	51.4	23.5	205.0	20.4	2.4	5.2	28.0
1998	74.3	67.2	67.0	42.4	251.0	23.9	0.2	6.5	30.6
1999	80.7	97.0	87.3	47.9	312.9	13.2	0.3	7.9	21.4
2000	70.1	194.3	109.5	53.8	427.8	16.1	0.4	15.1	31.6
2001	161.9	237.4	158.9	92.7	650.8	39.1	0.5	23.2	62.7
2002	269.7	355.3	228.8	104.5	958.3	81.0	1.3	25.2	107.4
2003	346.4	457.6	295.2	183.4	1,282.6	147.5	1.8	42.1	191.4
2004	526.7	568.1	395.6	211.5	1,701.9	189.7	1.7	31.4	222.8
2005	570.9	653.3	484.2	292.7	2,001.0	173.0	0.8	52.7	226.5
2006	803.1	902.4	694.3	466.8	2,866.6	251.1	1.4	70.5	323.0
2007	1,412.7	992.9	849.6	837.6	4,092.9	208.8	1.1	138.3	348.1
2008	1,686.6	1,816.8	964.1	1,246.1	5,713.6	406.2	1.3	231.2	638.7

Source: Bank of Ghana

The 2001-2008 period under the FINSSIP reform programme therefore, saw a major increase in private sector bank deposits when compared with the FINSAP period (1988-2000).

Interest Rates

An explanation of the increase in deposit mobilization observed under both FINSAP and FINSSIP may be found in interest rate developments in the pre and post reform periods.

A key driver of financial sector reform under FINSAP was the negative interest rates prevailing under the regime of direct controls and the disincentive to savings and deposit mobilization this provided. Average real savings rates reached -111.8 percent in 1983. The FINSAP reform programme, by liberalizing interest rates, resulted in an increase in nominal interest rates. However, as Table 12.6 shows, real interest rates continued to be negative, with bank savings rates averaging -10.0 percent between 1984 and 2000 and -8.8 percent between 2001 and 2008. Real bank lending rates on the other hand turned positive by 1989 (5%), increasing to 22.0 percent by 2000. Real lending rates however declined to 9.1 percent by 2008, following the general trend decline in interest rates between 2001 and 2008.

The post reform period however did not result in positive real interest rates on bank products. Real interest rates on savings deposit accounts for example increased from an average of -46.0 per cent between 1975 and 1986 to an average of -6.0 percent between 1987 and 2000.

Table 12.6 also shows that real interest rate spreads (i.e. the difference between banks lending and deposit rates adjusted for inflation) were on average negative between 1983 and 2008. The FINSAP period between 1984 and 2000 saw real interest rate spreads at an average of -20.0 percent. While real interest rate spreads during the FINSSIP period (2001-2008) were marginally positive, they averaged -0.9 percent. Economic theory[21] will therefore predict, as was observed, higher deposit mobilization and higher bank lending under the FINSSIP regime (2001-2008) than under the FINSAP regime (1984-2000) because real interest rates paid on deposits were higher.

---

[21] The Mckinnon-Shaw hypothesis

Table 12.6. Selected interest rates, Spreads and Inflation: 1975 - 2000

	12-month Deposit	Average Saving Deposits	Lending Agric	Lending Other	Treasury Bills	Inflation (cpi, 2002 =100)	Average Real Saving Rate	Average Nominal Interest Spread (Lend-Dep)	Average Real Interest Spread (Lend-Dep)
1975	8	7.5	6	12.5	7.8	40.4	-23.4	4.5	-25.6
1976	8	7.5	6	12.5	7.8	67.0	-35.6	4.5	-37.4
1977	8	7.5	8.5	12.5	7.8	105.9	-47.8	4.5	-49.3
1978	13	12	13	18.5	12	108.5	-46.3	5.5	-49.4
1979	13	12	13	18.5	12	18.3	-5.3	5.5	-10.8
1980	13	12	13	18.5	12	87.8	-40.4	5.5	-43.8
1981	19	18	20	25.5	18.5	100.2	-41.1	6.5	-46.8
1982	9	8	8	14	9.5	16.8	-7.5	5.0	-10.1
1983	12.5	11	12.5	19	13	142.4	-54.2	6.5	-56.1
1984	16	14.5	16	22.5	16.8	6.0	8.0	6.5	0.5
1985	17	15.5	18	22.5	16.8	19.5	-3.3	5.5	-11.7
1986	20	18.5	22.5	23	19.8	33.3	-11.1	3.0	-22.8
1987	22	21.5	30	26	19.6	34.2	-9.4	4.0	-22.5
1988	22	19.25	30	30.3	19.8	26.6	-5.8	8.3	-14.4
1989	20	17	30	30.3	19.9	30.5	-10.3	10.3	-15.5
1990	22	16	29.5	30.3	27.5	35.9	-14.6	8.3	-20.3
1991	24	15	31.5	31.5	18	10.3	4.3	7.5	-2.5
1992	22.5	13.5	26.5	29	25.4	13.3	0.1	6.5	-6.0
1993	32	18.75	39	39	32	27.7	-7.0	7.0	-16.2
1994	31	18.1	35.5	37.5	29.5	34.2	-12.0	6.5	-20.6
1995	31	26.25	38.5	40.5	33	70.8	-26.1	9.5	-35.9
1996	31.5	28.25	47	43	47.9	32.7	-3.3	11.5	-16.0
1997	32	28.5	49	44	45.6	20.5	6.7	12.0	-7.0
1998	25	16.5	42	38.5	28.7	15.7	0.6	13.5	-1.9
1999	18.75	13	36.75	34.75	34.2	13.8	-0.7	16.0	1.9
2000	26.25	18	47	47	42.0	40.5	-16.0	20.8	-14.1
2001	20	14.5	44	44	28.9	21.3	-5.6	24.0	2.2
2002	20	13	38.5	38.5	26.6	17.0	-3.4	18.5	1.3
2003	15.5	9.75	32.75	32.75	18.7	31.3	-16.4	17.3	-10.7
2004	11.25	9.5	28.75	28.75	17.1	16.4	-6.0	17.5	0.9
2005	9.5	6.375	26	26	11.5	13.9	-6.6	16.5	2.3
2006	8.75	4.75	24.25	24.25	9.6	10.9	-5.6	15.5	4.1
2007	10.75	4.55	23.75	24.25	10.6	12.7	-7.3	13.5	0.7
2008	15.5	9.0	27.25	27.25	24.7	18.1	-7.7	11.8	-5.4

Source: Bank of Ghana

Financial Deepening

Key monetary indicators often used in gauging the extent of financial deepening in an economy (Tables 12.7 and 12.8) point to significant deepening of the Ghanaian financial system over the past couple of decades, especially following the financial sector reforms. The indicators thus reflect the strong contribution of the financial system to the growth of the economy over the period. This has however happened with broadly unchanged interest rates spreads, a situation that has triggered the pursuit of vigorous market competition policies[22] by the central bank. In the process, money supply, broadly defined, rose consistently from an average of 17.2 per cent of GDP during 1990 – 1995 to 45.8 per cent at end-2008. This was reflected in a strong deposit mobilization over the period, rising significantly from some 11.1 per cent of GDP during 1990 – 1995 to 36.3 per cent of GDP at end-2008. The strong deposit mobilization supported increased growth of bank credit to the private sector from under 10 per cent of GDP during the 1996 – 2000 to 27.7 per cent of GDP by 2008. Currency outside banks remained broadly unchanged at an average of some 7.6 per cent of GDP over the period.

Table 12.7. Ghana: Indicators of Financial Deepening (Annual Growth Rates, Per cent)

	1991-1995	1996-2000	2001-2005	2006	2007	2008
M2+/GDP	17.2	23.5	31.0	36.3	40.8	45.8
Deposits/GDP	11.1	16.0	22.1	27.5	31.6	36.3
Currency outside banks/GDP	6.1	7.5	8.9	8.7	9.2	9.4
Currency outside banks/Deposits	54.8	46.7	40.6	31.8	29.3	26.0
Private Sector Credit/GDP	4.8	9.9	12.9	17.7	23.4	27.7
M1/M2	0.70	0.66	0.68	0.63	0.62	0.61

Source: Bank of Ghana

---

[22] Including the licensing of new banks and publication of annual percentage rates recently.

The data from Table 12.8 indicates that going by the traditional measures of financial deepening, M2/GDP, Bank Credit/GDP, Bank Deposits/GDP some financial deepening has taken place since the liberalization of the financial sector even though the pace was slower during the FINSAP regime.

Table 12.8. Financial Deepening Indicators (1970-2008)

	M2/GDP	Bank Deposits/GDP	Credit to the Private Sector/GDP
1970	19	12.4	8.2
1971	19	12.6	12.6
1972	23.7	15.2	10.1
1973	22.6	15.6	5.3
1974	21.6	14.4	5.7
1975	26.5	17	5.8
1976	29.1	18.3	5.9
1977	29.7	19.5	5.0
1978	36.6	16.6	3.5
1979	22.8	14.2	2.8
1980	20.4	12.4	4.1
1981	22.9	14.7	3.1
1982	19.8	12	3.7
1983	13.2	7.8	2.7
1984	12.5	7.4	3.0
1985	16	9.7	4.5
1986	16.6	10.4	5.2
1987	17.1	10.9	4.3
1988	17.3	11.2	3.6
1989	16.9	11.1	5.6
1990	13.6	9.7	3.9
1991	13.4	9.3	3.2
1992	17.5	11.8	4.6
1993	16	12.7	4.6
1994	18.7	12.8	5.3
1995	17.5	13.1	6.5
1996	19.4	14.5	8.3
1997	18	17.7	7.3
1998	22.7	16.8	10.6
1999	23.7	16.4	14.3
2000	26.7	16.9	14.2
2001	26.9	18.7	11.8
2002	31.5	21.8	12.3
2003	32	22.3	12.6
2004	33.4	24.1	13.1
2005	31.4	23.0	14.9
2006	36.2	27.3	17.7
2007	40.9	31.6	23.5
2008	45.8	36.1	27.7

Source: Bank of Ghana

The M2/GDP ratio was 19.0 percent in 1975 and by 1995; (twenty years later) it was 17.5 percent. At the beginning of FINSAP in 1988, M2/GDP was 17.3 percent, and after declining in the early 1990s, it increased to 19.0 by 1996, and increased significantly to 26.6 by 2000. However, this is still lower than the level of 29.6 percent attained in 1976. Under the FINSSIP reforms, M2/GDP increased from 26.7 % in 2000 to a record high 45.8 percent by 2008, indicative of a significant deepening of the financial sector.

Bank deposits to GDP increased from 11.2 percent in 1988 to 17.7 percent in 1997 and declined to 16.2 percent by 2000 (still lower than the 1977 level of 19.5 percent). Following the FINSSIP reforms, bank deposits/GDP reached a record level of 36.0 percent by 2008. Private Sector Credit/GDP increased significantly from 3.2 percent in 1998 to 14.0 per cent by 2000 (following the FINSAP reforms) and further to 29.7 percent by 2008. With the increase in bank credit, Ghanaians experienced the unusual phenomenon of banks pursuing customers at their work places and in their homes to offer credit.

The evidence therefore shows that Ghana's financial sector has been deepened by the two programmes of financial sector reform implemented between 1984 and 2008. However, it is clear that by all the relevant measures, more financial sector deepening occurred under the FINSSIP regime (2001-2008) than under the FINSAP reforms during the period of structural adjustment.

CONCLUSION

This book has examined monetary policy and financial sector reform in Ghana since independence in 1957. During this period Ghana has adopted three monetary regimes; direct controls, monetary targeting (indirect monetary instruments) and inflation targeting. Financial sector development and reform has also taken place alongside the monetary policy regimes. These include regulatory and legal reforms, capital market and money market reforms, banking reforms, currency redenomination, reforms, payment system reform, rural banking reforms, and accessing the international capital markets.

The choice of monetary policy regime in Ghana has generally been consistent with accepted economic thinking and central bank practice internationally. This was more so for the direct control regime as well as the indirect monetary instruments regime. The move towards inflation targeting was however different in the sense that it was not consistent with central bank practice in low income countries.

It is important to note that the link between a monetary policy regime and macroeconomic outcomes is a very complex one because there are so many other factors at play making it difficult to ascribe a causal relationship. However, the major lesson from the era of direct controls of prices and interest rates that were largely in place between 1957 and 1983 is that direct controls did not achieve the desired objectives of increasing credit or lowering the cost of borrowing. Direct controls in Ghana rather reduced savings, investment, and growth.

Did direct controls not help in their case of some of the East Asian countries like South Korea? South Korea inherited a legacy of direct controls from the Japanese colonial era. As with Ghana after independence, the focus was on rapid industrialization and growth. Without a well-established capital market, the Korean government played an important role in mobilizing and allocating financial savings for industrial investment through its control over the financial system. A major difference between the Ghanaian and Korean direct control regimes was that the latter mobilized financial resources at controlled prices to support export-led industrialization while the former supported import-substituting industrialization. Korean industry had to be efficient to compete internationally while Ghanaian industry wallowed in protective inefficiency (similar to the approach of the Soviet Union). The Ghana Cocoa Marketing Board is a successful example of how the government supported an export oriented industry with private-sector farmers growing the cocoa crop and the government marketing board assisting with inputs, research and marketing of the cocoa (a Private Public Partnership).

In Korea however, government intervention was not without its costs. By 1972, Korea's manufacturing industries as well as its financial sector were heavily indebted and had to be rescued (Cho, 2002). The Fifth Five-Year Plan (1982-86) for Korea marked a movement away from the state interventionist strategy with the government undertaking a liberalization of the financial sector. Commercial banks were denationalized, but the state retained the right to appoint boards of directors and senior officers. There was, however, an easing of direct government control of banks and nonbank financial institutions. This notwithstanding, the 1997 Asian financial crisis was to highlight major governance issues in the relationships between the large business conglomerates which were supported by government (the Chaebols) and the banking sector.

The era of indirect monetary instruments in Ghana introduced a more market-driven approach to monetary policy but the deviation of monetary growth targets from actual growth rates as well as inflation targets from actual was wide. The inflation targeting regime thus far has delivered the best results in terms of the deviation of inflation from its target as well as the volatility of inflation and other macroeconomic variables.

The financial sector reform programme (FINSAP) which was implemented between 1988 and 2000 achieved a great deal, including the:

- liberalization of interest rates and abolition of directed credit,
- restructuring of financially distressed banks,
- strengthening of the regulatory and supervisory framework,
- promotion of non-bank financial institutions: discount houses, finance houses, acceptance houses, leasing companies, mortgage finance companies
- liberalization of the foreign exchange market,
- establishment of forex bureaux, and
- the establishment of the Ghana stock exchange

The legal framework for the financial sector was enhanced with the passage of bills such as the:

- Banking Act 1989
- Bank of Ghana Law 1992, PNDCL 291
- Securities Industry Law 1993, PNDCL 333
- NBFI Law 1999, PNDCL 328
- Insurance Act 1989, PNDCL 227
- Social Security Act 1991, PNDCL 247

The Financial Sector reforms between 2001 and 2008 under FINSSIP built on these reforms with the goal of addressing many of the constraints in the financial sector and repositioning Ghana's financial sector as an international financial services center (IFSC) in the sub-region. In this regard, reforms introduced included the:

- Bank of Ghana Act 2002
- Monetary Policy Committee (MPC) process - Transparency
- Universal Banking
- Abolishing Secondary Reserve Requirements
- Banking Act 2004
- Banking Amendment Act 2007 – Offshore Banking
- Long Term Savings Act 2004

- Venture Capital Trust Fund Act 2004
- Payment System Act, 2003
- Foreign Exchange Act 2006
- Anti-Money Laundering Act 2008
- Credit Reporting Act 2008
- Licensing of first Credit Reference Bureau
- Establishment of a Collateral Registry
- Borrowers and Lenders Act 2008
- Insolvency Act, 2003
- Home Finance Act 2008
- Non-Bank Financial Institutions Act 2008
- Central Securities Depository Act 2007
- Insurance Act 2006 (Act 724)
- National Pensions Act 2008
- Treasury Single Account
- Rural Banking Reforms:
  - ARB Apex Regulations 2006 (L.I. 1825)
  - Governance Reforms,
  - Millennium Challenge Account – networking, computerization, etc.
- Payment and Settlement System Reforms
  - Real Time Gross Settlement System (RTGS)
  - Central Securities Depository (CSD)
  - Automated Clearing House (ACH)
  - Cheque Codeline Clearing (CCC)
  - National payment system with a common interoperable platform that is inclusive of the unbanked in rural and urban areas (e-zwich)
  - Ghana Interbank Payments and Settlement System (GHIPSS)

- Strengthening of the regulatory and supervisory framework
  - Risk Based Supervision

    o   Electronic Financial Analysis and Surveillance System (eFASS)
    o   Stress Testing
    o   Publication of Annual Percentage Rates (APRs) of banks

- ISO 27001 Certification for the Bank of Ghana
- Redenomination of the Currency
- Sovereign Credit Rating with Standard and Poors and Fitch Ratings.
- Issue of a sovereign bond on the international capital markets

The wide ranging reforms that were implemented in the 2001-2008 period, resulted in a significant deepening of the financial sector in the 2001-2008 period compared to the 1984-2000 period (using all key measures like deposit/GDP, M2/GDP, credit to the private sector/GDP, etc.).

The ability of the Bank of Ghana and the Government to undertake the wide ranging reforms between 2001 and 2008 was primarily because the reform programme was domestically owned and an independent Bank of Ghana was mandated to drive it. It is difficult to imagine a Bank of Ghana where Governors in the past constantly had look over their shoulders (sometimes literally at the barrel of a gun) with concern about the reaction of political authorities to various initiatives being able to move the financial sector reform process as quickly as the Bank of Ghana did in the 2001-2008. With its new found independence under a democratic political dispensation, the Bank of Ghana had a clear focus on the type of financial sector it desired and was willing to think outside the box to achieve this. The fact that a reform or policy had not been implemented before anywhere in the world was not a deterrent.

Throughout the reform process, the Bank of Ghana constantly drove home the point that Ghana should benchmark itself against the best in the world and move away from the "poverty mentality" to a "can do" attitude. It is this thinking that allowed Ghana to leapfrog many countries in the area of payment system development for example. It is the same thinking that made

Ghana the first post HIPC country to issue a sovereign bond (and the first country in Africa outside of South Africa and Egypt to do so), and it is this same thinking that made Ghana the first low income country in the world to adopt the inflation targeting monetary policy framework, and the first central bank in Africa and one of the few in the world to obtain ISO 27001 certification.

Furthermore, Ghana's financial sector reform programme was not donor driven. To the extent that donors helped (which was useful), it was complementary to ongoing efforts. With a lot more domestic ownership of its reform process, Ghana was able to move faster and accomplish a lot in the process. This reinforces the view (which I share) that the quicker Ghana and other African countries can wean themselves from donor dependence on a sustainable basis, the better would be their prospects for development.

Notwithstanding all the reforms in the financial sector however, the sector still faces fundamental problems that need to be addressed going forward, if Ghana is to obtain the financial sector development and low interest rate environment that other developed countries have become accustomed to. These challenges, many of which are not within the remit of central banks, include:

Durable Macroeconomic Stability

A key determinant of high nominal interest rates is inflation. This is why central banks have focused more narrowly on this objective recently. The experience however suggests that the fiscal and monetary policy framework must be consistent for low and durable price stability. Throughout the years, economies like Ghana have been able to attain short periods of macroeconomic stability punctuated by periods of macroeconomic instability driven by fiscal excesses. This means that market expectations are difficult to anchor around low inflationary expectations as the next bout of inflation and currency depreciation may just be around the corner. Single digit inflation was attained once in 1999 and twice in 2006 but was not sustained. Bankers have long memories, are particularly skeptical in this environment of uncertainty, and price loans accordingly.

What is therefore required is a period of macroeconomic stability long enough for it to be the expected norm by market participants. This requires a commitment to the goal of price stability and a monetary policy framework that is transparent and market driven to be able to anchor inflationary expectations. The historical experience of England and many other countries speaks to the very high priority attached to the maintenance of the value of money. So important was maintaining the value of coinage that by 1121 when there was a noticeable decline in the quality of England's silver, all the Mint Masters in England were assembled and punished by having their right hands cut off! (Davies, 1996). This was a rather draconian method of monetary control but it speaks to the importance attached to price stability for centuries.

The experience of Ghana shows that while monetary policy regimes matter (for example the inflation targeting regime has produced the lowest average inflation since the 1970s), fiscal policy regimes matter even more. There is yet to be invented a monetary policy framework in the world that can withstand a sustained onslaught from the fiscal authorities as we saw in Ghana in 2000 and 2008. It bears noting that historically, there has been no fiscal deficit in any country that cannot be explained by critical exigencies, including war. At the end of the day however, all governments are faced with critical choices in managing public finances which have to be made, failing which the economy suffers the macroeconomic consequences.

There is therefore a critical requirement by governments of a commitment to fiscal discipline beyond the electoral cycle. Governments and politicians have to realize that there really is no free lunch and political promises have to be paid for. Rather than eating the corn today, it should be planted for the future. This is especially important in the context of Ghana's discovery of oil as there will be a temptation as well as pressure to spend the oil revenues as quickly as they are realized or mortgage yet to be realized revenues. The passage and enforcement of a Fiscal Responsibility Act, and a law for the management and use of oil proceeds will be important in this regard.

Empowering the Private Sector

One of the keys to dealing with the problem of fiscal dominance and its threat to macroeconomic stability is empowering the private sector to deliver projects and services that can be done more efficiently by it or in partnership with government. An example for Ghana recently has been the discovery of oil which was done by the private sector in partnership with government. It required the investment of hundreds of millions of dollars (with the risk of not finding oil) which the Government of Ghana did not have. Left to the Government working alone, it is highly unlikely that oil would have been discovered in Ghana at this time. Many projects, properly structured will elicit private sector participation and reduce the burden of that expenditure on the budget. Ultimately, governments should always ask the question: "Why *can't the private sector undertake this project?"* or *"How can a private public partnership be structured"?*

For the private sector to play its proper role however, it is important that the rule of law prevails, property rights upheld, and contracts respected and political witch-hunting and vindictiveness avoided. Some private sector businesses collapse simply because of a change of government. Uncertainty about the rule of law or the respect for property rights informs the desire of private foreign investors in Africa to have the "blessing" of governments before undertaking any investment. While this may provide good photo opportunities for some African governments, it is symptomatic of an underlying problem of uncertainty over property rights. After all, how many foreign investors (with investments that dwarf those in Africa) troop daily to meet with President Obama or Prime Minister Cameron? At the same time domestic investors are denied the very incentives foreign investors are given as though they do not face the same risks. To reduce the overall cost of doing business, there should be a level playing field for domestic as well as foreign investors in terms of taxes, duty-free waivers, etc. The laws should be clear and applied fairly to all domestic and foreign businesses. Mauritius and Singapore provide good models in this regard. Without the private sector being assured of this type of certainty in the business environment, African countries cannot expect the low interest rate regime that prevails in the more developed economies given the risk premium that will be attached to operating in African business environments.

The relationship between government and the private sector is also very critical for the performance of the financial sector in many African countries. The situation where government delays payments for goods and services provided by the private sector impacts negatively on the ability of the private sector to service its loans from the banking loans, increases non-performing loans, and reduces the incentive of banks to lend to the private sector. This is a different form of crowding out the private sector.

It is also the case that government cheques have historically been dishonored because of "insufficient funds". This has led to a situation of distrust by banks of the ability of governments to honor its obligations to the private sector. Banks are therefore reluctant to lend to the private sector on account of future potential receivables from government. In any country where the word of government cannot be trusted, (given the importance of the government sector in the economy) the interest rate premium will be higher. It is therefore important that government restores the trust of the public in its ability to honor its financial obligations.

Historically financial systems have flourished in environments devoid of fear and insecurity; in environments of enterprise and innovation. This partly explains the inability of Ghana's financial sector to grow appreciably during the PNDC era of Citizens Vetting Committees. The lesson here is that policy makers in Africa should encourage and celebrate, and not demonize legitimate entrepreneurship, if the financial system is to play its facilitating role in growing the economy.

Unique Identification Numbers for the Population

A key ingredient underpinning financial transactions in any society is *trust* or what Fukuyama (1999) refers to as "social capital". For example, since 1801 the motto of the London Stock Exchange is "*My Word is My Bond*" and deals were made with no exchange of documents and no written pledges being given. Transactions are based on trust and anyone breaching this is ostracized with attendant consequences. In this type of environment, interest rates on loans would be lower than in an environment in which the word of the borrower cannot be trusted and the probability of default is high. Banks in Ghana have complained about customers who take loans for particular purposes only to do something quite different and unproductive. It is important to note that this does not mean that individuals in the U.K. and other developed financial centres are necessarily more trustworthy. The difference is that they have put in place institutions and technology (like CCTV) to engender trustworthy behaviour.

In the developed economies, the consequences of declaring bankruptcy for example are severe and will affect your job prospects, ability to obtain a loan etc. Everyone can be uniquely identified by a number on a database that is accessible for background checks. This means that the cost of loan default is high. In Ghana and many other developing countries, unique identification numbers on such a database do not generally exist and therefore the cost of loan default is low. Defaulters will generally switch to another financial institution or even change their name to access another loan. The establishment of a credit reference bureau, as Ghana has recently done, without a unique identification for market participants will not solve the problem either. It is therefore important to have a unique ID that cannot be faked and can also be easily authenticated offline as well as online. In Ghana, the biometric smartcard platform may provide an ideal solution.

Address System

The importance of a system of property addresses is probably one of the most underestimated requirements for the development of an economy and its financial sector. One can imagine what would happen if for example the address system in the United States, United Kingdom, South Korea or Japan disappeared overnight. These economies would basically grind to a halt because so much depends on residential or business addresses. For banks and other lenders, the question in Ghana and other developing countries is how to track down a defaulter. Borrowers are also aware that they cannot be tracked down and so are likely to default. It is very imperative that countries like Ghana put in place a comprehensive address system as a matter of priority. The United Kingdom for example developed its postcode system in the 15 year period between 1959 and 1974. This was in response with the increasing confusion with similar street names going back to the 1840s. The six-digit postal code was finally settled on after many experiments. The availability of GPS technology and Google maps today together with the experiences of various countries should make the task much easier for a country like Ghana. The absence of an address system increases the risk premium bankers attach to a loan.

Financial Inclusion (Banking the Unbanked)

The financial system cannot develop to its potential and monetary policy cannot be effective if the majority of the population continues to be excluded from access to financial services. The importance of this to the overall development of financial systems in Africa cannot be overemphasized. This is the reason why the Bank of Ghana has placed a high priority on banking the unbanked through the facilitation of a common platform and technology (the e-zwich biometric smartcard) for banks and other non-bank institutions to allow access to financial services by the unbanked in the context of overall payment system reform. Other technologies (like the mobile phone) are also available to deliver mobile banking services and should be encouraged in the context of the central bank's regulatory framework for branchless banking.

Unwritten Rules of the Game

International development is very competitive and therefore countries try to wrest a competitive advantage at every turn. Unlike the game of football where the rules are clearly defined for all participants, not all the rules of the international development game are written down. Indeed, economists are still searching for some of them. Developing countries are therefore able to compete on relatively more equal terms in sports like football than in the game of international development, where there are so many unwritten rules that countries have to figure out for themselves. A unique identification number, an address system and financial inclusion (banking the unbanked) are basically some of the key unwritten rules for effective monetary policy and financial sector development in particular and overall development in general.

Without these systems and institutions in place, no monetary policy framework will be sufficient in the long run to engender the type of financial sector that will be critical in the growth process. No donors have thus far required that countries put in place Address Systems, Unique IDs, etc. in place as conditions for aid for example. African and other developing countries have to put these systems in place themselves as a matter of priority and urgency to support the effectiveness of monetary policy and financial sector development as well as the wider goal of economic development, growth with stability, and jobs. In the presence of such market failure, there is an important role for the State, working with the private sector, to put in place some of these efficient rules or norms that underpin any modern society or financial system to allow for the efficient functioning of monetary policy and the financial sector within a market economy.

REFERENCES

African Development Bank (2009). "Africa and the Global
    Economic Crisis: Strategies for Preserving the Foundations of Long-
    Term Growth". Working Paper No. 98, July 2009.

Alexander, W.E., T.J.T. Balino, Charles Enoch et al, Adoption of
    Indirect Instruments of Monetary Policy, IMF Occasional Paper No.
    126, Washington DC. June 1995

Arango, Sebastian and Ishaq Nadiri, M., (1981). "Demand for
    money in open economies" Journal of Monetary Economics, Volume
    7, Pages 69-83.

Arize, A. C., J. Malindretos and S. S. Shwiff, (1999). "Structural
    breaks, cointegration, and speed of adjustment Evidence from 12
    LDCs money demand" International Review of Economics &
    Finance, Volume 8, Issue 4, , Pages 399-420

Aryeetey, E. (1994) *Financial Integration and Development in
    Sub-Saharan Africa:A Study of Informal Finance in Ghana*. London:
    ODI Working Paper No. 78.

Aryeetey, E. (1996).The formal financial sector in Ghana After
    the Reforms. Report of a Study Sponsored by the World Bank
    Research Committee and Administered by the Overseas Development
    Institute

Aryeetey, E and F. Tarp, (2000), "Structural Adjustment and
    After: Which Way Forward" in Aryeetey, Ernest, Jane Harrigan and
    Machiko Nisanke (Eds.) *Economic Reforms in Ghana: The Miracle
    and the Mirage*, Oxford: James Currey and Woeli Publishers

Attafuah, Kenneth A. . Criminal Justice Policy, Public Tribunals
    and the Administration of Justice in Rawlings Ghana (1982-1992): A
    study in the Political Economy of Revolutionary Social Change and
    Criminal Law Reform. Ph.D.   Dissertation, Simon Fraser
    University, Burnaby, Canada. 1993.

Balino, T.J.T., Carlo Cottarelli (eds.) Frameworks for Monetary
    Stability: Policy Issues and Country Experiences, IMF, Washington
    DC., 1994

Balino, Tomas J.T. and L.M. Zamaloa (eds.) Instruments of
    Monetary Management: Issues and Country Experiences,
    International Monetary Fund, Washington DC, 1997.

Ball, Laurence, and Niamh Sheridan. 2003. "Does Inflation
    Targeting Matter?" Paper for NBER conference on Inflation
    Targeting, Bal Harbor, Florida, January 23–25.

Bank of Ghana (2007). Commemoration of Fiftieth Anniversary.
    Edited by Edward Ayensu. Accra

Bank of Ghana (2009). Financial Stability Reports: Monetary
    Policy Committee Statistical Releases, 2002- 2009.

Bawumia M., Zakari Mumuni and Banjamin Amoah (2008).
    Choice of Monetary Policy Regime in Ghana. Bank of Ghana
    Working Paper.

Berg, Claes (2005). "Experience of inflation targeting in 20
    countries" Sveriges Riksbank Economic Review.

Bouey, Gerald, (1983). "House of Commons Standing
    Committee on Finance, Trade and Economic Affairs", Minutes of
    Proceedings and Evidence, No. 134, March.

Brownbridge, Martin and Fritz Gockel (1998) "The impact of
    financial sector policies on banking in Ghana" , in Banking in Africa:
    the impact of financial sector reform since independence Oxford and
    Trenton, NJ: James Currey and Africa World Press, 1998

Burnside, C. and Dollar, D. (2000) Aid Policies and Growth.
    Washington, DC: World Bank, Policy Research Department.

Carare, A. and Stone, M.R., (2003). "Inflation Targeting
    Regimes". IMF Working Paper, WP/03/9, January.

Cecchetti, Stephen G., and Michael Ehrmann, (1999). "Does Inflation Targeting Increase Output Volatility? An International Comparison of Policymakers' Preferences and Outcomes." NBER Working Paper No. 7426. Cambridge, MA: National Bureau of Economic Research.

Chenery, Hollis, and Strout, A. M. (1996) 'Foreign Assistance and Economic Development', American Economic Review Vol. 56: 679-733

Cho,Yoon Je (2002) "Financial Repression, Liberalization, Crisis and Restructuring: Lessons of Korea.s Financial Sector Policies" ADB Institute Research Paper Series, No. 47, November 2002

Corbo, Vittorio, Oscar Landerretche, and Klaus Schmidt-Hebbel, (2001). "Assessing Inflation Targeting after A Decade of World Experience." International Journal of Finance and Economics 6: 348–68.

Chibber, A., and N. Shafik, 'Exchange reform, parallel markets, and inflation in Africa: the case of Ghana,' World Bank Working Paper, WPS 427, World Bank, Washington DC., 1990.

Davies Glyn (1996) A History of Money from Ancient Times to the Present Day, rev. ed. Cardiff: University of Wales Press, 1996. 716p. ISBN 0 7083 1351 5.

Debt Relief International (2000), "A debt sustainability for Ghana". Mimeo

Dowling, J. M. and Hiemenz, U. (1983) 'Aid, Savings and Growth in the Asian Region', The Developing Economies, Vol XX1, No. 1, March.

Easterly, William (2001) "Growth Implosions and Debt Explosions" World bank mimeo. Washington DC.

ECA and AUC (2009) *Economic Report on Africa 2008*, Addis Ababa: ECA.

ECA, AUC, and AfDB (2009). *Assessing Progress toward Attaining the Millennium Development Goals in Africa 2009*. Report presented to the 2nd joint ECA/AUC Conference of Ministers of Finance, Planning and Economic Development and African Ministers of Economy and Economy, Cairo, Egypt, June 2009.

Edwards, S. and S. van Wijnbergen (1989) "Disequilibrium and Structural Adjustment" in Chenery and T.N. Srnivasan, Handbook of Development Economics, Vol. II, Amsterdam: North Holland.

Ewusi, K., The Determinants of Price Fluctuations in Ghana, ISSER Discussion Paper, University of Ghana, Legon, 1997.

Financial Stability Board (2009). Progress Report in Implementing the London Summit Recommendations for Strengthening Financial Stability. Report of the Financial Stability Board to G20 Leaders. September, 2009.

Fracasso, A., H. Genberg and C. Wyplosz (2003), "How do central banks write? An evaluation of Inflation Reports by inflation targeting central banks", *Geneva Reports on the World Economy Special Report 2*, International Center for Monetary and Banking Studies, Centre for Economic Policy Research (CEPR) and Norges Bank

Friedman, Miton and Anna J. Schwartz (1963). A Monetary History of the United States, 1867-1960

Frimpong-Ansah, J.H. (1991). The Vampire State in Africa: The Political Economy of Decline in Ghana. James Currey. London.

Fukuyama, Francis (1999) Social Capital and Civil Society. Institute of Public Policy, George Mason University,

Gray, Simon and Glenn Haggarth, Introduction to Monetary Operation in Tony Latter (ed.), Handbooks in Central Banking No. 10, Centre for Central Banking Studies, Bank of England, September 1996.

Green, John H., Repurchase Agreements: Advantages and
    Implementation Issues, IMF/Monetary and Exchange Affairs
    Department (MAE) Operational Paper OP/ April 1997.

Griffin, Keith (1970) 'Foreign Capital, Domestic Savings, and
    Economic Development', Bulletin of the Oxford University Institute
    of Economics and Statsitics, Vol. 32: 99-112

Gupta, K. and Islam, M. A. (1983) Foreign Capital, Savings and
    Growth: An International Cross-section Study. Dordrecht, Holland:
    Reidel Publishing Company

Haggarth, Glenn, Introduction to Monetary Policy in Latter, Tony
    (ed.) Handbooks on Central Banking No.10, Centre for Central
    Banking Studies, Bank of England, September 1996.

Hardy, Daniel C., Reserve Requirements and Monetary
    Management: An Introduction in Balino, Tomas J.T. and L.M.
    Zamaloa (1997).

Hayman, Catharina J. Use of Foreign Exchange Swaps by
    Central Banks, in Balino, Tomas J.T. and L.M. Zamaloa (1997).

Heikensten, Lars (2005): "Inflation targeting in Sweden –
    implementation, communication and effectiveness ".Conference on
    inflation targeting: implementation, communication and effectiveness,
    Stockholm, 10 June 2005

Herbst Jeffrey. 1993. *The Politics of Reform in Ghana. 1982-
    1991*. University of California Press Ltd.

Horská, Ing. Helena (2004). "Inflation Targeting in the Central
    Eastern European Countries – A comparison with the Czech
    Republic". Doctoral thesis, Faculty of Economics and Public
    Administration, University of Economics, Prague.

House of Commons Treasury Committee (2006). "Banking the
    unbanked": banking services, the Post Office Card Account, and
    financial inclusion. Thirteenth Report of Session 2005–06

Hu, Yifan, (2003). "Empirical Investigations of Inflation Targeting" Institute for International Economics.

Howells, Peter and Bain, Keith, 'The Economics of Money, banking and Finance'

IMF (1986). Ghana Stand-By Arrangement, Washington D.C. October

IMF (1987). Ghana. Recent Economic Developments, Washington DC.

IMF (1988). Ghana. Recent Economic Developments, Washington DC.

International Monetary Fund (2008) Ghana: 2008 Article IV Consultation—Staff Report October 2008, IMF Country Report No. 08/344

International Monetary Fund (2000) . Ghana: Selected Issues. , IMF Country Report No. 2

International Monetary Fund (1999) . Ghana: Selected Issues. , IMF Country Report No. 99/3

International Monetary Fund (2003) . Ghana: Selected Issues. IMF Country Report No. 03/134

International Monetary Fund (2008) . Ghana: Selected Issues. IMF Country Report No. 08/332
International Monetary Fund (2007) . Ghana: Selected Issues. IMF Country Report No. 07/208

International Monetary Fund (2001) . Ghana: Enhanced Heavily Indebted Poor Countries (HIPC) Initiative. Preliminary Document. June 2001. Washington DC

International Monetary Fund (1989), Monetary Management in Ghana, Central Banking Department, IMF, Washington DC.

International Monetary Fund. 1991. Ghana: Adjustment and
    Growth. 1983-91. Occasional Paper No. 86. Washington D.C

Kapur, Ishan; Michael T Hadjimichael; Paul Hilbers; Jerald Schiff
    and Philipe Szymczak (1991), "Ghana: Adjustment and Growth 1983-
    91", Occasional Paper No 86, International Monetary Fund,
    Washington DC.

Keynes, J.M (1936)., General Theory, Book VI, Chap. 23.

Killick, Tony (1978). Development Economics in Action. A Study
    of Economic Policies in Ghana. London Heineman

Krugman, Paul (1988) 'Financing vs. Forgiving a Debt
    Overhang', Journal of Development Economics Vol. 29: 253-68

Kwakye J.K., E.Y. Addison and H.A.K. Wampah (1996), Inflation
    Management by Bank of Ghana: the Strategies, The Difficulties and
    the Way Forward, A Paper Presented at the Inflation Management
    Roundtable at Akosombo, Research Department, Bank of Ghana,
    May 1996.

Latter, Anthony, the Interbank Market, Paper Presented at
    IMF/MAE Workshop on Monetary Operations at Joint Vienna
    Institute, Vienna, Austria, September 1997.

Laurens, Bernard J. Refinance Instruments: Lessons From Their
    Use in Some Industrial Countries, In Balino, Tomas J.T. and L.M.
    Zamaloa (1997).
Lawson, R.M., Inflation in the Consumer Market in Ghana,
    Economic Bulletin of Ghana, Vol. X, No. 1, 1996.

Leite, Sergio Pereira (1982), "Interest Rate Policy in West Africa"
    Staff Papers 29 (1), International Monetary Fund, pp48-76.

Leite et al (2000) Ghana: Economic Development in a Democratic
    Environment. IMF Occasional Paper, 199. Washington D.C.

Leith J. Clark and Soderling L. (2003) Ghana - long term growth,
    atrophy and stunted recovery (2003). The Nordic Africa Institute, The
    Nordic Africa Institute, Uppsala : Nordiska Afrikainstitutet

Loynes, John Barraclough . 1962. *The West African Currency
    Board 1912-1962.* London: West African Currency Board.

Martson, David, the Use of Reserve Requirements in Monetary
    Control: Operational Features and Country Practices, IMF/Monetary
    and Exchange Affairs Department (MAE) Operation Paper OP/ , May
    1996.

Masson, P. Miguel Savatano, Sunil Sharma (1997) "The Scope
    for Inflation Targeting in Developing Countries". IMF Working
    Paper, No. 97/130.

Maxwell J. Fry (1998) "Saving, Investment, Growth, and
    Financial Distortions in Pacific Asia and Other Developing
    Areas"International Economic Journal, 1 Volume 12, Number 1,
    Spring 1998

Maxwell, Simon (2005) The Washington Consensus is dead!
    Long live the meta-narrative, Overseas Development Institute, WP
    243.

McKinnon, Ronald I.(1973), *Money and Capital in Economic
    Development,* Washington, D.C.: Brookings Institution, 1973.

Mensah, Sam (1997) "Financial Markets and Institutions:
    Ghana's Experience." The International Programme on Capital
    Markets and Portfolio Management Indian Institute of Management,
    September 8-20, 1997

Mishkin, Frederic S. (2001). "Inflation Targeting". Columbia:
    Graduate School of Business, Columbia University.

Mishkin, Frederic S., and Klaus Schmidt-Hebbel, (2001). "One
    Decade of Inflation Targeting in the World: What Do We Know and
    What Do We Need to Know?" NBER Working Paper No. 8397.
    Cambridge, MA: National Bureau of Economic Research.

Mosley, P., Hudson, J., and Horrell, S. (1987) 'Aid, the Public
    Sector, and the Market in Less Developed Countries', Economic
    Journal Vol. 97: 616-41

Mosley, P. (1995) 'Aid Effectiveness: A Study of the
    Effectiveness of Overseas Aid in the Main Countries Receiving ODA
    Assistance', unpublished paper, University of Reading.

Nachega, Jean-Claude, (2001). "Financial Liberalization, Money
    Demand, and Inflation in Uganda," IMF Working Papers 01/118,
    International Monetary Fund, Washington D.C.

Neumann, Manfred J.M. and Jurgen von Hagen, (2002). "Does
    Inflation Targeting Matter?" Federal Reserve Bank of St. Louis
    Review 84 (4): 127–48.

Non-Performing Assets Recovery Trust (various years) Annual
    Report and Accounts Accra.

Orleans-Lindsay, J. K. 1967. *Bank of Ghana 1957-1967.* Accra:
    Bank of Ghana.

Page, Sheila (ed.) Monetary Policy in Developing Countries,
    Rotledge, London, 1993.

Papanek, G. F. (1973) ' Aid, Foreign Private Investment, Savings
    and Growth in Less Developed Countries', The Journal of Political
    Economy, No. 81

Polak, J.J. (1957). "Monetary Analysis of Income Formation and
    Payments Problems, IMF Staff papers, November, 1-50

Ray, Donald (1986). Ghana: Politics, Economics and Society. London. Frances Pinter Publishers Ltd

Shaw, Edward S. (1973), *Financial Deepening in Economic Development,* New York: Oxford University Press, 1973.

Schobert, Franziska (2001), The Change-over to the Euro in Montenegro: Causes and Consequences, ifo Studien 3/2001.

Sowa, N.K. and Kwakye J.K., Inflationary trends and Control in Ghana, AERC Research Paper Twenty-Two, Nairobi, 1993.

Sowa N.K. and Ivy Acquaye (1999), Financial and foreign exchange markets liberalization in Ghana". Journal of International Development, 11, 385-409

Steel, F., Hyperinflation in Ghana, Legon Observer, pp. 308-12., 1979.

Svensson, L. E.O., (2007). "Inflation Targeting". Princeton University

Tabatabai, Hamid, 1986. "Economic Stabilization and Structural Adjustment in Ghana" *Labour and Soceity* Geneva, Vol. II No. 3.

Tanner, Archibald A (1995), "Financial System Restructuring: An Overview of Ghana's Experience", The West African Banker No 5, pp5-11

Toye, J.F.J., Mosley, P. and Jane Harrigan, 1991. Aid and Power: The World Bank and Policy-Based Lending London and New York. Routledge.

Truman, E. M., (2003), *Inflation Targeting in the World Economy,* Washington: Institute for International Economics.

Uche, Chibuike Ugochukwu (1996) From Currency Board to Central Banking: The Politics of Change in Sierra Leone, African Economic History, No. 24 (1996), pp. 147-158

Van der Merwe, E.J., (2004). "Inflation targeting in South Africa".
    Occasional Paper No 19 July, South African Reserve Bank.

Weisskopf, Thomas (1972) 'Impact of Foreign Capital Flows on
    Domestic Savings in Underdeveloped Countries', Journal of
    International Economics Vol. 2: 25-38

Williamson, John (2004) John Williamson, (2004) "A Short
    History of the Washington Consensus". "From the Washington
    Consensus towards a new Global Governance," Barcelona, September
    24–25, 2004.

White, H. (1992) 'The Macroeconomic Impact of Developing Aid:
    A critical Survey', Journal of International Development, Vol. 4, No.
    3, February.

World Bank (1994). Ghana: Progress on Adjustment.
    Washington DC.

World Bank (1985). Ghana: Towards Structural Adjustment.
    Washington DC

World Bank (1986), Financial Sector Review, World Bank,
    Washington DC.

World Bank (1994), Ghana Financial Sector Review: Bringing
    Savers and Investors Together, Report No 13423-GH World Bank,
    Washington DC.

Yahya, Kassim (2001) Monetary Management in Ghana. A
    Paper Presented at the Conference on Monetary Policy Framework in
    Africa Pretoria, South Africa
Younger, Stephen D. (1992) 'Aid and the Dutch Disease:
    Macroeconomic Management When Everybody Loves You', World
    Development Vol. 20, No. 11

Younger, Stephen D. and Jane Harrigan (2000) "Aid, Debt and Growth" in Ernest Aryeetey, Jane Harrigan and Machiko Nissanke eds. Economic Reforms in Ghana, The Miracle and the Mirage, James Currey, Oxford.

Ziorklui, Sam Q. (2001) "The Impact of Financial Sector Reform on Bank Efficiency and Financial Deepening for Savings Mobilization in Ghana". African Economic Policy Discussion Paper Number 81, February 2001. , Howard University

Index

Lightning Source UK Ltd.
Milton Keynes UK
08 December 2010

163978UK00002B/11/P